Also by Sharo

Freedom Is a Psycho-Ki

Cats and Dogs Are People Too! (1999)
(Italian translation available)

Jivamukti Yoga: Practices for Liberating Body and Soul (2002)
(with David Life)
(German, Italian, Russian, Spanish, and Turkish translations available)

The Art of Yoga (2002)
(with David Life)

The Jivamukti Yoga Chant Book (2003)
(Chinese, German, Italian, Japanese, Russian, Spanish, and Turkish translations available)

Yoga and Vegetarianism (2008)

Yoga Assists (2013)
(with David Life)
(Italian and Russian translations available)

Simple Recipes for Joy: More than 200 Delicious Vegan Recipes (2014)
(Italian translation available)

The Magic Ten and Beyond (2018)
(German, Italian, and Russian translations available)

The Art of Norahs Nepas (2019)

Yoga and Veganism: The Diet of Enlightenment (2020)
(Audiobook narrated by author also available)

Magic Is a Shift in Perception: Poems 1972-2019, A Memoir of Sorts (2020)
(Audiobook narrated by author and Russian translation available)

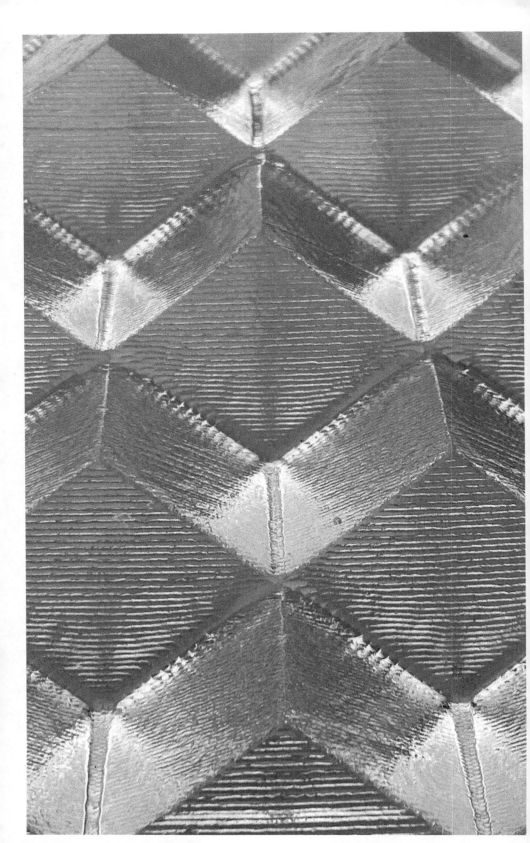

Eternity is Happening Now

Essays and Stories

Volume One

Sharon Gannon

Typeface: Georgia
Library of Congress Cataloging-in-Publication Data

Gannon, Sharon
Eternity Is Happening Now, Essays and Stories, Volume One

Cover photo by the author of the glass sculpture *Apsara,* by Frederick Gladding Kahl
Author photo by David Life, Woodstock, NY 2015

Book design and layout by David Life

Notes about the quotes that appear under the title of many of the essays and stories:
Citations that appear after a scriptural verse will indicate the name of the book, the volume, the chapter, and the verse, in that order. The name of the book will be spelled out when it appears under the title of an essay, but when it appears in the body of the text of an essay the name of the book will be abbreviated. For example: the Bhagavad Gita, BG; Patanjali's Yoga Sutra, PYS; Shrimad Bhagavatam, SB.

If a person's name is not given in the credit line after a translation of a Sanskrit quote, the reader should assume that the translation is the author's.

For all of us in time

To step into the atha, where eternity is happening—now. To be able to die to the past and give up the illusion of a future is to be born into the present.

Volume One Contents

Introduction

Most mornings she appears, eyes wide open, in a train of cloth, declaiming key words and phrases over and over with a sort of "Eureka!" mantra effect. She cannot be delayed in her trip to the keyboard until the essay, story, or poem is scribed. This writing is truly inspired!

In the time I have known Sharon Gannon, she has written every day. Don't get me wrong, she does many things in a day, but she writes every day too. Her work ethic would be considered grueling for most normal people, but her joyful, loving, devotion to God seems to allow her to float through each task effortlessly, unscathed, and in good humor. She doesn't labor over *what* to write, it seems preformed in her nervous system. Somehow, between the darkness of night and the first light of day clarity has dawned. Almost as if it were always there—for a very long time, lying in wait, only to be dispensed in quatrains, riddles, and islands of lucidity.

It takes a special combination of commitment to both the subject and the act of writing to become a prolific writer. To sustain oneself through all levels of critical thought, writing, and editing, and then promoting, an author must feel that what they have to say can have a good effect on the world—if they present it in just the right way. Writing in itself is a discipline in most cases (part of finding the right way), but in the case of Sharon's writing, it is a spiritual practice—the only right way is to benefit others.

Many Jivamukti Yoga teachers and students benefit from Sharon's writings in the form of the Focus of the Month essays—an invention of hers from early in the development of Jivamukti Yoga. Her dedication to written communication shows in the many years of contemplation, research, translation, reading, and practicing evident in hundreds of these wonderful essays. These regular missives are anticipated, translated, and read around the globe.

This book is a many-layered witnessing of life from a dazzling perspective. Dazzling in the sense of refracted glittering light. Whether she's relating an ancient yogic story from scripture (as in how Valmiki is transformed from a thief to a best-selling author, Vol Two, pg 276) or an event in her own life (like when her adventurous mother became a freight-train-hopping hobo—True! True! Vol One, pg 269), we can benefit from Sharon's fresh insights (like what *brahmacharya* has to do with veganism, Vol Two, pg 151), her ability to weave a tapestry of meaning ("Sex, Death, Sleep, Love, Magic, and Pratyahara," Vol One, pg 107), and to find new significance for multidimensional living (see Vol Two, pg 216, "Yoga and Money").

She is a philosopher and scholar—a thinker who has sought answers for the deep questions that rattle around in all our brains—questions about life, death, life after death, life after life, devotion, ahimsa, and liberated living.

She is a spiritual seeker who has immersed herself in the study and practice of yoga. *Yoga* means "to connect." The writings in this book reveal the many connections she has been able to make by looking at life through the lens of her soul and then writing about her findings. Her book illuminates a unique application of yoga philosophy for our daily lives. In translating the word *asana* (usually translated as "pose") to mean "seat"—or the quality of our relationship to others and the Earth—she provides both the means and the goal to strive for in our lives. In so many examples the stories and essays in this book will provide the essential guidance that is so necessary and so hard to find.

These beautiful words can inspire your day, or your book-discussion group, your online friends, or the students you teach. Sharon's insights and the clear way she can communicate those insights through writing have been my personal treasured daily dose of intelligence of treasured soulfulness for decades, and now they can be everyone's.

My suggestion is to open one of these volumes randomly and choose a piece to read or select an intriguing title from the Table of Contents and let the essay or story inspire. Of course, you may prefer to read the books from front to back. If you choose to do this, don't be surprised when you come upon ideas and phrases that are repeated, this is to be expected since each piece was originally written as a "stand-alone" rather than a part of a sequential collection. Even so you may discover, as I have, that the ideas that are repeated are things that we all need to be reminded of on a daily basis and be appreciative of hearing again and again.

—David Life

Author's Preface

I am always so grateful in the morning when I wake up. It is a time of great hope and euphoria. It is this time of the day when I feel most totally at ease. All the cells and tissues of my body seem to have been refreshed and reorganized, most likely because my consciousness was immersed in the wordless, imageless, deep-sleep state of union. In those first few moments of awakening, all parts of myself seem to be aligned with the source, resulting in such equilibrium that all I can feel is gratitude. Even my skin feels evened out, my breathing is peaceful, and my heart is filled with optimism. During this state of enjoyable receptivity, I am often blessed by insights. It is mysterious where the ideas come from. I don't know. Somehow it seems that the journey from deep sleep through dreaming and then waking causes a focused clarity, bringing my mind to a relaxed, effortless point of cognition about a particular subject.

The ideas contained in the writings in this book are the results of those insights—little realizations that occurred when I woke up in the morning. I can't take credit for these ideas, because I didn't think them up; they just appeared to me, and I was privileged to hear them when I woke. Then, later, after I got out of bed, I would do my best to write them down and fashion them into an essay or story or at least a quick note. Originally, I did that not so much to communicate to others, but rather to contemplate and organize the essence of the insight into something coherent, so that I could make sense to myself of what had occurred. This book contains essays and stories that are the result of that process.

Although the waking insights form the foundation of the writings, their final versions were not written in a vacuum, as if I were attempting to transcribe a memo from the deep. There were also other contributors that shaped the final content, such as the ideas of other writers, challenging people in my life, recollections, and direct questions from students and friends.

Like most writers, I read a lot and derive inspiration from reading the ideas of others. When you read a book, you are immersed in an intimate conversation with the author. I agree with Marc Bolan when he sings, "Book after book, I get hooked every time the writer speaks to me like a friend." Many of the ideas in these pieces were inspired by other writers, both contemporary and ancient. I immerse myself in an eclectic range of books, exposing myself to different perspectives daily. The comprehensions that arise from my reading stimulate contemplation that often reveals exciting underlying correlations between diverse subjects. Although I subsist on a varied diet drawn from the major intellectual food groups of both fiction and nonfiction, my bread and vegan butter is yoga philosophy. It is through the lens of the ancient scriptures that I see the world and attempt to incite solutions to its problems.

Other contributors come in the form of challenges I might be having with a particular person in my life whose ideas I find difficult to agree with. After many frustrating attempts to talk with them face-to-face, often the solution would reveal itself abstractly in my mind and I would then try to express in writing what I had been unable to express in person. This forced me to examine my point of view with the intention of elevating it to the level of communication, as opposed to mere self-expression— wanting to get my point across.

"Aha!" moments can occur when I am able to put something together that had eluded me before. A memory will sometimes visit me unexpectedly and prompt me to write an account of what happened, and in that process something that had been unsolved and mysterious is revealed and becomes clear. That is the case with the stories included in these volumes. Several of them relate events that happened to me, while others are accounts of ancient yogic stories I had heard or read about.

Many of these pieces started as letters in response to a question. As I sat at my desk and wrote in the morning, the mail would come, either in the form of a letter in an envelope that arrived in the mailbox or an email conveying a question from a friend or student. Often, I would discover that the answer to their question was to be found in the insight I was working on trying to expand into an essay at the time. In this way their yearning for guidance provided me something/someone tangible to relate to on a personal level, and that made the writing flow more easily and the ideas develop more meaningfully.

As a teacher, I am dedicated to the service of the students who see me as their teacher. Not all but many of these essays were written to be used as a Focus of the Month, to provide teaching themes to Jivamukti Yoga teachers, offering some direction for the classes they taught. Some of the essays that became a Focus of the Month were originally longer essays that had to be cut down to meet a word-count restriction. Here, in this book, many of those essays appear in their unabridged form, while others are new and have never been published before.

Working on this book, being immersed in the process of unpacking insights has provided me with clarity and direction to navigate through the rough waters of existence. I don't claim to be an educated philosopher, but like most people I do have a desire to understand and be understood, which leads me to question and examine my own ideas and perceptions and to listen to the ideas of others.

No matter what activities I may be outwardly involved in, in my heart I am trying to feel God's presence. In the Bhagavad Gita, Krishna gives Arjuna advice about how one should behave in the world, saying, in essence, "Do whatever you do in this world, but do it in remembrance of Me." And in the tenth canto of the Shrimad Bhagavatam we find this holy guidance regarding worldly activity: "You need to let go of everything that does not increase *bhava* (divine good mood)." The modern-day American saint Alice Coltrane taught that while we may engage in many activities throughout life, we actually "have only one job, and that is to get to God." These essays are part of my own work toward that aim. It is my sincere wish that others might find these offerings useful too, or at least entertaining.

Note: In these essays and stories there will be many references to God. In a universal way of thinking God is all-pervading and cannot be truly contained in one material form, claimed by one religion, or defined by a particular gender. The Bhagavad Gita says that God is "the father and the mother of the universe..." (BG 9.17). In the yoga sutra, Patanjali stresses the importance of devotion to God, but he does not suggest a particular form of God or Goddess to be devoted to—he leaves that choice up to the yogi and refers to God as *Ishwara,* meaning one's own choice. Although God is omnipresent, it is difficult to worship a ubiquitous, formless, no-thing. God appears to different people in different forms and each person should be respected for how they choose to worship Him/Her/It or That. Being a Krishna devotee, the form of God that I worship is Krishna, who appeared in an avatar form as a man and so, when Krishna is referred to in this book, the pronoun "He" will often be used. I hope that this is not offensive to any readers.

Essays and Stories

I

GOD

The cause of all causes,
love itself, eternal, vast,
limitless reality—
defying boundaries of religion, culture,
species, or gender.

One Job

abhyase 'py asamartho 'si / mat-karma-paramo bhava
mad-artham api karmani / kurvan siddhim avapsyasi
*If you cannot practice meditation, then think of My work and perform
your own work for My sake, and you shall attain enlightenment.*
—Bhagavad Gita 12.10

On a hot summer day in the East Side neighborhood of Detroit, some kids were outside playing in a gushing hydrant, shrieking, drenched with delight. One kid yelled into an open window on the first floor of the house where her sister was playing piano, "Alice come out and play with us." The young pianist inside responded softly, "I *am* playing!"

I was blessed to meet Alice Coltrane many years later when she came to play at the Jivamukti Yoga School, gracing us by leading an intimate kirtan gathering. Afterwards we were sitting together in a vegetarian restaurant, and she shared some stories from her childhood about how the other children were always trying to get her to come out and play. "They didn't understand that I was playing! she laughed. Not just the piano—I had discovered the joy of play, God's Lila, which is inside—inside one's own soul."

Shortly before her untimely death in 2007, I heard an interview on the radio with Alice Coltrane, whose spiritual name was Swami Turiyasangitananda. The interviewer was asking about her prolific musical accomplishments and had cited many recordings she had done and performances that had happened or were scheduled to happen, as well as a recent book she had authored. The interviewer then said, "You have been so busy, doing so many things, how do you keep it all together and get so much done?" To which Alice responded, in her characteristic voice, which was so slow and serene, "I only have one job and that is to get to God, and that is a full-time job!"

Alice's job description is meaningful to those who aspire to find God. Since God dwells within each one of us, we had better get inside as soon as possible if we want to find what we are looking for. Run for cover; seek the solace, which is always waiting for you inside. Don't spend too much time out there looking around trying to find it. Valuable things, the important things that we think we have lost, are always found in the least expected places, the last places we would think to look.

The storm is coming, it might already be raging, and you

just haven't noticed in a while, or you might even consider yourself aware that the storm is occurring, but you think it is like the weather and there is nothing you or anyone can do about it. You think things just happen to you, the world is coming at you, and you are a passive victim of circumstances, sometimes fortunate, sometimes unfortunate. You have heard optimistic people say that peace and love are possible. But the world is in such a mess, shouldn't we or somebody *do* something about all the violence, misery, and unfairness in the world, first, before we go inside?

If you want the world to be a peaceful place, you must be a peaceful person. The world mirrors your mind. A turbulent mind creates a turbulent world. The nature of the soul is peace. If you can allow your mind to dwell in the soul, it becomes peaceful. Everything you see is a projection coming from your mind. If you don't like what you see out there, change what's inside your mind. That change of mind must come from within—deep within. Once you have found the inner peace and joy of the soul—inside yourself—you are able to move in the world from a place of spiritual activation. You embody that which you want to see in others and the world. God is the source of that inner peace and joy; and God dwells within you as your very soul. When you act from that serene inner reality, you can then see the world realistically: you stop blaming others, you stop being angry, judgmental, or upset with others and instead find creative ways to increase your inner joy. If instead you insist on searching outside yourself to find peace and happiness you will eventually, but inevitably, become disappointed, disillusioned, and perhaps even cynical. When that occurs, you will lose your faith in life, feeling that it has no meaning and that there is no happiness to be found.

Often it takes a violent storm for one to seek shelter. There are many accounts of people who have gone through a traumatic experience—an accident, the death of a loved one, or a serious illness—that instigated a mystical or transcendental realization, forcing them to go inside and reevaluate the purpose of their life.

Okay, so you're convinced that it is important to go inside —you have answered the *why* of the situation, but what about the *how*? *How* do we "go inside"? Patanjali says, "Give up and take refuge in God" (PYS 1.23). But that brings us back to where we started, because we don't know how to find God. Patanjali, of course, gives meditation as a means to find the inner Self, as does Krishna in the Bhagavad Gita. But what if I'm a person who has a lot to do? I have children and a job and not much time, and I can't seem to meditate long enough or well enough to begin to feel that inner peace. Am I destined to be lost and unhappy? Is there something else I can do? Yes! Krishna says, "Keep doing what you do, but remember Me while you are doing it" (BG 12.10). You don't have to divide your day into spiritual activities at one time and mundane work or entertaining distractions at other times; all your life, every moment, can be a full-time job, a spiritual practice, if you can remember God.

Bhakti Trumps All

*The Lord does not reside in the heart of one who is always focused on
worldly affairs ... and is falsely attached to the path of action.*
—Shri Harirayaji's Shiksha Patra 32.4,
translated by Shyamdas and Vallabhdas

A practitioner must be careful not to lose sight of the ultimate goal of yoga, which is God-realization. Remembering God and being able to serve God should be foremost in our minds and hearts and should permeate all of our actions. When we ask, "Make me an instrument for Thy Will, not mine but Thine be done, free me from anger, jealousy and fear, fill my heart with joy and compassion," we are asking God to reside in our hearts and to use us as divine instruments. That plea invokes the arising of humility within our hearts and diminishes pride and with it the tendency to identify ourselves as the doer of actions and instead acknowledges God as the ultimate doer.

The simplest definition of Jivamukti Yoga is "a path to enlightenment through compassion for all beings." Even though *bhakti* and *ahimsa* are both tenets of Jivamukti Yoga, there could arise a tendency to forget bhakti, devotion to God, and become overly consumed with promoting animal rights, veganism, and environmentalism—or you could say saving the world—as a way to practice ahimsa (nonharming) and develop compassion in one's daily life. We must be careful not to allow our activism to take priority over our devotion to God. If we do, we will undoubtedly be bound by *avidya* and *asmita*—ignorance and ego identification, respectively, and all the debilitating vices that come with those hindrances, like pride, anger, revenge, and impatience, for example.

It is understandable that when a person becomes vegan and experiences the truth that has been kept from them their whole life it can be a huge, cathartic awakening. Realizing how caught they had been, how indoctrinated into a cultural system founded on unquestioned prejudice against other animals, on enslaving, exploiting, and eating them, as well as on consumption of the Earth's resources and the quest for money, it is not surprising that that awakening would come with a certain amount of zeal and a full-on commitment to activism. After all, to have your world turned upside down, to see that what you previously thought of as "normal" is in fact a lie, could certainly motivate a person to a life of action. Passion for compassion is a good thing and should be fostered and honored. But if you become too obsessed with thinking that it is up to you to save the world, you could easily become prideful and identify yourself alone as the one that must accomplish great goals.

Remember that Karma Yoga is the yoga of selfless service. As described in the Bhagavad Gita it can be truly practiced only by someone who is willing to relinquish the fruits of their actions. A karma yogi is one who acts selflessly for the greater good, is humble, and does not expect any reward, not even acknowledgment or appreciation from others for their good actions.

I am not saying that we should be apathetic and not aspire to live a committed life focused on uplifting the lives of others and making this world a better place. On the contrary, we should aspire to live in a way that enhances the lives of others and strive to abolish all forms of animal and Earth cruelty and selfish exploitation. I am only pointing out that if we neglect to remember God in our whirlwind of compassionate activism, we will lose sight of our ultimate goal and mire ourselves in undeserved fame, trapping us further in ignorance and ego identification. The solution is to devotionally offer every thought, word, and deed to God—striving to align with and love God more. Be humble and remember that the cause of everything is God. Don't try to do everything all by yourself. Let go and let God be the doer; be an instrument, a conduit.

When you can become a conduit for God's grace, then you "can-do-it." Allow God to work through you and give God credit for any accomplishments you may appear to have achieved. When others congratulate you, immediately defer to the real doer behind every action and proclaim, "All glories to God!" You could also be specific and insert your favorite name for God in the proclamation. But if you feel that invoking God's name out loud would cause too much alienation among the company you are with, then say the holy name silently. What's important is that you humbly remember God and are willing to defer to a power higher than your own limited, mortal self. In this way bhakti develops within you and you find interesting and effortless ways to incorporate your worship in everyday life.

Shyamdas would often quote from Rasakhan, one of his favorite bhakti poets, about effortless worship—how to balance bhakti with your everyday activities in the world:

Effortless Worship

Listen to everyone, but don't say a word.
In this manner,
remain in the world.

Perform your vows and practices with sincerity—
they will carry you across
the mind ocean.

Greet all without negativity, and
remain in the illumination of
devotional association.

Rasakhan says,
"Worship Govinda the way a village woman
balances a water jug upon her head,
with effortless concentration."*

*This is Shyamdas's translation of the poem "Effortless Worship," by Rasakhan, which appears on page 74 of The Poems of Rasakhan: Treasure House of Love, by Shyamdas, Krishna Kinkari, and David Haberman.

The Meaning of Life

yat karoshi yad ashnasi / yaj juhoshi dadasi yat
yat tapasyasi kaunteya / tat kurushva mad-arpanam
*Whatever you do, whatever you eat, whenever you give help to
another, even your own austerities (practices) and your hardships,
O son of Kunti,
do everything as an offering to Me.*
—Bhagavad Gita 9.27

The meaning of life is to drop all the meanness. When meanness drops away—what remains is kindness. To choose kindness over meanness is to live a meaningful life. The purpose of our lives is to remember who we really are—to remember our eternal connection to the supreme source—to God. This remembrance is called Self-realization, awakening, enlightenment, or Yoga. This awakening happens when the soul realizes that it is not just a separate skin-encapsulated ego, a mortal body and mind, but that it is the living residence of God.

To live a meaningful intentional life makes life worth living and gives our lives purpose. God is Love, and that great love lives within us as well as in each living being as the *atman*, the eternal soul. To awaken spiritually is to remember the presence of God in your life. In the Bhagavad Gita, Krishna suggests a simple practice to awaken this remembrance. He says: Remember Me in everything you do. Call My name. Before you eat or drink anything, offer it to Me first. Make every action an offering to Me, then I will be present in your life. This is how you consciously spiritualize your physical existence. Every moment that you engage in the remembrance of God causes your soul to awaken to *prema,* divine love, and with that great love all is possible.

The yogic scriptures say that the nature of God is *satchidananda*—truth, consciousness, and bliss—actually, *mostly* bliss. A blissful, happy person, one who shines with an inner divine light, is naturally kind to others. Their bliss radiates and overflows from the atman. When they interact with others it is a magnetic soul-to-soul attraction. They look for a deep connection with another. They are not mean-spirited, nasty, callous, miserly, judgmental, or self-centered. They are other-centered. They are compassionate and friendly, exuding warmheartedness toward everyone. Their very presence brings the promise of happiness to every situation, subtly reminding the rest of us that happiness is possible—that we too can remember who we really are.

Patanjali, in his Yoga Sutra, tells us that avidya is the biggest obstacle to this remembrance. Avidya means "ignorance," as in not knowing, or rather forgetting, the divine, blissful nature of your soul, being in denial that God lives within you. Avidya gives rise to other obstacles that keep the soul in bondage and makes the experience of true happiness difficult to feel or experience. According to Patanjali, the other obstacles to the remembrance of your true nature are: *asmita* (egoism, arrogance), *raga* (attachment to likes), *dvesha* (aversion to dislikes), and *abhinivesha* (fear of death). Yoga practices help us overcome these obstacles.

Yoga is a practical science that provides us with ways to interact with others and the world around us. The method gives us suggestions to improve our behavior toward others so as to free us from fear and suffering and liberate us from the wheel of *samsara* (repeated suffering), so there is no cause for future rebirth in the cycle. Practicing *ahimsa*, nonharming, is the first recommendation to the aspiring yogi who desires to discover how best to relate to others. The best way to behave is to refrain from harming them. This is one of the reasons a serious spiritual practitioner would choose a vegan diet, because to eat meat and dairy products is a mean thing to do, as it involves tremendous cruelty. Choosing a compassionate diet is a big step toward purifying ourselves from meanness and opening us up to the flow of kindness. Our actions are powerful. Whatever we do will come back to us. How we treat others will determine how we are treated.

There is nothing that we actually own—all we really have in life is our effect upon others. A happy person is a person who brings happiness to others. Because happiness dwells within us, when we engage in making others happy, we draw from that inner well, we pull it up to the surface and release it to benefit others. But in the process, we experience that happiness—it transforms us as it comes through us. It is God's gift moving through us. To live in a way that our lives enhance the lives of others and increase God's bliss in this world is to engage in the project of remembering who we really are—remembering our connection to God and the goodness of our eternal souls. We have two jobs in life—to remember God and to be kind to others—and they go hand in hand.

If we can be daring and courageous enough to let go of meanness, let go of complaining, blaming, and seeing ourselves as victims, then we have a real chance of feeling God's mercy. We embark renewed every moment on the adventure of discovering happiness. We live a blissful, delightful, meaningful life filled with purpose. *Jivanmukta* is the Sanskrit term used to describe a person who is living such a liberated life.

The Uninvited Guest

bodhi-rupam bodhi-sattvam bodhi-gamyam anamayam
parama-satyam parama-shantam parama-brahma parat-param

*It is of the form and essence of intelligence, and it is experienced through
intuition. It is pure, simple, and transcendental. It is ultimate reality,
ultimate truth, and ultimate tranquility, which is called Brahman.
It is smaller than the nucleus and greater than the greatest.*
—Shri Brahmananda Sarasvati

Lana Turner was a highly successful, glamorous Hollywood actress who achieved enduring movie stardom in a career as a leading lady. The story of how, as a beautiful sixteen-year-old high school student sitting at a soda fountain counter sipping a Coke, she was spotted by a talent scout and instantly signed to a film studio contract is show business legend. Afterward, thousands of wannabe actresses flocked to Hollywood and posed in various drugstores hoping to be noticed by a film director. Simply sitting pretty and waiting to be discovered may have worked for Lana Turner, but it won't work for an aspiring yogi who wants to attract the attention of God. You see, God is not like a Hollywood talent scout. You must invite God into your life—not wait coyly for God to notice you and send you an invitation. *You* must make the first move and open the door of your heart to God.

The cultivation of Divine intention is the most important activity anyone can engage in. The first step to knowing God, the prerequisite, is to have a desire to know God. The spiritual aspirant must desire God above all other desires. The aspirant must have a heart burning with love, a heart filled with *shubheccha*—one-pointed yearning to know God.

God is the true ground of being—existence itself, that which has always been, the eternal reality. God is Love. Love is the Truth—it is consciousness itself. Its nature is boundless and limitless joy. The ancient scriptures describe God as *satchidananda*—truth, consciousness, and, mostly, bliss. But if God is mostly bliss and is present everywhere, why then is there so much suffering in this world? Why is life filled with disappointment, exploitation, violence, disease, starvation, poverty, war, pollution, and death? Why isn't everyone overflowing with happiness? Has God forsaken us? Where is God when you need Him/Her/Them the most? These are commonly asked questions used to justify the nonexistence of God and the dull acceptance of life as mundane.

We blame God for the lack of love in our lives, all the while shutting our hearts to love. We have free will—we can decide whether to love or hate, to focus on the positive or dwell in the negative—the decision is always ours. Although God is always present everywhere in all beings and things, God is also hidden in every form and in every sound. God is always waiting at the doorstep of our hearts, but God will never step through that door as an uninvited guest. Because the nature of God is love, like love, God will never force Him or Herself upon us. Love is not aggressive; love is very polite. It is up to us to open the door of our hearts and invite love to step inside. God remains hidden unless we reach out and call to Him or to Her. Only then can we feel God's presence. This can be done through prayer, meditation, chanting mantras, singing the holy names of God, and even asana, but underlying all those *sadhanas* (conscious spiritual practices) must be the sincere intention to know God.

When God-realization is your intention, then any activity you engage in has the potential to invoke God, to reveal the presence of God. But simply performing asanas, or even meditation, without the conscious intention to know God will not yield Divine rewards. In fact, performing so-called yoga practices without a Divine intention could even take you far away from Yoga and bind you tighter to *avidya*—ignorance and delusion. But if yoga practices are done lovingly, with Yoga, enlightenment, and God-realization as the intention in your heart, then there is a good chance you will find that love has crossed the doorstep and become an invited and most welcome guest. You will even find that you can see that love in the hearts of others. The hidden Divinity becomes revealed in all forms, in all beings, in all things, and in all sounds, and the futility of negativity, sadness, and despair becomes completely obvious. You will no longer feel a need to ask, as Michael Franti sings, "Love, why did you have to go away, leave us here all alone. / To survive these crazy, crazy days."*—for you will know that it was actually *you* who went away, and knowing that, you can invite love back into your heart to stay.

*Lyrics from "Love, Why Did You Go Away," by Michael Franti, from the album *Everyone Deserves Music.*

Intention

The power of intention is a critical factor in all areas of life.
—Deepok Chopra

An aim that guides an action is an intention. To do something intentionally is to act on purpose. To act on purpose means that you act consciously. To pay attention is to act consciously, to act deliberately—to aim toward a goal. It is said that those who believe in coincidence aren't paying attention. Practicing yoga with a high intention is very important because what determines the outcome of any action is the underlying intention. Practicing asana with an elevated intention could make the difference between achieving mere gymnastic strength and flexibility or enlightenment.

I was just reading an online article about the growing popularity of yoga in America. It stated that twenty-two million people are practicing yoga! The top six reasons people practice yoga according to the statistics are to gain flexibility, to lose weight, to increase muscle tone, to relieve back pain, to look younger, and to reduce stress. In the millions of statistics gathered, no spiritual intention seems to have emerged. People weren't citing as their reason to practice yoga to become enlightened or to get closer to God or to better contribute to the happiness and freedom of others.

Yoga certainly doesn't care why you are practicing. Yoga will give you any result you intend if you do it long enough. What you are thinking about when you perform an action will determine the result of that action. You become what you contemplate. If you want yoga (the practice) to bring you to Yoga (the goal—enlightenment), then the intention underlying your practice must be Yoga. You are not going to achieve Yoga as your goal accidentally—you must desire it with your whole being.

Yoga means "enlightenment," or to link to the higher Self. Just as each of us must find our own way to relate to God, each of us must find our own way to articulate an elevated intention. Offering your practice to God is one way of establishing a high intention. For many that is a tall order. Offering your practice to your teacher is another. Wanting your teacher's enlightenment, you dedicate the efforts of your practice to that aim. That will give you a break from thinking about yourself. Offering your practice to a person you know is another way to establish a high intention, because other-centeredness takes us out of our egoic self-centeredness and awakens compassion, which is the cause of enlightenment. What is realized in the enlightened state is the Oneness of Being—where otherness disappears. So, if you can find a way to set an intention for your practice that helps you to get past your preoccupation with your small personality self, then you are on the path that will lead to Yoga.

In the Jivamukti Yoga tradition we often set the intention for a class by chanting *lokah samastah sukhino bhavantu* and then add the translation, "May all beings everywhere be happy and free and may the thoughts, words, and actions of my own life contribute in some way to that happiness and to that freedom for all." The Bhagavad Gita teaches that one who desires Yoga must renounce the fruits of their actions. This does not mean that you don't do things on purpose or set enlightenment as your goal. The wise practitioner has faith in God and knows that their main duty is to act with the utmost integrity, with the highest selfless intention, and at the same time to not be concerned with the outcome of their actions, but to leave that to God.

The Magic of Cooking

brahmarpanam brahma havir / brahmagnau brahmana hutam
brahmaiva tena gantavyam / brahma-karma-samadhina

*See God everywhere: God is the ladle; God also is the food; God is the
fire; God is the preparer; and God is the eater of the food.
God is the reason for eating and God is the goal to be reached.*
—Bhagavad Gita 4.24

I asked my first spiritual teacher, "How do I become enlightened?" And he said, "The first thing you need to do is to learn how to cook." I was incredulous at his response; it disappointed me. I couldn't embrace his advice seriously as it didn't seem "spiritual enough" for me. Cooking? I was an impatient, skinny girl who found disdain in eating and was trying to reduce her food to a minimum and eventually live on air. How did he think I could get into cooking? What could possibly be the point?

Over the years I've come to see the extraordinary wisdom of his advice. Traditionally, alchemists, magicians, and wizards used the kitchen as their laboratories to prepare potions. The cauldron or cooking pot was seen as a tool of magic that could heal and alter perception. Preparing and cooking food can be a magical act, a potent, alchemical process through which one form is transformed into another. Varied selected ingredients are deftly combined and subjected to the elements of water, fire, and air in just the right proportions, with just the right timing and with appropriate spells—consisting of good mental intentions. Everything in the kitchen must be clean. The atmosphere in the kitchen must be purified, with no gossip or small talk going on. All ingredients, both subtle and overt, must combine harmoniously to manifest a delicious meal that is first offered to God. Krishna says to Arjuna in the Bhagavad Gita that a yogi offers all their actions to God, including preparing, cooking, and eating food. The mindful, devotional ritual involved in the preparation, offering, and eating of the food transforms what could be a mundane activity into a religious practice that increases *bhava* (the ultimate good mood) and satisfies both body and soul.

A cookbook can be seen as a book of formulas for this magical process, complete with how-to instructions, suggestions, and advice, which, if followed with a cheerful heart and sense of adventure, could result in the most delightful culinary experience manifesting on the dinner table. Food prepared in this way can even produce a shift in perception of oneself and others, yielding hope and encouragement to move forward through life.

To make this magic happen most effectively, it is essential to bring consciousness to what we eat and how we prepare it. When we eat meat, eggs, and dairy products, we are buying into a cultural conditioning that has disconnected us from the natural intelligence of our bodies for the purpose of generating profits for the animal-user industries, we are destroying the health of our bodies and our environment, and we are participating in horrific enslavement, cruelty, exploitation, and slaughter of other animals, which will eventually, but inevitably, come back to us. When we adopt a vegan lifestyle, we bring respect and kindness into the kitchen and into our lives—respect and kindness to our bodies and to our relationships with others and the world. Yoga teaches that whatever we want in life we can have if we are willing to provide it for others first. If we want to be free, then depriving others of freedom and utilizing so many resources that others are left impoverished cannot lead us to our goal. Making kind choices when it comes to the food we eat is one of the most basic ways to begin to ensure our own happiness and freedom.

The most courageous act any of us can do at this time is to dare to care about others—other animals, the Earth, and all beings. To be more other-centered than self-centered is the first step to being God-centered. Choosing vegan ingredients and cooking them yourself with a pure intention will not only help you create tasty meals but will help you start your own radical movement of peaceful, joyful coexistence with all of life.

In the Mahabharata, Yudhishthira, the eldest of the Pandavas, discovers that all four of his brothers are apparently dead, having drunk poisonous water from a lake that is presided over by a *yaksha* (nature spirit) who has taken the form of a crane. The yaksha strikes up a deal with him. If he answers a series of questions correctly, the lives of his brothers will be restored. One of those questions is, "Who is truly happy?"

Yudhishthira answers, "One who cooks their own food."

The state of mind of the cook influences the food. If we eat food that someone else has cooked, we don't know what kind of intention was put into the preparation of the food. For example, food prepared in a restaurant. To most cooks it's a job—they are getting paid to prepare food for customers; they are not preparing offerings to God. While food is being prepared it is very susceptible to vibrational influences in the kitchen. When we eat that food, we pick up those vibrations. They enter into every cell and tissue of our bodies.

Our state of mind when we cook impacts the outcome of the food. If we are in a bad mood, it is best to stay out of the kitchen. To cultivate the highest intention and clear any negativity in our minds, praying or chanting mantra before we start to cook and while we are cooking can be helpful. To pray is to set a high intention, to implore the divine forces to come to our aid for a good and selfless end. As we approach the cooking process, we make sure that our minds and hearts are centered in an elevated intentional mood. When we participate in the practice of cooking as an act of worship—an offering to God—this purifies the whole experience, ridding our minds as well as the kitchen of subtle toxins, like selfishness, worry, anger, and impatience.

Such a purified atmosphere will lead to a cleaner kitchen, free from dirt on both the subtle and gross material level. It is for this reason that when I cook, I don't allow anyone else in the kitchen, because I know that we will most likely become engaged in talking—chatting about this or that—and this will affect the food and infuse the offering with unrelated intention. Cooking is a yogic practice like meditation. You must stay single-pointed in your focus. When you are sitting on your meditation mat, it is best not to be carrying on a conversation with your friend. The same holds true with cooking. For you to see cooking as a yogic practice, as a magical act, you must respect and treat it as such.

See the kitchen as part of God's abode, as a sacred space, as a doorway to enlightenment. The kitchen is a temple, and all the pots, pans, spices, grains, fruits, and vegetables, as well as the stove, spoons, knives, bowls, and plates, are all divine objects, full of consciousness, waiting to become part of the divine, alchemical process of creating a meal to be offered to God. Allow the fire of your soul to become part of the heating element that cooks the food.

When mantras and prayers are used as a blessing over food, the result is that the preparing of the meal, the one who is preparing and offering the meal, and the eating of the offered meal all become merged, and the experience exudes a magical potency that can bring one closer to the knowledge of the transcendental Divine Reality. Offered food is known in the yogic literature as *prasad,* which means "blessed food." The so-called simple act of preparing and eating food can be a spiritual experience if the intention is there. The yogic scriptures warn against eating food that has not been offered to God first as ingesting poison that will only fuel the disease of *avidya*. If we want to increase our humility and devotion to God, then using practices that diminish our identification with our ego are helpful to this aim. Most people eat to satisfy their own selfish appetite, while a yogi eats to remember God.

When every action we take is in remembrance of God, as an offering to God, then we are acting with the highest intention. The purpose of our life according to the spiritual traditions is to become God-realized, to remember God. When we dedicate every action to God, we come closer to that remembrance. The seemingly mundane actions of everyday life, like cooking and eating food, become transformed into prayer.

I would like to share with you my personal offering prayer, what I say before I eat:

Om lokah samastah sukhino bhavantu, Om shantih shantih shantih, Hari Om. Jai Shri Krishna! I offer this lovely meal to you, my beloved Lord Krishna, as an offering of my sincere devotion. [Then I describe the meal, naming each item that is being offered.] May you accept and be delighted with this offering. May we be blessed by your mercy in the form of this prasad. When we eat it may we be filled with your light, your love, and your joy and feel your presence inside our hearts as well as all around us, and because of that may we be able to enhance the lives of others, but most importantly may we increase your bliss in this world or in any other where you would want it to be increased. Jai Shri Krishna, Radhe Shyam, Shri Krishna sharanam mama [three times], Hari Om!

Here's one of my favorite recipes. It is easy to prepare, colorful, and nutritious, and it has everything—protein, omega-3 fatty acids, and chlorophyll—and, of course, it's delicious! It's great as a side dish and even as a paté, when, spread on bread or toast, it evokes the taste of an aged cheese.

Spirulina Millet

>1 cup uncooked millet
>2 cups water
>4 tablespoons flaxseed oil
>4 tablespoons powdered spirulina
>1 tablespoon soy sauce, tamari, or Braggs Liquid Aminos

Place the millet and the water in a medium pot over high heat and bring to a boil. Reduce the heat to low and simmer, covered, for 15 to 20 minutes, until most of the water is absorbed. Turn off the heat and let stand, covered, for 10 minutes. Transfer the cooked millet to a large bowl, and fluff with a fork. Add the flaxseed oil and, using a fork, mix well to coat the millet. Little by little add the spirulina, using the fork to mix. Add the soy sauce, mixing well until the millet is bright green.

Makes 2 to 4 servings

*Recommended Reading: Simple Recipes for Joy and Yoga and Veganism, both by Sharon Gannon.

Serene Intelligence

mayy eva mana adhatsva / mayi buddhim niveshaya
nivasishyasi mayy eva / ata urdhvam na samshayah

*Keep your mind on Me alone, your intellect on Me; thus,
you will dwell in Me from now on.*
—Bhagavad Gita 12.8

In this age of struggle known as the Kali Yuga, it can be very difficult to maintain a serene mind. Conflict between nations, conflict at work, conflict with enemies, conflict with friends, conflict at home, and even conflict within oneself can disturb one's mind and destroy one's happiness. It is common to be suspicious of someone who is happy and calm, thinking they must be ignorant, uneducated, living in a bubble, or even mentally ill, and that to be an intelligent, caring human being one must be disturbed and filled with anxiety—and further, that if you seek solace in spiritual practices, you are an escapist living in denial and burying your head in the sand.

Buddhim or *buddhi* means "intelligence." The highest and most important aspect of the intellect is its ability to grasp and understand the truth. Many people focus their minds on relative truth, that which is bound by the transient comings and goings of temporal existence, while the spiritual practitioner aims to comprehend or dwell in absolute truth. Absolute truth is knowledge of the supreme Self, or God. Krishna, in this verse from the Gita, tells Arjuna that if he is able to focus his intelligence on Him, on God, then without a doubt (*samshayah*), he will gain access to the heart of God. God is Love. God is Great. With great love all is possible. To know God is to love God, and this is the yogi's purpose.

To realize that purpose one must devote their whole being to that aim. As Patanjali advises in the twenty-third sutra of the first chapter of his Yoga Sutra, *Ishvara-pranidhanad va*, which means, "Offer your whole life (*pranidhanad*) to God (*Ishvara*) and absolutely (*va*) you will come to know God." Patanjali promises that success in Yoga will be absolutely guaranteed to the one who surrenders to God with loving devotion. The Sanskrit word *Ishvara* means "one's own choice of Lord." It is significant that Patanjali uses this word. He is not naming the Lord; he is leaving that up to the yogic practitioner to choose their own form of God to surrender to.

A blessed mind is a serene mind. *Chitta* means "the

content of the mind"—the mind's intelligence—and *prasad* means "blessed." Because so much of our anxiety seems to be caused by other people—they make us mad, they act in deceitful ways, they are unfair, they are unkind, and on and on—Patanjali tells us in sutra 1.33 that *chitta-prasadanam,* or "serenity," is our mind's innate state. Hey, that's good news! We should have faith in that truth and do all we can to protect that blessed condition from defilement. Patanjali gives some advice as to how to accomplish that: Be happy for those who are happy, compassionate for those who are unhappy, delighted for those who are virtuous, and indifferent to those who are wicked. If we choose to ignore this advice, we will become entrenched in our own negative emotions and be unable to remember God or devote ourselves to His service. Our intelligence will be consumed by anxiety, and we will be unable to enjoy anything in this world or in any other.

Finding fault with others is a sure way to disturb your mind and destroy your intelligence. When judgment of others arises, strive to let it go. Let God take care of things. If you remember that God is the supreme doer, you will be able to surrender and let go of your ego's tendency to try to control the outcome of a situation. Your job is to protect the serenity of your mind. As my teacher Shri Brahmananda would say, "Mind, your own business!" Follow the dictates of the *yamas* (restrictions) and relate to others with kindness, truthfulness, caring, respect, and generosity. Rid your mind of the diseases of pride, envy, anger, laziness, lust, greed, and gluttony. No one is saying this is an easy task and that we can accomplish it alone, so to provide help in times of need we would be wise to contemplate the practical suggestions given to us by holy beings and do our best to implement them.

Keeping good company, the practice of *satsang,* can assist the arising of serene intelligence through the study of the Self. *Svadhyaya* means "study of the Self." It is one of the five *niyamas* (observances) outlined by Patanjali. He suggests that svadhyaya be part of every yogi's *sadhana.* But because satsang—association with saints, sages, and enlightened beings in the flesh —is hard to come by these days, the next best thing is to immerse yourself in their holy teachings. Fortunately for us, these once-secret teachings are now readily available in the form of books and audio and video recordings. Reading holy books is a form of satsang. It is best to set aside some time every day to read a holy book or listen to elevated teachings.

Another meaning of intelligence I found in the dictionary is "secret information." I think Harirayaji, great-great-grandson of Vallabhacharya, thought of intelligence like this when he spoke about the importance of protecting the most secret information, your devotional *bhava*: "The age of struggle has arrived and can destroy everyone's intelligence. Be careful! This Kali Yuga can swindle you, so secure your devotional mind, guarding it like you would keep a precious jewel in a vault. Safeguard your bhava."*

In the Path of Grace, Vallabhacharya outlines practical means to protect one's chitta-prasadanam: Eat only prasad, food that has first been offered to God, and even water should be offered before drinking; keep good association (satsang); listen to and recite the stories of Shri Krishna (*katha*); sing His praises (*kirtan*); and always chant the refuge mantra, *Shri Krishna sharanam mama*.

As you can see, there are many sources of holy advice. It seems that if we were able to incorporate at least some of the precious jewels offered by blessed beings into our daily lives, we could experience a little serenity during these difficult times.

*Shiksha Patra, by Harirayaji, page 225, chapter 29, verse 1 commentary, translated by Shyamdas and Vallabhdas.

What Does Love Have to Do with It?

*sarva-bhuta-stham atmanam / sarva-bhutani chatmani
ikshate yoga-yuktatma / sarvatra sama-darshanah*
Through the practice of yoga,
the yogi sees the Divine Self in all beings and things
.—Bhagavad Gita 6.29

*The person who can sacrifice everything,
who is standing on the platform
and dropping everything, declaring, "God here I stand.
I will never misuse any power. Therefore come. Make me your
instrument." That person will have transfer of power
from the divine source.*
—Shri Brahmananda Sarasvati

I think when you look at the Yoga Sutra deeply enough, you discover that Patanjali's yoga is Bhakti Yoga, a devotional practice. Patanjali suggests that the most direct way to attain God-realization is to surrender yourself—body, breath, heart, mind, and soul—to God. Sutra twenty-three of the first chapter states, *Ishvara-pranidhanad va*, which means, "By giving your life and identity to God, you will come to know God." Surrendering to God is *bhakti*. Patanjali gives this directive as the most direct means to Yoga—to *samadhi*, the attainment of eternal happiness. We could refer to it as the one-step path. When you can unabashedly surrender all to God, your small, conditioned self, with all of its negative emotions, frustrations, and disappointments, is left behind, and you become an instrument for God's will. This is expressed in the prayer "Make me an instrument for Thy will; not mine but Thine be done; free me from anger, jealousy, and fear; fill my heart with joy and compassion." The nature of God is unconditional love.

So why is it so difficult for us to surrender to this eternal love? *Avidya* is the cause of our reluctance. Avidya is when we are ignorant of who we really are. Instead of remembering our true nature as connected to God, to eternal joy, we insist on a mistaken identity—one that revolves around our body, mind, and emotions, as well as the unresolved issues with others, frustrated ambitions, complaints, and blame that are housed in our body. Our body is the storehouse for our unresolved karmas—all of our unfinished business with others. All of our small-self concerns make up our individual self, or *jiva*, whereas our true Self, the *atman*, is eternal, bliss-filled—free from all suffering.

All great beings have eventually realized that only through surrendering to love is anything of real and lasting importance attained. The inspiring words of Dr. Martin Luther King, Jr., come to mind: "I have decided to stick with love. Hate is just too big of a burden to bear." It is difficult to have love for God when you are filled with hate, anger, disappointment, and blame toward others. Our negative karmas are intertwined with our relationships. For example, we get angry with someone, and it is our anger that disallows our experience of happiness, joy, or love. If we can't resolve our relationships with others, we have no chance of happiness and certainly no chance of relating to God. But how do we let go of hate and all the other negative emotions that afflict our souls so that we can surrender to love, to God?

Someone recently asked me if asana practice could be a bhakti practice. Asana practice *must be* a bhakti practice; it must be done with loving devotion to God if the ultimate aim is to be reached. The ultimate purpose of asana is to purify the body, to purify your negative karmas, so that you can open to Love, which is God. You cannot love God and hate God's creation. When we can love all beings and things, the veil of ignorance will be lifted, and we will be able to see clearly the Truth—the omnipresence of God. Through loving devotion, we will feel the presence of God within us. The more we remember that presence in our own heart, the more we will be able to recognize it all around us. When we see that divine presence in others, we will naturally feel an affinity toward them, which will give rise to kindness and friendliness.

Each asana is connected to a chakra and to specific karmic relationships. Asana practice can be a magical practice that can shift our perception of self and other. Through asanas we can resolve the negative karmas involved in our relationships. Asanas are a very exacting science in this respect: standing asanas provide us with opportunities to purify our body by resolving issues with our parents, home, and money; forward-bending with romantic, sexual, and creative partners; twists with those we have hurt; backbends with those we feel have hurt us; the shoulder stand series helps us resolve our relationship with ourself; bowing our head to the ground in child's seat helps to awaken respect and love for our teachers; and headstand provides us with access to the *sahasrara* chakra (the crown chakra) and our relationship to God.

If you practice asana to purify your body of the negative

emotions associated with your relationships and release your soul of the burden of ignorance, the gateway to true love and happiness will be available to you. As you practice asana, remember to think of those with whom you have unresolved issues and send them love and good wishes. Through regular practice this love will become more and more sincere. Love is the only power strong enough to resolve negative emotions. It is only through the act of love that we come to the realization of Love—the goal of Bhakti Yoga. Practice asana so that you will be able to love God more. There is no greater goal to strive for in this lifetime.

With Great Love All Is Possible

There is really no good reason to be unhappy.
—Jerry Garcia

Suffering, unhappiness, fear, and disappointment all seem to be the natural condition of life. Even when a bit of joy comes through, it seems so fleeting, and we feel betrayed when it evaporates. Early on in life we learn to blame others or the world in general for our disappointments. We habitually look for the downside, and in doing so mire ourselves in negativity. We even learn how to derive a sense of cynical pleasure from our suffering. From the point of view of an angel on a heavenly planet looking down upon this world, it might appear that the world loves suffering more than any pleasure. Is this truly the way it is? Is life equated with repeated suffering and unhappiness, punctuated with random pauses when we get something we want? Is there no alternative?

Life is what you make of it, it can go any number of ways, according to the condition of your own heart and mind. What you hold dear in your heart will be how the world appears to you. If you hold tight to unhappiness, the world will be an unhappy place. But if you have a sense of adventure and are willing to surrender to Love, then a multitude of possibilities await you. When you are willing to let go, renouncing everything that hinders your ability to feel happiness and allow love to work through you, you start to feel the presence of your own eternal soul. You let go of the heaviness of feeling that you must do everything yourself, along with all the other burdens you have been carrying. You let go of negativity—and instead offer yourself as an instrument for God's will, so that all your actions are purified through the radiance of the Divine working through you. The nature of God is Love. When you let go and let God, all of your actions become loving actions. Then, with this Great Love, all is possible. This is the formula. Let's investigate *how* it works, starting by breaking down each word to contemplate the meaning of this phrase.

With: *to align side by side together, diminishing a sense of separation from or opposition to.*
Great: maha, *big—bigger than a transient, mundane, ego-centered love, which can easily flip into its opposite when we are triggered by negative emotions.*

Love: *eternal, all encompassing, unconditional acceptance. In this context, love refers to Shri Krishna, to God, the Supreme Being, who is Love itself, boundless and limitless,* satchidananda: *truth (*sat*), consciousness (*chit*), and bliss (*ananda*)—in fact, mostly bliss, joy, and happiness. The name* Krishna *means "the most attractive." Love is the most attractive force in the universe. To love and be loved is the blissful pleasure we seek. All beings and even seemingly inanimate things gravitate to it. We may think and say that we want other things, material things like money or stuff or to be acknowledged, but ultimately, we are looking for love, even in those temporary diversions. In our hearts we all want to fall into love. We all want to experience the eternal joyful core of our being. Shri Krishna as Love itself is the ultimate destination.*
All: *without exception.*
Is Possible: *likely to happen.*

When you align with God, with Love itself, the possibilities are limitless. To surrender to God, to feel the divine presence in your eternal soul, is to let this great love work through you. This is the underlying request in the prayer "Make me an instrument for Thy will, not mine but Thine be done."

How do we know if our actions are being motivated by the *atman*, the divine soul within, or by our own ego? Are we doing God's work or being fooled by the ego? The ego is incapable of compassion, self-centered, and craves personal rewards, even if they come at the expense of others, while the soul is other-centered. We all have these two voices operating within us. Some refer to them as the good and bad angels or the light and darkness in our minds. Love and light is the essential nature of the soul, whereas ignorance and darkness are impositions.

George Harrison sang, "Beware of darkness / Watch out now, take care / Beware of the thoughts that linger / Winding up inside your head / The hopelessness around you / In the dead of night / Beware of sadness / It can hit you / It can hurt you / Make you sore and what is more / That is not what you are here for."*

The ego identifies with negativity. Even though we all know that love feels better than despair, we often tend to hold on with dear life to our negative feelings. Why? Out of habit—we have been accustomed, and for the most part unconsciously, to identify ourselves with our past negative karmas. "Oh, you know that is just how it always happens," "I can't seem to win for losing," "It's the story of my life!" But we must break through the chains, the habits of negativity, that bind us if we are to be free of suffering. If we insist on seeing ourselves as a victim, enlightenment, peace, and joy will forever be out of reach. If we want happiness, we must choose it over unhappiness. The choice is ours.

The presence of God, Love itself, is always within us as well as in the core of everyone and thing. But often it is buried over with so many layers of negativity that the experience of it is negated. We would be wise to remember that where there is fear, blame, jealousy, anger, hate, sadness, and despair, great love is hidden. Life can be viewed as an immense skyscape filled with possibilities. The blue sky, like true love, is the eternal, ultimate truth underlying all of existence. Love is eternal. Negative emotions are not permanent but can appear that way when we choose to hold on to them.

`Negative emotions are actually like dark clouds that obscure the radiance of the sun and turn the blue sky gray, but only temporarily. Because negativity is impermanent, those clouds will pass, so it is best to let them go and not get pulled into identifying with them. When we insist upon identifying with the negative dark clouds and deny the existence of the blue sky and the sun underneath, we maintain the shrouds of darkness within us, and that darkness permeates into our perception of ourselves and the world around us. The choice is ours.

Yoga teaches us how to exercise choice; how to embody eternal love by letting go of temporary dark, negative emotions. When we remember that divine love is always within us as the core of our being, we can even enjoy the darkness when it visits. For example, when sadness clouds our sky, we feel the sadness deeply, but experience it as a witness and don't get lost in its darkness. The samsaric world is a place of suffering. But there is a way out of this suffering. Love is the way out of samsara and into the discovery of our ultimate destiny. With great love all is possible, because love is the way to Love—the blue sky of infinite possibilities.

---

*Lyrics from "Beware of Darkness," by George Harrison, from the Album *All Things Must Pass.*

Krishna's Appearance

yada yada hi dharmasya / glanir bhavati bharata
abhyutthanam adharmasya / tadatmanam shrjamy aham
Whenever there is a decrease of righteousness in the world
and unrighteousness is on the rise, I will manifest Myself.
—Bhagavad Gita 4.7

Krishna explains in the Bhagavad Gita that whenever virtue declines and evil dominates, He, the omniscient, omnipotent, omnipresent divine Lord, will appear, manifesting Himself as an avatar, an embodied being. The word *avatar* comes from the Sanskrit *avatara,* meaning "to descend." It refers to the descent of a cosmic spiritual entity into an earthly physical form. It is Vishnu, the preserving aspect of the Divine, who most often appears as an avatar. Many people insist that since God is omnipresent, meaning all-pervading, God cannot be contained in one form, so God must be formless. But it is difficult to relate to nothing, so a form is helpful. An avatar can take a human form but is not restricted to only a human incarnation. An avatar appears in a form that resembles the people He/She wishes to help and in a form those people would most likely trust.

In the past Vishnu appeared on Earth as a fish, turtle, and a boar. Many millennia ago when the fish avatar, Matsya, appeared, humans had not yet arrived. The inhabitants of planet Earth were living in the water, and so He appeared as a water creature, a form that was most appropriate and relatable. Two aspects that facilitate relatability are name and form, known by the Sanskrit words *nama* (name) and *rupa* (form). To be able to recognize God as a person and to be able to call Him by name increases our ability to communicate and to develop a relationship with Him.

The form of an avatar may appear to be physical, made of flesh and blood, and have the look of a male or female animal or human, but that is only the outer appearance. The form of an avatar is totally spiritual. Unlike you or me, who reincarnate into physical forms that are products of our past karmas, an avatar is not compelled by their karmas to take birth. They are not subject to nature (*prakriti*) and the three *gunas*, the constituents of nature that govern existence. An avatar comes into the physical world to counteract evil and awaken souls to their true spiritual eternal identities. Over the eons of time, the outer look may take on many disguises, but the inner intention, the purpose for the avatar's appearance, is always to encourage and protect that which is good, for the sake of love, light, and balance. One such divine incarnation was Krishna, who appeared as a human being more than five thousand years ago. A unique aspect of the avatar Krishna is that He is the *avatari*, the complete manifestation; all the other incarnations are said to have been partial manifestations of Him, even Lord Vishnu.

As Krishna, He manifests a multifaceted nature. He tells Arjuna, in the Gita, that He appears according to how one understands and worships Him (BG 4.11). His different *lilas*, or plays, can be seen as roles He assumes for our sake. He shows how we can develop a relationship with God that could take various forms, according to our individual perception of God. Krishna's different relationships mirror the various relationships we encounter in our own lives. Those relationships could be seen as basically falling into the following four categories: master, child, friend, and lover. Master, or parental, is when we see ourselves as a child and relate to God as a father or a mother or as an authority figure, a master or boss we are working for.

In the religions that stemmed from Abraham—Islam, Judaism, and Christianity—God is most often seen in this way, as God Almighty, a master, a father figure, who demands obedience and punishes His children or servants if they break the rules. Christianity expands to allow us to also worship Jesus, the son of God, an avatar who took a human form to bring the message of love. Most Christians prefer to worship God in the form of Jesus dying on the cross. Although for a couple of weeks out of the year, God as a vulnerable baby—lying in a manger protected by his parents and a few caring sheep, cows, and donkeys—takes precedence.

The most popular form of God worshiped by millions of Hindus today, is Krishna as an adorable baby endowed with superpowers known by such names as Lalan, which means "little lad," or Gopal, "the friend of the cows." This kind of relationship with God allows the devotee to assume the role of a parent, who takes care of a child. This reversal of roles is unique in Hinduism and causes the devotee to be responsible for the happiness and well-being of God. Such a relationship can pull you out of self-centered concerns, which tend to propagate a victim mentality in which you blame God for your misfortunes or pray to Him for rewards or to fix things in your favor, much like the demands children make on their parents.

Relating to God as a friend, someone you share everything with, a close companion, promotes trust. With a friendly God as your companion, you are better able to accept what happens in life; you can even develop a sense of adventure, enabling you to explore new possibilities as you might with a friend. With a friend, you feel comfortable, because you know they like you as you are; they don't judge you. There is no need to impress them or win their approval. You feel stable, secure in your relationship, knowing they are on your side and are rooting for you. Friends are well-wishers of each other.

The relationship with God as your lover is thought to be the most exalted, because it encompasses the best of all the other types of relationships and brings the highest reward. The *gopis* (dairy maids) of Vrindavan personify this type of relationship. They experienced Krishna as their lover and knew themselves as His beloveds. Even when they first encounter Him as a one-day-old baby in a cradle in the house of His foster parents, Nanda and Yashoda, they see Him as their lover. This perception occurred on a transcendental level of reality not easily understood by ordinary people. The lover-beloved relationship is also found in some forms of Christianity. Catholic nuns, for example, become brides of Christ. Saint Teresa of Avila had this type of ecstatic liaison with Jesus—a deep mystical communing that satisfied her completely, leaving no room for any mundane, worldly, sensual pleasure.

To develop a relationship with anyone on any level, mundane or transcendental, knowing the name of the person is an important first step. For one thing, it allows you to call out and get their attention. When you name someone, you will then be able to see them, a picture of them will appear in your mind and perhaps eventually lead to your actually seeing them appear before you. In many respects what happens in ordinary life mirrors how things happen in the otherworldly realms. The name of God is the same as God; it is the vibrational form of God. Saying the name of God invokes or awakens the presence of God in your heart and mind and eventually in the world around you. The name Krishna means "that which is all attractive; that which is attracting you and has always attracted you; your innermost heart's desire." Krishna is love itself.

We all want to be loved and to love. It doesn't matter what religion you follow, or if you don't consider yourself religious or even spiritual, everyone has this desire toward love. The name

Krishna means "that which pulls you, attracts you to eternal reality, to love itself, boundless, limitless joy, which exists inside your own heart." The name of Krishna is the same as Krishna, so to say His name is to invoke the presence of divine love. The sound of His name will trigger a remembrance of love deep within you. The presence of that love has the power to dissolve ignorance, fear, doubt, anger, confusion, as well as all negative emotions, revealing your connection to your own eternal soul. Once that reconnection is made, your destiny is brought to light. It is akin to a rebirth. To remember your identity as an eternal soul is the purpose of your life. In the words of the great *bhakta* Shyamdas, "Your true wealth is the remembrance of who you really are."

To celebrate God's birthday is to celebrate our own potential for awakening to the light of love. Although God was never really born and never dies, nor does He reincarnate. In His avatar form He appears. The appearance day, or birthday of Shri Krishna, the eighth avatar of Lord Vishnu, the eighth child born to Vasudeva and Devaki, is known as Janmashtami (*janma*, "birth," plus *ashtami*, "eighth") and is celebrated on the dark moon of the eighth day of the eighth month. According to the Hindu lunar calendar this would be in the month of Shravana or Bhadrapada (which, corresponding to the Gregorian calendar, falls in August or September, depending on the moon's cycle). It is a big holiday, akin to Christmas, and is celebrated in India as well as in other parts of the world where Krishna devotees live. On Janmashtami, as well as the days preceding it, the stories of Krishna's birth are told. The account of His life has been written in the Shrimad Bhagavatam, a Sanskrit text comprising eighteen thousand verses spanning twelve hefty volumes. The tenth volume deals specifically with the stories of Krishna's life and His pastimes starting with the details of His birth, His appearance.

The setting is a prison in the bustling city of Mathura in the northern Indian state of Uttar Pradesh, around 3000 BC. It is the rainy season, and midnight. The rains have been heavy, the Yamuna River is restless and overflowing her banks, the sky is stormy. Vasudeva, the prince of the Yadava clan, and his pregnant wife, the princess Devaki, were put in prison on their wedding day by Devaki's brother, King Kamsa, after it was prophesized that his sister's eighth child would kill him. Devaki has already given birth in prison to seven children, who have all been killed by Kamsa shortly after delivery.

Now, with the assistance of only her husband, Vasudeva, she gives birth to their eighth child, a beautiful baby boy. They can see that this baby is special, glowing with an otherworldly luminosity. Their dingy cell is filled with light as if a thousand warm suns had descended into the dark and putrid dungeon. Devaki, overwhelmed, falls into a deep slumber. Vasudeva hears a divine voice telling him to take the newborn baby out of the dungeon and across the river to the village of Gokul and place him for safety in the home of the cowherd Nanda and his wife, Yashoda, who has just given birth to a baby girl. The voice instructs him to exchange the babies while Yashoda is sleeping and bring the baby girl back to this cell. The voice demands that he go now!

Vasudeva does not hesitate. He picks up his baby boy, and as the iron door miraculously swings open, walks out of the prison cell. He is surprised to see the guards slumped against the walls and on the floor sleeping as if under a spell. He makes his way undetected through the town to the banks of the river. The heavy rain has caused the river to swell, making it seem more like an ocean. He is determined to cross, so he lifts his baby above his head, holding him above the waves with his left hand, and starts wading across. Somehow, he will make it to the other side.

Vasudeva is having some difficulty navigating the turbulent water when he feels the presence of a creature swimming underneath him—a large serpent, his scaled body becomes a sort of boat that carries Vasudeva and baby Krishna above the waves. The serpent's cobra-like hood becomes an umbrella protecting them from the torrential rain. No ordinary mortal snake, he is Adishesha, a celestial being also known as Ananta, the endless one. After delivering father and son safely to the other side of the river, he waits, coiled patiently on the bank, for Vasudeva to return.

Vasudeva goes to Nanda and Yashoda's home, where everyone is sleeping soundly, and exchanges the babies. Although he is devastated by having to relinquish his precious, luminous boy, he feels that he is part of a master plan and summons the strength to follow through. Holding the quiet, smiling baby girl in his arms, he makes his way to the river, where the enormous serpent is waiting to carry them back across. After successfully accomplishing the safe transport of Vasudeva and the baby, Adishesha will later assume a human form as Balarama, Krishna's brother, and will be His companion for the duration of the avatar's stay on Earth.

Vasudeva walks back into the prison cell, undetected by the slumbering guards, and places the sleeping infant in the arms of Devaki, who immediately wakes up with a scream. Her voice breaks the spell that has immobilized the guards, and they rush into the cell to see the newborn. Kamsa is informed and is instantly standing in the cell demanding that Devaki give over the baby. She of course doesn't, and he violently pulls the baby out of her arms, intending to smash her head against the stone wall. As he hurls the baby girl toward the wall, she stops in midair, suspended above his head. She laughs and assumes her true transcendental form as the eight-armed goddess Durga, riding a lion and holding weapons in each resplendent hand. With an irresistible voice that resounds with heavenly musical cadence, she proclaims: "Kamsa, your slayer has already been born and is safe and well. There is nothing you can do. Your days on this Earth are numbered. You are destined to be killed by Him, who is the liberator of all souls." And with a delightful laugh she disappears!

Kamsa is dumbstruck. In a rare moment of mercy, he releases Vasudeva and Devaki from their imprisonment. Meanwhile, early the following morning, Yashoda awakes to find the adorable baby Krishna in her bed. She has no recollection of the baby girl born the night before, the memory having been deleted from her mind through celestial means. Nanda prepares to celebrate the arrival of their son and invites everyone around to come and meet the entrancing dark-skinned baby, who never cries but smiles and laughs all the time and in whose presence all hearts are uplifted. Nanda and Yashoda love Him as their child. Radha and the other young gopis come that first morning to meet Krishna. Their meeting is one of recognition. They see their deepest heart's desire before them and do not need anyone to tell them that Krishna is God. Seeing through His infant form, they know Him as the Supreme Lord, the capturer of their hearts.

Krishna spends His childhood in Gokul, frolicking in the forest, playing with His friends, the cows and other animals, as well as the young village children, including His favorite girlfriend, Radha. The deer, the birds, the insects, and other animals, flowers, trees, bushes, and clouds seek His companionship and all love Him and see Him as their best friend. Besides engaging in childlike activities, He also faces many challenges and is quite busy combating demons and performing miracles, like lifting up Govardhan Hill and balancing it on the tip of His little finger, using it like an umbrella to protect all the residents from a torrential rainstorm. When He is eleven years old, he goes to Mathura and kills King Kamsa, fulfilling one part of His plan to rid the world of evil. Although Kamsa's relationship with Krishna was not a loving one, as he saw Krishna as his enemy, when he dies at the hand of Krishna, he realizes Krishna as his supreme master and attains liberation. So even that kind of relationship brought something good in the end.

When He grows into a ravishing young teenager, Krishna expands His territory to include Vrindavan, a nearby town surrounded by forests. Thus begins the next phase of His avatar life, the Vrindavan lila, in which He enchants and enraptures. He plays the flute, dances, and makes dalliances with Radha and the other gopis in and around the forests of Vrindavan and along the beloved sandy banks of the river Yamuna. The gopis desire Him as their lover. As the lover of Radha and the gopis, Krishna exemplifies the most exalted of relationships that the soul can have with God, that of a lover.

The Shrimad Bhagavatam describes the appearance of Krishna in Vrindavan in detail. He is adorned with a peacock feather and His ears are graced with flowers and exotic ornaments. Krishna's clothes are the color of bright gold, which offset His dark blue-black skin. He wears a garland of fragrant forest wildflowers. His lotus-like feet appear splendid and cause the soil to tremble with delight wherever they touch the ground. He fills the holes of His flute with the honey nectar from His lips. As He walks through the forest, the trees bend their limbs low to bow to Him, while the clouds hover above to provide cooling shade. The birds harmonize with the melodies of His flute. He is followed by the deer and other forest animals, whose eyes never leave His form. He is surrounded by the gopis, who vie for His attention.

By the time Krishna reaches adulthood, He has fully established His transcendental presence in the hearts of Radha, the gopis, and all of the inhabitants of Vrindavan, and He has rid the land of His childhood of demons. It is time that He moves on. Along with His brother, Balarama, He travels to the island of Dwarka. He rules that kingdom and lives lavishly with His eight main queens—Rukmini, Jambavati, Satyabhama, Kalindi, Mitravinda, Nagnajiti, Bhadra, and Lakshmana—as well as the sixteen thousand other queens He rescued from the clutches of a demon. Each queen lives in her own palace.

During this time, Krishna meets and becomes friends with His cousins the five Pandava brothers, whose mother, Kunti, happens to be His aunt, as she is the sister of Vasudeva. Krishna has a special friendship with Arjuna, one of the brothers, who asks His help in fighting a great war. Krishna will not wield a weapon but agrees to side with the Pandavas and become Arjuna's chariot driver. Krishna does not let on to the Pandavas or anyone else involved in the battle that He knows the outcome of this war because He is the mastermind behind it. It figures in His plan as an avatar to annihilate evil. The corrupt greed-driven *kshatriya* (warrior caste) rulers of the world would meet on the battlefield and by the end most would have been killed. The war would end the reign of tyranny, and Yudhishthira, the son of Dharma, Arjuna's elder brother, would be established on the throne, where he would rule righteously and restore balance to the world, at least for a while.

But before the battle begins, there is an incident involving a conversation between the two friends that will become one of the most important philosophical discourses to affect human beings for centuries to come. Krishna and Arjuna are on the battlefield, Kurukshetra, before the sound of the conch triggers the beginning of the war. Arjuna is in a state of despair, overwhelmed with anguish at seeing the faces of the opposing armies, each made up of friends, relatives, and teachers anxious to fight one another. Arjuna experiences great trepidation and tells Krishna he can't fight. This provides Krishna with an opportunity to fulfill another part of His role as avatar—to give the famous discourse on Yoga that will become known in centuries to come as the Bhagavad Gita.

As Krishna appears differently to different people, He gives examples of the various relationships through which one can approach God. They reflect the same relationships that exist in "ordinary" life, but when they are used by the soul to know God, they become elevated and lose their mundane nature. Whether we cultivate a relationship with God as master, friend, child, lover, or even as an enemy, it will be a transformational experience, able to alter our perception of what is possible. As Shri Krishna gently reminds us, "Any way that you choose to approach Me, I will surely come to you."

II

OTHERS

When otherness disappears,
only love remains.

Someone to Talk To

*The key which unlocks the door to happiness in this world
is to let go of finding fault with others.*

I have friend who is a world-renowned rock star. Sting once said to me: "I put on a better show when someone I know and love is in the audience. It's only natural, isn't it?" I think he's right; it is natural. It is difficult to communicate to an empty room or a room with frowning or indifferent faces. Usually those who live as recluses don't have much chance for personal growth. Others who insist that they don't need anyone and would do what they do regardless, okay, what to say? Perhaps some people can do fine relating to nothing or to the impersonal, but for most of us, the development of our talents, intelligence, emotions, and spiritual awareness depends on our having others in our life to relate to.

A performer who steps on stage and faces a sea of indistinguishable faces, or a teacher who teaches a roomful of strangers, will do their best to find someone to address themselves to. That someone might be a person they are imagining is in the room—someone in their mind or in their heart. But it is more difficult to sustain yourself for a long time when you are speaking to an imaginary listener. It is always better to have a real flesh-and-blood person in front of you. One of my dearest friends, Shyamdas, who was a kirtan singer and spiritual teacher, often said to me, "When you sit in the front row, I can sing and teach better, because I see your face and it gives me instant feedback as to how I'm doing, and since I know you love me and are not finding fault with me, I am encouraged to go deeper."

Accomplished performers will tell you that they could not have gotten where they are without the support of at least one person in their life whom they knew without a doubt loved them unconditionally. Great teachers will relate similar accounts of how they were compelled to teach because of the unconditional love of one devotee who was always sitting nearby eager to hear what they had to say.

Good performers and distinguished teachers are endowed with gifts of communication. They can engage an audience because they are masters of communication. Someone who is good at communication not only knows how to speak, but also how to listen, how to pick up on someone's reactions to what they are saying and adjust their own delivery accordingly. A master communicator is a channel for nourishment from a cosmic source. In other words, the best communicators do not toot their own horns and demand that others listen to them because what they have to say is more important than anything else; actually, they aren't even interested in expressing themselves. Good communicators are servants who serve the yearning for happiness in the souls of others. They always ask themselves before they speak, "How will my words make people feel about themselves?" They then choose their words with care to bring about the most elevated experience.

Our time is precious, and we should not spend it in unhappy situations. This is a simple idea but often difficult to know how to put into practice. When you attend a performance or a lecture, if you want to get the most out of your experience, then as an audience member, your job should be to remain in rapt attention, hanging on every word or every note. Don't be a smug or passive observer, sitting in the audience waiting to be entertained. Instead, become like a puppeteer pulling their puppet's strings. If you want to have the most meaningful experience, you should actively participate in making it so. Project love and support directly to the person before you. See them as a holy, intelligent, and profound being. Know that you have that much power, because you have the power of love in your heart. It is the divine power of love, and it is our true nature, the nature of our *atman*, our soul.

All is God, there is nothing but God, and everything comes from God. Any bliss that we experience in this material world is a reflection of divine bliss. Love is the magical elixir that has the power to draw the sweetest essence from our hearts. God is Love. God is the only real doer. God's nature is bliss-filled. God is attracted to and by love. God loves the one who loves God. God enjoys being with *bhaktas* (those who love, cherish, and are devoted to God). Because bhaktas recognize divine bliss, their attraction to the Supreme personality causes bliss to expand and be drawn forth out of God's cosmic body to merge with the bliss of the devotees' hearts, resulting in a full-on bliss-filled experience. May all our encounters with others be magically transformed into bliss-filled experiences through the power of love being drawn from us outward into the world. Magic, after all, is a shift in perception, and that shift is waiting within all of us to happen.

Union Through Others

The world you see outside of you will always be a reflection of what you have inside of you.
—Cory Booker, US senator

The state of *Yoga*, or union, is when the individual self reunites with the infinite, undifferentiated, eternal Self. Yoga has been described as *samadhi*, or blissful ecstasy, because it is such a relief to finally reconnect with your whole being after so many lifetimes of wandering in the illusionary world of disconnection. The methods of yoga help to bring together that which appears to be separate.

Enlightenment is the goal of all yoga practices. Perceiving others—that is, perceiving ourselves as separate from others—is the biggest obstacle to enlightenment. For a yoga practice to work, it must address how to dissolve the illusion of otherness in our lives. Yoga teaches us that in truth there is only oneness; others are a projection coming from our own minds, from our own past *karmas* (actions). The practices help us to purify our karmas, which involve our relationships with others, so that we may perceive the Oneness of Being.

In the Yoga Sutra, the sage Patanjali shares a few practices that may bring us closer to union. He is speaking to those who are still seeing others but who are interested in dissolving the disconnection between self and other.

Patanjali suggests that if you are still seeing others and not the divine Oneness of Being, then: 1) Don't hurt them (*ahimsa*); 2) Don't lie to them (*satya*); 3) Don't steal from them (*asteya*); 4) Don't manipulate them sexually (*brahmacharya*); and 5) Don't be greedy, taking so much that you impoverish them (*aparigraha*). He gives these directives in the second chapter, the chapter on practice, and he refers to them as the five *yamas*—five ways to restrict your behavior in regard to the others you may encounter in your life.

On an immediate practical level, how we treat others will be reflected in our own experience of life. The others in our lives reflect us. If we ourselves desire happiness and liberation from suffering, then our relationships with all beings and things should be mutually beneficial. No true or lasting happiness can come from causing unhappiness to others. No true or lasting freedom can come from depriving others of their freedom.

Patanjali tells us what we can expect to happen when we

become established in the practices of the five yamas. When we stop harming others, others will cease to harm us. When we practice telling the truth, we will be listened to. When we stop stealing from others, prosperity will come to us. When we treat others respectfully and don't manipulate them sexually, we will enjoy good health and vitality. And when we let go of tendencies toward greed, we will come to know the reason we were born, and with that our destiny will be revealed to us.

If we want to know who we are, it will have to start with how willing we are to look at the way we are treating others, because how we treat others determines how others treat us; how others treat us determines how we see ourselves; and how we see ourselves determines who we are.

The simple but powerful gesture of placing our two hands together in front of our hearts in a prayer position (*anjali mudra*) when we greet another expresses reverence. Two hands coming together: the left and the right—representing the Sun and the Moon, the *ha* and the *tha*, the self and the other. This humble gesture speaks without words of our willingness to see past outer differences and acknowledge the soul of the other.

Identity

tat tvam asi
That thou art, or you are that.
—Chandogya Upanishad

To see yourself in others, in all others, to see so deeply that otherness disappears—when that happens, only One remains and *that* is Love. You are *that*. In the words of the Chandogya Upanishad: *tat tvam asi*. This is what it means to be enlightened. An enlightened being is one. One what? One who has dropped the pretense of self, one who does not see themself as separate from other selves. One who has lost themself in Love, lost themself in Oneness. Lost themself in God. One who has found themself in the *atman*. My goodness, how to get there?

Two important practices that can bring about a shift in identity away from the small self to the enlightened Self are remembering God and being kind to others. A person is either actively seeking knowledge of the small, "lowercase," self (*jiva-jnana*) or knowledge of the "uppercase" Self (*atma-jnana*). The Sanskrit term *jiva* refers to the individual self, *atman* refers to the eternal soul, the cosmic Self, and *jnana* means "knowledge." To seek *atma-jnana* is to seek for who we really are beyond our individual body, mind, and personality. As we do, we awaken to the presence of God and let go of the cravings of I, me, and mine. We feel more at peace and able to expand that peace. Our hearts become more embraceable as our ability to love expands. When we become more other-centered rather than self-centered, we naturally become kinder to others. Through kindness we will begin to remember God.

Yoga teaches that to realize the eternal Self, we must first come to terms with our seemingly individual self, and that means having a tranquil mind and becoming comfortable in our own skin, with who we are as a person, with our relationships with others and the experiences of our life. No one can escape their destiny. A person must acknowledge the karmic seeds they have planted in the past and when they come to fruition do their best to work through the ripening process.

The Bhagavad Gita is a story of the necessity of doing our duty, as well as a manual on how to reshape our destiny by planting the right kinds of seeds to help us evolve and eventually be liberated from the wheel of *samsara* and the illusion of the separate egoic self. In the Gita, Krishna instructs Arjuna to do his work but at the same time to think of God; in that way our karmas become purified, as selfish motivation is overwhelmed by selfless action. Misidentification (*avidya*) is cleansed from our souls, and the atman, the presence of God, is revealed in our hearts as well as in the hearts of others.

Before we can awaken and know the divine Self, we must have knowledge of the small self—jiva-jnana. Everything in our lives revolves around identity. We spend the first part of our lives trying to find an identity and the rest of our lives doing our best to defend that identity. We are attracted to certain things, people, situations, music, books, food, clothing, lifestyles, etc., because these fit in with how we would like to see ourselves and how we would like others to see us. How can we avoid becoming trapped in the prison of our identity, disconnected from the eternal essence that feeds and connects us all as one complex cosmic entity?

The yoga teachings are quite clear about the importance of bringing past actions to completion before we can realize our true identity. To resolve an action is to bring it back to its original nature, and love is the original nature of all things. The practice of vinyasa recognizes that in order to bring a heightened level of consciousness into our lives we must be able to be fully present and embrace each moment as it is and let it go without regret, holding on, or apologizing; in this way we free ourselves to be present for the next moment, and the moment after that. Living our life with the intention of contributing to the happiness of others will help us break the habit of doing things unconsciously, which often results in regret and guilt.

In the twelfth chapter of the Bhagavad Gita, Krishna tells us that the one He holds dear has a serene mind and naturally looks to the welfare of all other creatures and promises that that one will come to remember Him.

sanniyamyendriya-gramam / sarvatra sama-buddhaya
te prapnuvanti mam eva / sarva-bhuta-hite ratah
—Bhagavad Gita 12.4

Extending kindness to others as Krishna suggests also includes caring for all animals, not just human beings: eating a vegan diet; being more ecologically orientated (for example, not wasting water or paper); going out of our way to make others more comfortable, listen to them, speak well of them, not engage in gossip; feed the wild birds and other animal neighbors; if we live with a cat or dog, feeding them good, nutritious food that we cook for them ourselves; doing things for others anonymously so as not to inflate our egos by expecting acknowledgment. When we care for others, our own obsession with ourself begins to diminish.

There are many ways we can facilitate the remembrance of God while we are engaged in our ordinary life. For example, chanting God's name out loud or silently while we cook or clean the house; saying a prayer, such as, "Not my will, but Thy will, be done," before we take any action; meditating to connect to God; listening to or reading spiritual texts such as the Bhagavad Gita, Patanjali's Yoga Sutra, the Narada Bhakti Sutras, the Shrimad Bhagavatam, Bible, or Koran, etc., or biographies of saints that put us in a good mood by increasing our *bhava* for divine subjects; seeking out the company of others who are interested in elevated topics and engaging in uplifting conversation with them. All of these types of practices can bring serenity to our minds, take us out of our small, mundane self and put us in touch with our higher potential.

In the Yoga Sutra, Patanjali suggests that if we offer ourselves to God, our success will be assured: *Ishvara-pranidhanad va* (PYS 1.23). When we ask to be made an instrument for God's will, we relinquish our "own" will. Becoming a divine instrument is to identify with the atman. A *jivanmukta* lives in the world and might appear to be a normal person—a separate individual—but in fact lives liberated from that separateness, because they don't identify with it, but rather with the atman. The key to this shift in identification is to strive to become more other-centered, to awaken compassion, which will bring the clarity needed to see through otherness. With this clarity we will recognize God's presence in others and in turn feel it in ourselves.

If we live to enhance the lives of others, by doing our best to contribute to their happiness and freedom, then eventually but inevitably there will be a shift in our perception of ourselves and others. We will begin to see in a more expansive light and perhaps get a glimpse of who we really are—*tat tvam asi*—and that is when the magic begins. Or as Bob Dylan might advise, "So when you see your neighbor carryin' somethin' / Help him with his load / And don't go mistaking Paradise / For that home across the road."*

*Lyrics from "The Ballad of Frankie Lee and Judas Priest," by Bob Dylan, from the album *John Wesley Harding*.

With That Moon Language

Admit something:
Everyone you see, you say to them, "Love me."
Of course, you do not do this out loud, otherwise
Someone would call the cops.
Still, though, think about this, this great pull in us to connect.
Why not become the one who lives with a
Full moon in each eye that is always saying,
With that sweet moon language, what every other eye in
This world is dying to hear?
—Hafiz

What you desire most for yourself, why not provide it for others first? Life offers us infinite opportunities to see ourselves in others. When we look into the eyes of another, see our reflection, and ask of that other to "love me," we have ventured into the realm of Self. To get a secure footing into that, we must leave our selfishness and self-loathing behind. Love is not something we can do or something we can give; it is all-inclusive. We cannot love anyone or anything—Love is too big to be controlled like that by us. Love has nobody, nobody has Love. We can only *be* Love itself.

When we take the time to sit with someone quietly, both of us being still and close enough so that we can see into each other's eyes, we will see ourself reflected. We mirror one another. It takes a certain amount of daring to do such a thing—it is so intimate. Even with someone we know and consider a friend, for most of us it is awkward to get that close. Of course, there are times and occasions when this type of intimacy is accepted. It most often happens with mothers and their babies; when lovers are first getting to know each other they often spend long periods of time in this type of reflective moonglow. But it certainly isn't a common daily practice among most of us. We are either too busy to be bothered with looking that closely at the others in our lives, or afraid of the potential consequences, and instead seek ways to avoid interaction with most people we encounter during our day, our week, or our entire lives. Has it always been like this? Is this a natural way to live?

Some people say that there are only two kinds of beings in the world—predator and prey. They will draw parallels with wild animals and point out that carnivores never look directly into the eyes of anyone unless it is to challenge them to a fight or to hypnotize and frighten another animal they intend to eat.

50

Vegetarian animals on the other hand tend to have large eyes and are constantly on the lookout for enemies. Many human beings identify themselves as predators because they insist it is the better option. I don't agree with that, but I will say that if we acknowledge it as a fact for some people, it may help us begin to understand the fear and paranoia that permeate our social interactions with others. Cultural conditioning can lie deep, but the good news is that it is learned and so it can be unlearned.

Philosopher Ken Wilber says that, generally speaking, men and women are biologically under the influence of two very different chemicals and that over many thousands of years, our patriarchal-, meat-eating-, military-power-based culture has utilized this to advance its exploitation. Testosterone basically, at its worst, expresses itself as sexual aggression, manipulation, and violence. The counter influence is oxytocin, a hormone that induces strong feelings of attachment, nurturing, holding, and touching. Although most of us (at least those who are reading this essay) don't live in a world where we are constantly being chased by an aggressor and have to run for our lives or turn and engage in combat, many men and women behave as if this were the case. But as spiritual practitioners looking to evolve, we investigate other modes of relating to one another and in doing so we uncover more possibilities within ourselves. Perhaps yoga allows a man to become more of a shaman, tuning into his feminine side and thereby discovering less competitive, aggressive ways to relate to others.

The word *shaman* is composed of *sha*, which means "she," and *man,* which means "mind." Many shamans are healers who can walk between worlds and shape-shift. For a man to be able to assume the position of a shaman he has to expand beyond the testosterone-powered "normal" male gender role and incorporate a feminine way of thinking and being. Thus his mind becomes a she-mind or a she-man, a shaman, enabling him to perceive the world more *feelingly* and so relate more sensitively. A shaman could be seen as a yogi—one who has joined (yoked) their male and female aspects into one central unified whole. Perhaps for women, yoga can help to develop more fearlessness and confidence without compromising nurturing. Yoga can help us all feel more relaxed and at ease with ourselves and others.

A spiritual seeker is someone who is looking to find themself. If we want to embark on the spiritual adventure of daring to look into the eyes of another and feel comfortable about it, without having any ulterior motive other than pure perception of being, we can start by practicing with kindred spirits—other yoga practitioners—in the safe and sanctified space of the yoga classroom, a place put aside for the investigation of such matters. The quest is this: To see ourself in others—to look so deeply that otherness disappears—leaving only the Self, Love itSelf.

The Moon orbits around the Earth and pulls us—the ocean tides reflect this pull of the Moon. Hafiz says, in the poem at the beginning of this essay, "Think about this, this great pull in us to connect." An intelligent person is someone who can make connections. We increase our intelligence as we stretch our minds and hearts to connect and communicate with others. As the Moon reflects the Sun's light, we all reflect one another—the whole world is a mirror. As mirrors that can be set up in such a way as to reflect each other, providing a visual experience of endlessness, the eyes of the other can reflect back the infinite possibilities of life. Ultimately, no matter how you look at it, all the reflections come back eventually to the perceiver—as the seer sees, so the seen is seen.

Yoga philosophy states that the world is a projection coming from our own mind—for better or for worse. If we have negative thoughts in our mind, we see negativity in others. We could remember that harboring negative thoughts is optional and choose instead to embrace positive ones, and then these positive thoughts would radiate from us into the world and affect all the other beings that we "see." Eventually through this practice we will realize that there are no others—and it is at this point that Self-realization arises.

We all want to be loved, we want people to like us, we want to be acknowledged, and we don't want to be ignored or made to feel insignificant. A yogi knows this truth—that all beings matter, and when we dare to care, dare to reach out toward another for the sake of pure love, with that "sweet moon language," it transforms ourself and the other.

Recommended Reading:
• *Love Poems from God,* translated by Daniel Ladinsky. This book includes the Hafiz poem "With That Moon Language," as well as poems by other mystical poets.
• *The Gift, The Subject Tonight Is Love,* and *I Heard God Laughing,* all by Hafiz and translated by Daniel Ladinsky.
• *A Brief History of Everything,* by Ken Wilber.
• *A Garden of Forest Flowers,* by Swami Nirmalananda

Progressing Toward Kindness

sanniyamyendriya-gramam / sarvatra sama-buddhayah
te prapnuvanti mam eva / sarva-bhuta-hite ratah
Those who are able to control their senses, have equanimity of mind,
and rejoice in contributing to the welfare of all creatures are dear to Me.
—Bhagavad Gita 12.4

We all sometimes fall into negativity and despair, particularly when the news is filled with tragedies like school shootings and senseless wars, harsh political rhetoric, and the atrocities we humans are committing against ourselves, other animals, the oceans, forests, and the body of the planet herself, which are bringing us all closer and closer to an environmental, physiological, and psychological collapse. From one perspective, things seem to be getting worse and worse. But is that the only perspective, and do we have the power to change it?

We can look to popular culture to get a picture of what is in our psyches—what fears and longings lie beneath the surface of our consciousness. For example, if you read eighteenth and nineteenth-century literature, you will find a lot of class struggle and emotional unfulfillment. Think of the novels of Charles Dickens for example. The characters are mostly dissatisfied and feel victimized by society. But there is little, if any, mention of the real slaves of the system—the horses who are harnessed to the carriages pulling human beings to this party or that, or the cows who are tied up in the back alleys of tenement buildings anemically producing blue-tinged milk. The animals appear only as extras, insignificant to the important stories that are being enacted between human beings.

When I was growing up in the 1950s, war and science fiction, monster and alien films were very popular—*The Killer Shrews, Earth vs. the Spider, Godzilla, Creature from the Black Lagoon,* and *The Body Snatchers.* In *The Incredible Shrinking Man,* the hero has been shrunk down to half an inch and must battle a "giant" spider with a sewing needle. Many, if not most, of the films of that era reveal a deep mistrust of Nature and a feeling of human fragility and vulnerability. The protagonist resorts to annihilation and conquering of the invading enemy, rather than communication, collaboration, or finding ways to understand and get along. The narrative is about "us against them," with us always winning in the end through violent means. In *King Kong,* the giant gorilla climbs the Empire State Building, holding the human woman with whom he has fallen in love. He gently places her on a ledge for safety while military war planes come out in force and shoot him down. In *Them*, a government task force with an arsenal of machine guns and flamethrowers annihilates the giant ants threatening to devour all the human inhabitants of Los Angeles.

More recently, films like *The Matrix*, which asks questions about the nature of reality, and *Cloud Atlas*, which explores the concepts of karma and reincarnation, introduce characters who are empowered to work within the reality they know to solve problems or improve their situations. There is an increase in screenplays that portray individuals conquering themselves, rather than the world or beings from other worlds. Films that inspire empathy and compassion and show the good results that come from being kind and understanding of others are on the rise, bridging the perceptual chasm between self and other. Think of the Steven Spielberg movie *E.T. the Extra-Terrestrial*, in which a young child befriends an alien. In the twenty-first century we are seeing more and more stories entering into the mainstream that emphasize kindness as the key to overcoming prejudices based on race and gender—movies like *Hidden Figures* and *Moonlight*, for example.

It is inconceivable that works like these would have been understood and accepted in the 1950s; it would have been over people's heads. In this regard I would say we are making good progress. Hopefully, after these human rights are addressed, we will further evolve to address animal rights and seriously acknowledge speciesism as the ugly debilitating prejudice it is. When this happens, it will signal a cultural milestone for humanity. Perhaps we will finally understand what it means to be human—to be humble, close to the earth, willing to work together with other species to maintain a vibrant environment where all forms of life can thrive. Kindness is the key to inclusiveness.

Often when I talk about animal rights, people ask me, "Why care so much about animal abuse when there is so much human abuse in our world?" I care about animal abuse because we are all animals, and I choose not to be locked into the prejudicial system that proclaims this animal to be more worthy than that animal. Human beings are animals too—that is a biological fact—and the systematic and unquestioned abuse of nonhuman animals creates a cultural environment in which abuse is accepted, which in turn results in the abuse of humans.

If we want to solve a problem, it is best to look for the root of it and address that; otherwise, our efforts will be limited to the surface and the problem will inevitably recur. As my holy teacher Swami Nirmalananda said: "This picking and choosing who to love promotes schisms and prejudices and causes us to feel separate from all of life. We should be more cosmopolitan and feel ourselves as a citizen of the cosmos—a friend to all." Kindness can lead us in that direction.

We all want to be successful. Yoga teaches that success comes to those who are friendly and kind to others. For Yoga to happen—for us to experience freedom from the urge to exploit, dominate, and annihilate others, for us to experience the joy of "needing nothing and feeling whole," as Shri Brahmananda Sarasvati described the state of Yoga—we must explore kindness. We cannot remain tight and miserly, doling out kindness only to those we like or are like us, or to those who will give us something in return. When we begin to shed the limits of our kindness, we begin to understand our potential for being the limitless beings we really are. This is truly the great adventure: To break the self-centered chains that bind our hearts and begin to see the other as our own self. This equanimity of mind will lead to God-realization.

Love Everybody and Tell the Truth

vitarka-badhane pratipaksha bhavanam
When disturbed by disturbing thoughts, think of the opposite.
—Patanjali's Yoga Sutra 2.33

Ram Dass asked his guru, Neem Karoli Baba, known affectionately as Maharajji, about enlightenment: "What can I do to get enlightened?" Maharajji replied, "Love everybody and tell the truth." So, Ram Dass, taking what his guru said in earnest, tried this practice. But after a couple of days, he came back to Maharajji and said, "I tried it and found out that the truth is that I don't love everybody."

The kind of truth Ram Dass was talking about is the lie— the lie that lies between you and your enlightenment: identifying with your negative emotions, believing that your anger, disappointment, hatred, aversion, or sadness is the truth. Even making statements like, "I am angry" or "I am disappointed" or "I am sad" is a way of convincing ourselves—lying to ourselves— about who we really are. Most of us do not have training that helps us understand where negative emotions come from or that we can choose to feel them or not—that they are an option, not a given. Nonetheless, because of our conditioning and our own reinforcement of that conditioning through habit, when they *do* arise within us, we actually *do* feel them, and at that moment they *do* seem pretty real. Their presence is so strong that it is not easy to ignore them. Just as when a person is aggressively coming at us, the classic bully, for example, it is difficult to ignore them and walk away, because we get caught in the web of their energetic vibrations—we feel their anger and it makes us feel afraid. So, as bullies identify with a negative emotion like anger, we, while in their presence, can also identify with a negative emotion like anger or fear. Emotions can be contagious and can influence the way others feel about themselves.

Why are negative emotions so popular? Because they feel satisfying—at least temporarily, because they make you feel alive. This is one reason they can become so addictive. You become addicted to anger because it pumps you up. There is a corresponding chemical release of adrenaline—your heart beats faster, blood rushes through your veins, and you feel empowered. Sounds good, eh? Well not for someone who is searching for enlightenment, the realization of the Oneness of Being, because that empowerment also feeds your sense of isolation as it gives validity to your separateness. Negative emotions always affect you psychologically by intensifying feelings of separateness and isolation from others.

Most of us are brought up to feel disempowered: "It's me against them," "I need all the strength I can get to fight against the odds—the whole world is against me." And as with most addictions we build up tolerance, so that we need more and more stimulation to feel the rush—it is a downward-pulling spiral. Anger can lead to disappointment, which can lead to frustration, which can lead to sadness, which can lead to depression, and on and on it goes. With each downward spiraling we train our mind, our body, and our endocrine and nervous systems to meet the requirements of our craving, and eventually we are caught in a dark place of confusion, self-absorption, and self-loathing—the antithesis of enlightened awareness, which is typified by freedom, serenity, and ease of being.

Anger and other negative emotions may feel right and justified at the time, but Ram Dass eventually realized, as he continued to practice what his guru had suggested, that "it was more interesting to be free than it was to be right."

Spiritual practice is about letting the sunshine in—or shedding some light into the darkness—or expanding that which before appeared narrow and constricting. This growing into wholeness will be difficult as new ways of reacting to situations are tried—growing pains tend to be painful. The goal of spiritual practice is mind expansion, or cosmic consciousness, where your sense of self becomes so large that it incorporates all of existence —dissolving boundaries between self and other. Deep in our hearts we all basically want the same thing. It doesn't matter who we are. We may be temporarily in the body of a human being, or a dog, a cat, a bird, or a cow, but beyond outer differences, all souls yearn for love.

To start to see yourself in others cultivates positive emotions like friendliness and compassion. This will lead to tolerance and the ability to recognize commonality rather than differences, which will bring you to love—the experience of connection. Love will bring us to the truth—the real truth that we are One.

Satsang

sat-sangatve nissangatvam nissangatve nirmohatvam
nirmohatve nishchala-tattvam nishchala-tattve jivanmuktih
bhaja govindam bhaja govindam bhaja govindam mudha-mate
—Shri Adi Shankaracharya, from "Charpata Panjarika"

"Good and virtuous company gives rise to nonattachment. From nonattachment comes freedom from delusion. With freedom from delusion, one feels the changeless reality. Experiencing that changeless reality, one attains liberation in this life. I-AM is the ocean of awareness. Realizing this, one feels, 'I am not the body and mind, although I have a body and mind.' Realize Govinda, realize Govinda, realize Govinda in your heart, O wise one!" This is Shri Brahmananda Sarasvati's inspired translation of one verse from Shankaracharya's poem.

The verse is inspiring on many levels: it suggests that through good association—attaching yourself to others who believe that awakening is possible—your awakening will be possible. When you associate with others who are focused on enlightenment, then your own progress toward that goal will not only be encouraged but also assured. You *can* live as a liberated soul—a *jivanmukta*. Yes, enlightenment is a possibility for you in this lifetime! God dwells in your heart as your own self—so let your heart sing. *Bhaja* means "to sing and celebrate the glories of God," and as you do you are able to enter your own heart and come closer to your beloved. This adventure is only for the wise ones, not for those who are deluded and still feel their body and mind is separate from the cosmic unchanging reality-body of the Divine.

Keeping good company, or *satsang*, can be considered a practice of *shaucha*, one of the *niyamas* that Patanjali gives as a means to hasten awakening, or the experience of Yoga. *Shaucha* means "cleanliness." To keep yourself and your surroundings clean is one way to practice shaucha. But shaucha means more than physical cleanliness. It also means cleanliness of mind and heart. To a yogi, the only real dirt is the dirt of *avidya*, or ignorance of the true Self. When you are ignorant, you are deluded and mistake who you are for your temporary body and mind. Delusion prevents you from recognizing your Divine Self and so you are also unable to see the Divine in others.

One of the best ways to clean your mind is to be careful about what you expose it to. The mind is like a clear crystal. A crystal will take on the color of whatever it is near—it will reflect its surrounding environment. In the same way your mind is colored by what you expose it to. If you hang out with criminals, you will most likely become a criminal yourself and land in jail. But it can work in more subtle ways than that. For example, if you watch television or movies or read magazines or books with disturbing content—violence and/or gratuitous sex—your mind and your thoughts will become tainted by those images, and your life will thereafter be negatively affected. But if you instead immerse yourself in reading uplifting books and even watching movies that inspire, educate, and uplift, you will begin to purify your mind. Consciously purifying your speech will also positively affect the content of your mind. Refraining from "swear words" (words that defame God, natural bodily functions, or sex), as well as from gossip and hurtful words that are used divisively, will purify your mind.

Sat means "truth" and anga means "attachment," so the word satsang means "to be attached to the truth" (sangha is the Buddhist equivalent). Traditionally, satsang meant to keep the company of the enlightened, to spend time with your guru or a saint or to make pilgrimage to a holy place where a saint may have lived or taught. Of course, it is not always possible to live 24/7 with a saint, so the practice of satsang involves doing your best to make the most of your time. It doesn't mean that you must immediately quit your job, move away from your family, or divorce your husband or wife because they are not yogis. What it does mean is that when you do have a choice as to how to spend your free time, you spend it with kindred spirits. You go to a yoga class every day before or after work, you attend evening meditation classes or join a kirtan group and chant God's name, or attend a weekly lecture on the Bhagavad Gita, or sign up for Sanskrit lessons, or go to a spiritual retreat for a weekend. Satsang can also take more subtle forms, like surrounding yourself with inspiring books and reading scripture or biographies of saints and yogis or mystical poetry. You can also start your own satsang, by inviting people to your house to practice meditation together once a week or form a study group around a book that has inspired you.

Above all, be careful not to fall into the holier-than-thou trap of using satsang to segregate yourself from others, to criticize or judge others as unconscious, ignorant, bad, worldly, or unholy. Remember that the purpose of satsang is to increase your bhava, strengthen and broaden your mind and heart, so that ultimately you will be able to see clearly and perceive the divinity in all beings and be comfortable in all situations—being yourself the illuminated crystal that radiates the light of love, O wise one.

Living Wild

I am at home in the entire universe.
—Swami Nirmalananda,
the anarchist swami who lived in peace
deep in the wild forests of South India

Tompkins Square Park is near my apartment on Seventh Street in the East Village of New York. In the middle of the park there is a famous tree, where, in the 1960s after arriving in the United States, Bhaktivedanta Swami Prabhupada first chanted the Hare Krishna mantra. Lots of pigeons and other smaller birds often gather around the base of that tree, sometimes several hundred. One day as I was walking toward the tree, I saw many birds walking and quietly pecking at the ground. A group of three or four children came rushing by me toward the birds, screaming and laughing. They ran at full tilt, right into the peaceful demonstration. Of course, the birds, alarmed and frightened, flew off immediately, circled around overhead, and landed again, this time in another place not far off. The kids took off toward them with the same intent to disrupt and cause havoc. I turned to see who I assumed were the parents, who giggled and said, "They've been cooped up all day at school—how can you blame them for wanting to go wild?"

Is wildness synonymous with the freedom to do whatever you want, to whomever you want, whenever you want? Contrary to popular belief, to be wild is not to be selfish, chaotic, and unorganized. If you observe wild beings in a wild environment, you will see that orderly coexistence among all is the norm. To be wild is to be anarchistic—a state in which your actions are derived from the essential transcendental Self. That Self is the same in all beings. It is what holds us together and connects us to one another. To be an anarchist is to be ruled by the Self—to live your life so as to enhance the lives of others—even to enhance the world and perhaps even the greater universe. To be an anarchist is to know yourself as one with all of life—all animals, plants, water, even the Sun, Moon, and stars. The laws dictated by the Self are the natural harmonious laws of love. The Self is described by the yogic texts as *satchidananda*—ultimate existence, knowledge, and bliss. This happiness is our true nature.

Civilized ordinary people are kept apart from the deep joys that living a wild, free, and fully engaged life offers; instead, they live in fear—fear of others. So, governments with laws and militaries and police forces are employed to protect the people from the people—human people that is. Certainly, man-made laws cannot be read by wild animals like wolves or bears, because they aren't written in a language that any wild being can understand; laws are meant for human beings, who have forgotten the universal laws of nature. A yogi is someone who has moved away from the laws of civilized life, which justify the exploitation of others, and is trying to live by the laws of nature. The path of renunciation involves self-discipline to become freed from the man-made restraints imposed upon the Self. As the poet Gary Snyder suggests, "You first must be on the path, before you can turn and walk into the wild."

When engaged in the disciplines of yoga, the practitioner transforms. A dramatic alchemy is undergone that changes a person from a cultured, civilized, hypnotized robot into a cosmic being wild and free. As they drop the superficial, artificial restraints imposed by culture's attempt to tame and urbanize them, the yogi is able to reclaim wildness from within. All our man-made achievements are just tiny reflections gleaned from a glimpse of the vast intelligence and organizing principles inherent in the wild universe. Perhaps we should be humbler in our relationship with what is wild instead of taking a stance of arrogance and dominance—attempting to harness and lord over others.

A realized yogi is not bound by the false fences and demarcations constructed by prejudiced minds that insist on differences. A true yogi has equanimity of mind and can, as the Bhagavad Gita describes, perceive a lump of clay, a stone, or a nugget of gold as the same (BG 6.8). When the shackles of religion, nationalism, racism, sexism, and speciesism are broken, one is released from a ten thousand-year prison sentence and able to walk as a cosmopolitan citizen—a citizen of the cosmos—no longer taking pride in the things that separate one from another, like the confining traditions of language, sex, dress, and diet. A yogi moves comfortably as a free spirit easily through walls— those physically constructed as well as those mentally constructed. When one is truly filled with joy, no boundaries can contain them. They live as a friend to all, independent— dependent on no one in particular, as they find their sustenance at the eternal flowing fountain that sustains and nourishes all— God's radiant love. A yogi lives wild in the light of love.

The Magical Power
of Giving Blessings

For it is in giving that we receive.
—Saint Francis of Assisi

What is realized in the yogic state of enlightenment is the Oneness of Being. In this state, all separation between self and other dissolves. The yogi realizes themself as one with all that is. Then the world no longer appears as *out there* and coming *at you*. I once received a letter from a person who was considered by many to be a saint. Instead of opening the letter with a normal salutation like, "Dear Sharon," he opened it with, "Dear me in the form of you." Reading that simple yet direct salutation left a profound, positive imprint in my heart.

For a yoga practice to be helpful, it must acknowledge the obstacles to the goal of Yoga and provide the practitioner with a means to overcome those obstacles. The main obstacle to the realization of the Oneness of Being (Yoga) is perceiving others and yourself as separate. So, the practices must give you a means to dissolve the others in your life, or at least to purify your perception of who those others really are. When perception is purified, then you realize that everyone in your life is arising from inside you. What occurs inside you is reflected in the people who appear in the world outside you. So, if you don't like the way someone else is behaving and you really want them to change, then you need to recognize that they are only acting as phantoms arising from your own past actions. You should not bother trying to insist that they change; instead, you should initiate the change you want to see in them by changing your own behavior toward them now. The practice of giving blessings is a good way to start.

There is great power in giving blessings, not just for the recipient of the blessings, but also for the one giving the blessings. To bless someone is to enchant them. Through the act of blessing, unconditional love is transmitted energetically from one being to another. Through blessing another, you can transform them into a holy being by becoming a channel for love, and in the process you become blessed, because the blessing in a psychic way moves through you first. Uttering the name of someone is tremendously powerful. Most people can't help responding when their name is called. When you give a daily blessing along with someone's name, the specificity of the action yields positive results that over time can transform you and the people in your life into holy beings. Here is how it works; I call it the "blessing meditation":

Sit comfortably, close your eyes, and become aware of your breathing, feeling each time there is breathing in and breathing out. Start with the people you know and love, as it is easier to give blessings to them. Silently say the words, "Blessings to" as you inhale, and as you exhale say the name of someone you wish to bless. Continue for several minutes, extending your blessings to include your family and friends; then move on to others, such as your past boy or girlfriends, neighbors, bosses, and coworkers. Make sure to include others with whom you have, or in the past have had, more difficult relationships. You will find that as you say their names, their images will appear to you. With consistent practice over time, you will be able to not only see them, but also feel their blessed presence when you name them.

Over time, difficult issues that you may have with them will begin to resolve themselves. Over time, you will find that when they make an appearance in your dreams they will appear as benevolent, positive presences. Over time, you will find that when and if you do encounter them physically, your relationship with them will have magically and dramatically changed—you will feel that there is a new ease in your interactions with them. They will seem friendlier toward you. The feeling that they are coming *at you* will be lessened as your awareness of where they are coming from grows. They come from inside you.

No matter how many good deeds you do or the many profound and intelligent words you may say, what people will remember most about you is how you made them feel. If you really want to live a life of service to others, it is helpful to learn ways to make others feel good. Learning how to give blessings in an anonymous way is a powerful means to transform your world and the world of others. Because it is done anonymously, you don't run the risk of inflating your ego, which could happen if you were to give the blessings in person. Also, it would probably be impossible to contact each person in person, or even by phone, text, or email, every day to tell them you love them and bless them, and it would also surely become annoying to most of them. And since they live inside you anyway, the most direct means to contact them is to go within your own heart. When you say their name in a sincere, loving way, you both fall into love, dissolved into the universal heart—your own true being—the eternal reality of the *atman*.

But don't expect immediate results. Patience is important when you are cultivating your new reality. Every action, whether it is as subtle as a thought or more formed as a word or a deed, is like a seed being planted in the soil that will become the ground of your being. Seeds take time to grow. And it is not only time that will ensure healthy growth: a seed must be nourished by light, moisture, the right nutrients. Consistent loving care will yield positive results. When the seeds you have planted begin to sprout, you will enjoy watching how the people around you will begin to grow and blossom into the people you wish them to be, and you will discover yourself as the person you always knew you could be.

Man of Peace

*The nonviolent approach does not immediately change
the heart of the oppressor. It first does something to the hearts and souls
of those committed to it.
It gives them new self-respect; it calls up resources
of strength and courage that they did not know they had.
Finally, it reaches the opponent and so stirs his conscience
that reconciliation becomes a reality.*
−Dr. Martin Luther King, Jr.

The teaching of yoga as found in Patanjali's Yoga Sutra does not say that violence is wrong or right or good or bad or justified or not. Patanjali does not pass a value judgment on any action for its own sake. He speaks to those who seek enlightenment, to those who want to disentangle themselves from the cycle of birth and death. To them he says, choose your actions wisely, according to the results they will bring; be sure that those results are in alignment with your aims. Yogic discernment is known as *viveka*. Viveka doesn't only mean being able to divide right from wrong or black from white, it is knowing what will increase *bhava*, one's awareness of the loving presence of God, or what will not.

A yogi is not so much interested in being "right" as in being free. You can (and many do) justify violence from a perspective of being right: if someone hurts you, you can feel justified in retaliating, lashing out. Or when someone flies a plane into the World Trade Center, you, along with most Americans, may feel completely justified in engaging in some type of revenge. When push comes to shove, habits are hard to break—and so the world goes round and round and round. In Sanskrit this is referred to as the wheel of *samsara*. A yogi is committed to *moksha,* which is freedom from this karmic cycle of repeated suffering. You start out on that journey to liberation by ceasing to react to outer symptoms and instead directing your actions toward discovering the causes of the obstacles to freedom.

Gregory David Roberts spent time in India locked up in one of the worst prisons in the world, notorious for its filthy conditions and the violent, sadistic brutality inflicted upon the incarcerated. From his experiences, he wrote the book *Shantaram.*

The Sanskrit title translates as "man of peace." Chapter 1 of the book opens with this paragraph:

It took me a long time and most of the world to learn what I know about love and fate and the choices we make, but the heart of it came to me in an instant, while I was chained to a wall and being tortured. I realized, somehow, through the screaming in my mind, that even in that shackled, bloody helplessness, I was free: free to hate the men who were torturing me, or to forgive them. It doesn't sound like much, I know. But in the flinch and bite of the chain, when it's all you've got, that freedom is a universe of possibility. And the choice you make, between hating and forgiving, can become the story of your life.

If your goal is to perpetuate violence, then by all means react to violence with more violence, and you will see it will work every time. But if you have another aim in mind—for instance, peace or liberation—then your strategy must be more radical, as it must address the root cause of the issue. You must ask yourself what actions would result in peace. You must plant the best seeds to achieve your goals. If you want to eat apple pie, you don't start by planting a pumpkin seed. You must plant the kind of seeds that will in turn create the kind of karmas that are "good" for achieving your desired result. And if you are still living in a time-bound reality, you must be patient, as there really is no such thing as instant karma; seeds take time to grow.

When in the throes of suffering we can easily feel like victims and think that the violence is being inflicted upon us. At that time, it is difficult to reflect on possible causes, much less to calmly act from a causal place. Most of us react to symptoms, not to causes, and in doing so perpetuate the very things we want to be rid of. We attack the common cold with medicines that get rid of the symptoms, but does the cold go away? We view diseases like cancer and diabetes in a similar way by fighting the symptoms of the diseases but not addressing their causes. We say we want an end to terrorism, but how many of us are willing to look in the mirror and see where we ourselves may be contributing to terrorism? We say we want peace, but are we willing to live peacefully?

It is common practice for generals, soldiers, presidents, murderers, slaughterhouse workers, vivisectionists, and meat-eaters to justify violence by rationalizing that it will bring about something good in the end. Many who perpetuate violence against animals say, "Yes, it is evil, but it is a necessary evil."

Necessary for what? When is evil ever *really* necessary? Can we truly afford its consequences? The fact is that violence brings only more violence.

Roberts could not physically run away from his oppressors, because he was chained to a prison wall, but he could have reacted with violence by thinking violent thoughts about his tormentors, which is what most "normal" people would have done under the circumstances. Instead, he realized that if he really wanted to change the course of his life and be free of violence, *he* had to make the first move toward that freedom. He addressed the root cause, not the symptom. He did this by first acknowledging the subtle violence within his own mind, and then he refused to allow the *thought* of violence to grow. He used magical means to shift his perception of violence as coming from outside himself to recognizing it within himself. He then courageously turned the situation upside down by mentally/psychically showering his tormentors with forgiveness, and thus meeting violence with compassion. With this action he freed himself; no longer did he see himself in the role of the victim. He became the master of his circumstances by changing his perception of where things were coming from.

Panoramic World

devan bhavayatanena / te deva bhavayantu vah
parasparam bhavayantah / shreyah param avapsyatha
When humanity honors and cherishes the devas,
the devas in turn will cherish and nourish humanity.
—Bhagavad Gita 3.11

I've always believed in experiencing everything in life.
When you walk out with blinders on,
you cut yourself off from the angels and the fairies.
—Alyssa Milano

In this verse, the Bhagavad Gita teaches that cooperation with nature (*prakriti*) is essential: without acknowledging and caring for the devas, the agents of nature—life is not possible. In his book *Gita Wisdom*, Joshua Green describes devas as "empowered beings entrusted with regulating air, light, water, and other natural functions." Through a mutually beneficial relationship with nature, a person will be able to discover the Supreme being, who is the cosmic reality behind nature, including all beings and things. It is interesting to note that the Sanskrit word *bhavayata* ("may you cherish, may you increase the well-being of"), which is found several times in this verse, is a causative form of the verb *bhu*, which means "to be" or "to exist." The verse is saying more than that through cooperation, both humans and the devas will prosper; it is saying that their very existence is mutually dependent.

This message is urgently relevant to our times—a time when humanity has become out of balance with the world of nature, the world of the devas. Yoga seeks to regain that balance by striving to live life in harmony with the natural world—the *real* world. What *is* reality and where is it? Does it exist only in the sights and sounds we can see and hear with our physical eyes and ears? Can we really communicate with it?

There are other worlds, multidimensional realities. These worlds exist in the winds, in the ethereal, subtle atmosphere. Most humans cannot see the other beings who live in these worlds, but nevertheless they are there—devas, elemental beings, angels, elves, and fairies. They are the ones who take care of the living world. They are the guardians of the rivers, oceans, mountains, forests, flowers, and all physical forms in the natural world. They are also the guardians of the animals, helping them to live in ways that are sustaining.

Pan is one of the many names for the god, or deva, of the world of nature, including the elemental, animal, vegetable, and mineral kingdoms. Pan *is* nature. The prefix *pan-* means "all; to be everywhere," to exist beyond the confines of three-dimensional space and time, with no limitations on form. We acknowledge Pan when we use words like *panacea, pandemic,* and even the brand name Pan American Airways, the airline commonly known by its abbreviated form: *Pan Am* (*pan*, "everywhere," and *am*, "being"; also short for "American"). Nature exists everywhere. Even though we may not be able to see all of it, that doesn't mean it is not there; it only means that there are limitations to our perception. There are other ways of seeing besides through physical sight. We can perceive through feeling. It is possible to see the world through feeling. In Shakespeare's play, King Lear asks Gloucester, who is blind, "How do you see the world?" Gloucester answers, "I see it feelingly."

Many humans think that while we are also animals and part of the natural world, we are a special case and can live above the laws of nature. We exploit the natural world as if we had a right to, without thinking about the happiness or welfare of the Earth and her creatures. We enslave animals, destroy, and manipulate the plant world, strip-mine for minerals, dam waterways, and poison the air. We act as if the Earth belongs to us. But before we can act that way, we must think that way.

Our thoughts are very powerful. Thoughts can create their own elemental beings who will be set loose to inhabit the atmosphere around the person who is thinking these thoughts. A person who cannot see devas and fairies will also not be able to see their own thoughts manifested as elemental forms around them, but nonetheless they will feel the presence of these subtle forms. These forms will affect how they feel about themselves. They may have days when they feel under the weather, stressed, or bored. They may find themselves in a state of anxiety, thinking that someone else has caused a problem in their lives, when in fact it was they themself who set loose a negative thought that swirled around itself and formed into an elemental spirit who is now harassing them.

If we want to live a happy life, we must take care with how we think, speak, and act, not just toward other people but also toward nature. We must continuously strive to have good, kind, helpful, benevolent thoughts and to express those thoughts in sweet speech and song that honors and enhances. Our physical reality is made of these subtle vibrations solidified. Most people aren't aware of how powerful their thoughts and words are; they go on day after day living in realities they don't like and spending their time blaming others for the things in their world they don't like, when all along they are the ones who have created these things by thinking, speaking, and acting selfishly and destructively.

The other inhabitants of our physical, natural world—the other animals, trees, plants, rivers, etc.—seem to have more of an understanding of the multidimensional complexities of reality. Perhaps that is why most animals would never do the kinds of terrible, hurtful things to others that we humans seem to do without a second thought. Perhaps the other animals realize clearly how thoughts, words, and actions impact upon all of creation, seen and unseen.

The health of the many components of the living world that we can all see—the plants, trees, rivers, lakes, animals, and all that is—is possible only because of their connection to the nature spirits of the "unseen" worlds. It is with the help of these spirit beings that the natural "seen" world can flourish. It is the same with us—without the help of the nature spirits, we will not be able to flourish, and as the passage from the Gita implies, ultimately we will not be able to exist unless we can develop a mutually cherishing relationship with nature and nature's caretakers—the *pan*oramic world.

Nonviolent Communication

*It is the acid test of nonviolence that in a nonviolent conflict
there is no rancor left behind,
and in the end the enemies are converted into friends.*
—Mahatma Gandhi

*Criticism or condemnation born of hate cannot remove
the wrongs of the world.*
—Swami Nirmalananda

The key to effective spiritual activism is nonviolent communication. An activist is someone who actively works for change, and to be spiritual is to feel your connection to all living beings. Spiritual activism is working actively to further the conscious connection of oneself to others in a positive, life-affirming, mutually beneficial way. To be a spiritual activist is to be activated by spirit rather than by a skin-encapsulated ego. Through nonviolent communication, a spiritual activist pursues liberation, or enlightenment, for the benefit of all.

The biggest obstacle to our spiritual evolution currently is our perception and treatment of animals and the natural world. When people learn of the horrible animal abuse that goes on day after day, they often feel despairing, overwhelmed, and helpless, or they get angry and want to attack the perpetrators. Neither of these reactions will bring about a positive transformation that will benefit the animals. Only through active, conscious compassion can you affect people's minds and hearts, with the result that they find it in themselves to be compassionate and to extend that compassion to all beings, including animals. In other words, change must start with you—you must become the embodiment of compassion. Patanjali advises: *vitarka-badhane pratipaksha-bhavanam* (PYS 2.33)—"when disturbed by disturbing thoughts, think of the opposite."

When destructive emotions like hate, anger, or the desire to do violence arise within you, cultivate the opposite state of mind. See the other person's potential for kindness and bolster your own expression of kindness. View others with hope, seeing them as having overcome their own ignorance. If you see them in a negative way, the power of your perception will only help to keep them that way as you polarize yourself from them, and assume a superior role. You may at first encounter ridicule from others when you speak up for animals, but this ridicule can help you to hone your skills, enabling you to become better at articulating the message of veganism and animal rights in an informed and compassionate way. If you have a desire to be an effective speaker on the subject of yoga, animal rights, and veganism—that is, if you have a desire to be a spiritual activist— then these ideas may help you achieve your goals:

1. **Listening: The *Heart* of Communication.** Be sure you want to *communicate*, as opposed to merely express yourself. Strive to be a communicator not a professor. To communicate, you must be able to listen and hear where the other is coming from. Through empathetic listening, you will be able to change underlying causes, not just outward symptoms. Nonviolent communication with others you would like to inspire toward change will transform you in the process, as it will develop compassion, which dissolves differences and leads to an enlightened existence.

2. **Feeling: The *Means* of Communication.** Before you speak to others, ask yourself, "How do I want them to feel about themselves when I talk to them?" Strive to empower the people you talk to. Martin Luther King, Jr., understood the importance of this when he spoke to African Americans, he did not see black people as victims, but as strong, whole, and complete. He didn't have time for hate, recognizing that it would slow him down on his way to his goal. He envisioned a new world in which all people were respected and lived together in harmony, and he spoke from that elevated dream. Black people who heard him felt themselves to be as Dr. King saw them, empowered with vision and hope to take their rightful place in society rather than remain victims of an unjust racist system. Only through humility and respect will you be effective in communicating. When conveying the messages of yoga and vegetarianism to others, don't make them feel condemned or judged, but rather empowered to make conscious choices that will lead to liberation.

3. **Seeing: The *Expression* of Communication.** To separate the world into good guys and bad guys or victims and perpetrators will result in only more division, not the peaceful unification we seek as yogis. When you speak to others about vegetarianism or animal rights, you must not view them as stupid, callous, or evil. Instead, see them through your eyes of

compassion as holy beings, capable of kindness. If the person eats meat, why not view that as a temporary condition? If you can't see others as potentially kind and compassionate beings, how can you ever expect them to see themselves that way?

4. **Bliss: The *Result* of Successful Communication.** Joy is the true ground of being, and it pulsates within you at all times. Recognize it and celebrate it in others, and you will find it in yourself. By not trying to tame, enslave, and exploit others, you give them access to the right to pursue their true natures and, in doing so, you allow yourself the same adventure into bliss. If we are to spiritually evolve and survive as a species, we must liberate ourselves from the lie that we are separate from the rest of life. Recognize the potential within yourself to become liberated and for your life to serve as an instrument of liberation for others. Cultivate your vision by infusing yourself with compassion so vast that it includes everyone. Liberation, or *moksha,* is the goal of yoga, and blissful joy, is its experience.

The Unfolding Life

purushartha-shunyanam gunanam pratiprasavah
kaivalyam svarupa-pratishtha va chitti-shaktir iti

*When Self-realization comes, what seems like a great achievement
from an individual's perspective
is a nonevent from the perspective of the Self.
All the ups and downs, struggles and joys of countless lifetimes exist
on a finite level only. To the eternal, ever-present Self,
the one who is forever free, enlightenment is a nonevent,
as there was never ever any un-enlightenment!*
—Patanjali's Yoga Sutra 4.34

All that we see or seem is but a dream within a dream.
—Edgar Allen Poe

Life is a dream whether we are awake or asleep. What makes it a dream is that the images are manufactured in the processing plant of our own mind. Whatever we have experienced we store in our own being. It doesn't matter much to the mind if the experience is actual or virtual. To our mind, and ultimately to us, it is real. Life is real. According to the English dictionary, the word *real* means "something actual; of this earth." This definition is opposite of the Vedantic idea of what is real. To the Vedantist, anything that can be perceived in earthly terms of time and measured in space is anything but real. Real, according to Vedanta, is that which is eternal, limitless, blissful, and changeless and cannot be bound by time or space. *Brahman*, God, is real. The aim of yoga is to realize this true reality, to reconnect with God, the *paramatman*, the supreme soul, *purusha*, the primal being.

Patanjali uses the term *kaivalyam* to describe the state of Self-realization. Kaivalyam is that which remains after the mind and *gunas* have been dissolved into true eternal reality. Shri Brahmananda describes it like this: "Kaivalyam comes when the gunas become devoid of any motive of action for the small self and return to their original forms; or when the Self is established in its own nature, in absolute purusha, Brahman" (PYS 4.34).

As yogis we desire to be released from *samsara*, the wheel of time, and move beyond the biological to the eternal—outside time and space—but to do that we must perfect that which is manifest within relative time and space. We need to purify our *karmas*, our actions of thought word, and deed. To do this we need the help of the Divine Mother, Mother Nature, *prakriti* and her agents, the gunas: *sattva*, *rajas*, and *tamas*. Nature has qualities. These qualities are the gunas, and they are inseparable from Nature.

Our actions in the material world are colored by the gunas. *Sadhanas* are designed to provide us with practical means to enable us to transcend the limiting aspects of the gunas. To do that it is necessary to cultivate sattva guna, which is typified by goodness, purity, illumination, and equanimity. Rajas is characterized by passion, possessiveness, and attachment to likes and dislikes. Tamas is exemplified by darkness, inertia, selfishness, and the need to manipulate. Tamas is overcome by rajas, and sattva arises when rajas is transcended. Ultimately, even sattva guna will be transcended when kaivalyam arises, but to move toward that enlightened state sattva is vitally necessary. The sattvic quality of illumination will provide the aspirant a glimpse of reality.

We are born into Nature; it is our means for movement and change. Through Her blessing, we evolve. She gives us our unfolding life as a means for spiritual realization. As preparation for birth takes place in utero, the preparation for the spiritual or nonbiological state must be made while alive in the physical state. We can move into the transcendental only by going through that which is flesh and blood and seems actual. Through the experiences of life, the soul evolves and becomes purified. When the purified soul arrives in a state of sattvic balance, then the self may begin to gain perception of the absolute Self. On an absolute level there is only One, only Love, but to realize that one must awaken to the dream of relative existence. One must transcend the illusion of separate selves to know the truth of the Supreme Self.

Asana practice provides the means to purify our relationships with the world of others. Patanjali suggests that our relationships with others should be mutually beneficial and be based on steadiness and joy: *sthira-sukham asanam* (PYS 2.46). Our biological systems are made of the accumulation of all our past karmas. Every thought, word, and deed from every relationship from countless lives can be found in our body-mind personality self at this very moment—in the movement of our muscles, bones, and joints, as well as how our blood flows and our lungs breathe, and certainly in how our mind thinks and heart feels.

Individual consciousness evolves the way a baby develops,

moving from concrete to abstract, dense to subtle, diversity to oneness. Each moment in our lives presents an opportunity for growth. Everyone we meet reflects to us something of our own limitless possibility for exploration. Without interaction with others no evolution is possible for the individual self. How we treat others will determine how others treat us, how others treat us will determine how we see ourselves, how we see ourselves will determine who we are.

We see the everlastingness in everything that's passing. We become that everlastingness through everything that's passing. Life is continuously unfolding, never arriving for longer than a moment. The present moment emerged from the moment before it. The next moment can come only from the one preceding it. Life is process. We are life, as we live.

To gratefully embrace each moment and each person and situation as wondrous is to move toward true reality. There is no one in your life standing in the way of your happiness. Each person in your life, each moment in your unfolding life, is showing you the way to enlightenment.

The Secret to Love

Love is the expression of the one who loves,
not of the one who is loved.
Those who think they can love only the people they prefer
do not love at all.
Love discovers truths about individuals that others cannot see.
—Soren Kierkegaard

Being deeply loved by someone gives you strength,
while loving someone deeply gives you courage.
—Lao Tzu

Love is the most attractive force in the universe—we all gravitate to it. In our hearts we all want to go there—into love. We look for it everywhere except in our own hearts. Without love a person shrivels and dies. Love is the most powerful force in existence. It is a healing force and can protect us from the two kinds of evil. The negativity coming from within our own psyche in the form of poisonous negative emotions, as well as the negativity that seems to come from outside ourself—from others and the world.

To have been loved, truly and deeply loved, unconditionally for oneself by another is the most valuable gift anyone can experience. This love can be like a lifeline to a drowning person. It can provide not only protection in times of attack from destructive energies like hate, anger, jealousy, sadness, and violence, but also actual nourishment for one's soul. With such nourishment, a person will become strong and able to manifest into their full potential as an enlightened, radiant being able to bring happiness and liberation to all.

This type of nourishment goes beyond the physical body and can permeate into one's spiritual, or subtle, form as well. It will help a person while they are navigating through their own subconscious demons in the dream state while sleeping or while traveling through death and the between states that follow. Because of love, a person will have the health and strength to be able to fearlessly and compassionately throw off attacks of fear, sadness, doubt, etc. at the time of death and beyond and move toward the clear light of wisdom into their next incarnation—in the physical realm or an otherworldly one.

But what if we don't feel loved? Is there anything we can do to make ourselves more lovable? If we are suffering from a lack of love, the remedy is to love. Love exists within us. When we extend love to another, we will feel that love as it moves through us to that other and we cannot help being benefited by it. If we do not feel loved, we should make every effort to put aside self-pity and instead do all we can to bring out the love that is buried within us. We can cultivate love through sincere caring, devoid of selfish motives, by letting go of expecting to be loved in return or even of being acknowledged for our caring. We must recognize that our main job is to love. We shouldn't wait for someone to love us or waste our time measuring how much someone loves or doesn't love us, or feeling sorry for ourself because someone doesn't love us anymore or perhaps never did, or being disappointed because we think we love someone more than they love us. Forget it—let it go. Remember that our job is to love.

Where to start? Start by loving someone you feel you can love and then move toward enveloping those you may harbor disdain for. Love unconditionally without expectations or rewards in mind. If you dedicate yourself to this practice, you will gain valuable insight about your own capacity for love and what love is. Keep practicing no matter what. Allow the practice of love to consume you and become you. Be love itself, boundless and limitless—only then will you be able to attract the very source of love itself, the cause of all causes, God, *adipurusha*, the paramatman, ultimate reality, the Divine Self, a Love Supreme.

Dr. John Nash's Beautiful Mind

Happiness runs in a circular motion
Thought is like a little boat upon the sea
Everybody is a part of everything anyway
You can have everything if you let yourself be.
—From the song "Happiness Runs," by Donovan

While still a student at Princeton in the 1940s, Dr. John Forbes Nash, Jr., presented what was considered an original idea to the scientific community, which inaugurated a slow revolution in fields as diverse as economics, political science, artificial intelligence, mathematics, sociology, and biology. He was awarded a Nobel Prize in 1994 for this contribution, which has been referred to as governing dynamics, game theory, equilibrium theory, and Nash equilibrium.

Sylvia Nasar's biography of Nash, *A Beautiful Mind*, was published in 1998. Ron Howard made a movie based on the book in 2001, which starred Russell Crowe as Nash. Although the movie focused mostly on his mental breakdown and schizophrenia, his brilliant theory of governing dynamics was presented in a two-minute very clear and easy-to-understand way twenty minutes into the film. Most readers will have seen the film; if not, you can easily find it online. To understand the significance of Nash's original idea, it is first helpful to put it into context. Before Nash, the scientific idea put forth by Adam Smith (1723-1790), father of modern economics, that "in competition, individual ambition serves the common good, or in the pursuit of happiness, every man for himself," went unchallenged. Nash challenged that idea.

Here's a brief synopsis of the movie scene that illustrates how Nash did this. Through the medium of the film, we the watchers can grasp the elegance of Nash's idea and how it can be applied to real life. He is in a bar with his high-level-testosterone college classmates, and a group of girls walk in. There is a particularly striking blonde, whom all the boys go gaga over. They each verbally start knocking each other and scheming how to be the one to win her attention—acting out in the habitual sexist, competitive ways that men have been doing for eons to get what they want. Nash describes to them how their self-centered competitiveness illustrates Smith's outdated theory. He says, "Adam Smith needs revision," and explains how it can be applied to their situation, right there in the bar:

If we all go for the blonde, we block each other. Not a single one of us is going to get her. So then we go for her friends, but they give us the cold shoulder, because nobody wants to be second choice. Well, what if no one goes for the blonde? We don't get in each other's way, and we don't insult the other girls. That's the only way we win [a date with a girl tonight]. Adam Smith said that the best results come from everyone in the group acting on what's best for himself, right? But that's incomplete, because the best results will come from everyone in the group doing what's best for himself—and the group.

Nash's revolutionary new paradigm is an upsetting notion for a culture based on defending an individual's right to be selfish. We live in a culture that tells us that "the Earth belongs to us"—the Earth, meaning all beings and things. We are encouraged to exploit others under the dictum that "might makes right." This has led to the current situation on this planet of slavery and exploitation of animals as well as all of Mother Nature (all species of animals, plants, soil, water, forests, air, etc.). We have been conditioned to view other animals and nature as exploitable resources. We are taught as human beings that our actions involving interactions with others must serve only our own purposes. If an action promises to make us healthier, happier, wealthier, or more powerful, then we have the right to pursue it regardless of how it may impact others. We are taught that to create a happy society, each individual should be allowed to pursue happiness for themselves. Nash's new paradigm views this old paradigm as flawed, because on a basic level it doesn't perceive the happiness of every individual as essential to the happiness of the whole.

The American Dream as put forth by our Founding Fathers in the Declaration of Independence was heavily influenced by the ideas of Adam Smith. Primarily written by Thomas Jefferson, it was adopted by the Second Continental Congress on July 4, 1776, and reads: "We hold these Truths to be self-evident, that all Men are created equal, that they are endowed, by their Creator, with certain unalienable Rights, that among these are Life, Liberty, and the pursuit of Happiness."

Thomas Jefferson, along with many others who signed the Declaration of Independence, felt that an important purpose for creating the new country—the United States—was so that everyone could be free to pursue happiness. If we analyze our present society, we can easily conclude that we have not achieved a happy society based on the old paradigm. In fact, we are amid a global crisis, caused by our crass disregard for how our individualist, selfish pursuit of happiness has resulted in the unhappiness of other human beings, animals, and the devastation of the entire planet. We have impoverished fellow human beings and enslaved billions of animals, depriving them of their right to life, liberty, and the pursuit of happiness.

The cruel enslavement of animals, raising them for food and other exploitative purposes, has resulted in the devastation of our environment. It has also resulted in the moral and economic devastation of other human beings who make up the work force necessary to raise and slaughter animals. It is an ugly truth that poor people, paid low wages, are the ones employed to do the dirty work of killing the lowest members of our society, the animals. Although animals outnumber human beings, they don't really count. They, along with slaves, other people of color, and women were not thought by our Founding Fathers to be "endowed by their creator with certain unalienable Rights ... Life, Liberty, and the pursuit of Happiness."

We have reached a tipping point, where if we do not find a different way to live with one another, meaning all others, all earthlings, all forms of life on this planet, then we may all perish. Nash's idea offers a radical message to us: To create a happy society, everyone, each individual, in that society should be allowed to pursue happiness for themselves, if and only if it does not cause unhappiness to any other member of the group. Nash's so-called original idea had already been voiced in the Yoga Sutra of Patanjali, written thousands of years ago.

The Yoga Sutra is a manual for attaining happiness. The realization, which comes in the enlightened state, *samadhi*, is the realization of the Oneness of Being. All disconnection is eradicated in the enlightened state. The profound interdependence of life is revealed. What each of us does affects the whole. Every action is rewarded by a reaction. Whatever we do to others we eventually but inevitably do to ourselves. There are many teachings in the Yoga Sutra that are aligned with Nash's brilliant idea. Patanjali tells us that as long as we are unenlightened and are still seeing others, as separate from us, then we should treat those others kindly. He gives the five *yamas* as directives for how to do that: Do not harm them, do not lie to them, do not steal from them, do not rape them, and do not impoverish them (PYS 2.30-39). He also speaks about our relationship to others in the sutra *sthira-sukham asanam* (PYS 2.46). *Sthira* means "steady and consistent." *Sukham* means "joy, happiness, and ease." *Asanam* means "seat, connection, relationship with the Earth." The sutra could read as, "Our relationship to the Earth, to all members of this planet, should be mutually beneficial, should be steady, coming from a consistent place of joy and good intention—if, that is, we want to be truly happy."

There are two more sutras that reflect the idea that good things come to those who want good things to come to others too. *Maitry-adishu balani* (PYS 3.24) says that through friendliness, kindness, and compassion, strength and success are assured. In the last chapter we are warned that our own prejudices are the greatest obstacle to Yoga: *hanam esham kleshavad uktam* (PYS 4.28). Our prejudices against others that allow us to justify exploiting them are learned. The cruel ways we treat other human beings, animals, and the living Earth have been taught to us. Violence, rape, and meat-eating are not hard-wired in us; they are learned behaviors. The good news is that something that is learned can be unlearned.

Most people's relationships with animals occurs three times a day when they sit down to eat them. "That's a horrible way to define a relationship," says Ingrid Newkirk, founder of PETA. It certainly isn't a mutually enhancing relationship. It ultimately will not lead to happiness for anyone.

What we do to others we ultimately do to ourselves, eventually but inevitably. Another great scientist, Albert Einstein, also a mathematician, like Nash, reminded us of this law of karma when he announced that space is curved. Whatever we throw out there, comes back. Every action, even a subtle action like a thought, causes a ripple in the universe, and because of the curvature of space that action will find its way back to whoever instigated it. It is wise to be careful with what we throw out there. Whatever we want in life we can have if we are willing to first provide it for someone else. In fact, whatever we are experiencing in life has come from how we have treated others. If we want to ensure a happier reality for ourself and others, then we should treat others as we would like to be treated.

Yes, the message is an old one, but could never be more relevant. *Ahimsa*, which means "nonviolence," is not a new concept; in fact, it forms the foundation for all spiritual traditions

83

and most all religions in the world today. But extending ahimsa to include other animals and the Earth, that's a concept as radical as Nash's. Let us be courageous enough to move forward as radicals during this time and live our lives to enhance the lives of others and planet Earth. The governing dynamics of love, compassion, and kindness will create a new society, a global society in which we not only pursue life, liberty, and happiness, but all of us experience it as reality.

Where Have All the Fairies Gone?

The world is not only stranger than we suppose,
it is stranger than we can suppose.
—J. B. S. Haldane

Watch with glittering eyes the whole world around you because
the greatest secrets are always hidden in the most unlikely places.
Those who don't believe in magic will never find it.
—From *The Minpins*, by Roald Dahl

Devas are elemental nature spirits that protect and nourish the living world and sustain its diversity and happiness, ensuring harmony. They assist the blooming of flowers, the growth of trees, the songs of birds, the joy of rivers, and the lightness of air. They are essential to sustain a healthy, balanced ecosystem. They are excellent singers, musicians, and dancers. Endowed with artistic skills, they nourish our world with beauty, and they know how to add just the right amount of fun and mischief so we never become bored or complacent. They have been known by all of the world's cultures since the beginning of time. They are often referred to in the ancient scriptures of India as *gandharvas* and *apsaras*. Celtic lore abounds with stories of supernatural beings made of light who move easily between the material and spiritual worlds. The British originally called them *elves,* while the French called them *sylphs*, Italians *fatas*, Spanish *hadas*, and Russians *feyas*. But when Shakespeare called them fairies, all of England did the same.

The "fairy craze" reached its heyday in the nineteenth century—what has come to be known as the Romantic Era—but was still going strong into the early twentieth century. It was quite a cultural phenomenon to believe in fairies. Many highly respected members of society did. Sir Arthur Conan Doyle (1859-1930), author of the Sherlock Holmes mysteries, was one of the leading advocates of fairies. He liked to describe them as "dwellers at the border." Doyle insisted that there was an occult influence connecting us with an invisible world where these elemental spirits lived, and that children, artists, and mystics were able to access that world easier than adults. In 1911, anthropologist and writer W. Y. Evans-Wentz (1878-1965) published his book *The Fairy-Faith in Celtic Countries*, which made a credible case for the existence of fairies.

The highly respected Theosophical Society, founded in 1875 by H. P. Blavatsky and Henry Olcott, promoted the existence of angels, as well as fairies, calling them astral natural spirits or elementals. Fairies populate the verses of much poetry of the time. Percy Bysshe Shelly (1792-1822) sought guidance from the fairy world: "Teach us, Sprite or Bird, / What sweet thoughts are thine: / I have never heard / Praise of love or wine / That panted forth a flood of rapture so divine." Irish poet W. B. Yeats (1865-1939) felt that fairies held the keys that could transport us out of our miseries: "Come away, O human child! / To the waters and the wild / With a fairy, hand in hand, / For the world's more full of weeping than you can understand."

In 1904, the play *Peter Pan*, by J. M. Barrie, debuted on the London stage. In the first act, Peter, played by the actress Nina Boucicault, explains to Wendy, one of the children, that when a baby first laughs a fairy is born and there ought to be one for each child. Peter goes on to say that every time a child says they don't believe in fairies a fairy falls down dead. Later in the play, when the fairy Tinker Bell is dying, she tells Peter that she could get better if children believed in her. Peter then asks the audience imploringly: "Do you believe in fairies? If you believe in fairies clap your hands. Don't let Tinker die." All the children and most of the adults clap their hands and Tink is saved.

Everyone, child and grown-up alike, knew in their hearts that dying fairies heralded a different kind of life—a world dominated by industry's callous mechanization. Although people were embracing progress and all the comforts and profits it promised, they were also nostalgic for the old ways that were slipping away quickly. Our partnership with animals and nature was becoming way out of balance. We were losing all respect for the Earth and turning animals, nature, and even elemental forces into resources, commodities for profit. Most members of society agreed that nature, animals, and savages had to be controlled and dominated by our obviously cultured, superior Western human intelligence. With this human-centered, exploitative attitude, we were unabashedly severing our once copacetic ties with the natural world, and we were arrogantly relishing our ability to do it!

Our wanton disregard for and cruelty toward wild beings had been the norm for thousands of years. Imperialistic conquests of land, enslavement of animals and other human beings, fueled by a "might makes right" attitude, had prevailed from the dawn of history. The difference now was that our weapons of mass destruction had just received a huge upgrade.

New technological innovations, such as the spinning jenny, sewing machine, water frame, cotton gin, and power loom, gave a boost to the textile industry as well as to the slave trade. The steam engine, which powered locomotives and ships, revolutionized transportation. Goods could now be bought and sold far more efficiently. Bessemer's converter made steel mills possible. With the invention of dynamite, mines could be dug deeper, and minerals extracted, making it easier to fuel the steel mills, which in turn sped up the process of building railroads and making guns and cannons. The telegraph upgraded communication and laid the grounds for the future telephone and even the Internet. And with the harnessing of electricity, light bulbs allowed for factories to operate around the clock. The assembly-line method, first used in the slaughtering of animals, was extended to factory production. These innovations and more were seen as progress and increased our exploitative power over nature.

Fairies, those delicate, etheric creatures once entrusted with the care of nature, could not survive in such a harsh world where science had no regard for the supernatural and humans were at war with nature. The war on Mother Nature, which began thousands of years back, took an unprecedented turn during the nineteenth century that would have dire consequences on the lives of animals and the environment. Although human beings seemed to glory in the triumphs and products of the Industrial Revolution, the cost for these victories was a disconnection from the natural, as well as the supernatural, world. This riff was to infringe upon the innate tranquility of our very souls and fuel the digital age of the twenty-first century, in which people stay indoors all day, completely cut off from nature.

Artists, mystics, and children of the nineteenth century didn't concede so readily and embrace the new inventions and the culture that supported them. They were seen as dreamy, starry-eyed, and idealistic. The Romantic Era was born at that time. Romantics formed the counterculture to the mechanization of the Industrial Revolution. Their ideology fueled a passionate quest for what was natural, harmonious, gentle, delicate, etheric, and beautiful. They believed in the existence of the unseen real, a world beyond that which could be explained scientifically but could be felt with a heart aligned with beauty. This Romantic ideology was expressed by the poet John Keats (1795-1821) as, "Beauty is truth, truth beauty,—that is all / Ye know on earth, and all ye need to know."

When an established culture is challenged, the phenomenon of inversion often takes place. The threatening aspects of a growing counterculture are then incorporated into the mainstream to be appropriated by it. What is seen as a threat to the status quo is neutralized and becomes part of it. The opposing attitudes of the growing minority are thus rendered ineffectual. Historically, inversion has happened often. In the twentieth century, for example, as the antiwar, nonviolent ideology of Dr. Martin Luther King, Jr., grew in popularity, the United States government perceived it as a threat and orchestrated an inversion.

First, he was assassinated. The assassination was an act of state. The government executed him, effectively stopping him and his movement dead in its tracks, then made him into a cultural hero.* Dr. King's birthday is sanctioned as a federal holiday. Most cities and towns in the United States have a street or school named in his honor. This is an example of a cultural inversion and is, in some respects, similar to what happened to the Romantics of the nineteenth century. Their noble attitudes toward the beauty of the natural world and its connection with the spiritual realms became consolidated into the standards of the establishment.

The focus on fairies was one aspect of the cultural phenomena informing the arts of the Romantic Era. Art has a way of expressing deep psychological drives and suppressed yearnings. As the Industrial Revolution took hold, nature paid a price. Trains, factories, assembly lines, machines and the products they produce, and the money that was made superseded the losses endured by the natural world. This exploitation and desecration of nature took its toll on the subconscious mind of people. Artists, as the spokespeople for society, expressed this loss in various ways. Theater, dance, music, painting, poetry, fashion, and architecture, as well as the decorative arts of interior design, drew their inspiration from nature. To understand the arts of this time, we must look at the sociological, political, economic, and environmental situation permeating the atmosphere shared by all.

It was a time when the last great forests of the Western world were being cut down for use by the railroad. Trains run on tracks made of steel, laid over heavy wood supports. The miles and miles of railroad tracks being laid down demanded that millions of trees be cut down to support those tracks. Wood was also used to fuel the trains, as was coal. Wood used to build factories was also contributing to the disappearance of forests.

Forests were disappearing and people were disappearing from the forests. More and more people were moving from the country to the city, relinquishing their once close association with nature. Cities were teaming with people living close together, competing for jobs, food, fresh air, and sunlight. Unless you were wealthy and could live sheltered from what was going on in the streets, life in the city was harsh, unhealthy, dirty, and unnatural. The city was an artificial place. The promise of a better life came with a price. That price was the loss of the natural world. Grieving over a loss can instigate some unusual behavior and often take ironic turns.

Fashion

Cutting down forests meant that wild animals were losing their habitats and sources of food. Rivers were being polluted with runoff from the newly built factories. Very few cities had adequate sewer systems to accommodate their growing populations. The access to wild animals in America and Canada, as well as other countries, prompted a hunting frenzy, and an export business that supplied the fashion industries in metropolitan areas with hides, furs, and feathers. Beaver top hats and fur stoles made of whole foxes, minks, marmots, and other small, furred animals were all the rage, as were full-length bear coats. The Buckingham Palace royal guards wore twenty-one-inch-tall fur hats made of bear skin. These hats are still an essential part of their uniforms, although because of pressure from animal rights groups like PETA and fashion designers like Stella McCartney, they may soon be replaced with faux fur. In fact, the use of faux fur is becoming more and more popular in fashion today.

To wear the skin, fur, fins, and feathers of dead animals is seen by many today as cruel and certainly not as a declaration of one's love of animals and kinship with nature. Whereas during the Industrial Revolution, to wear parts of dead animals was seen as effecting a sympathetic affinity with nature. Today we may scoff at this ludicrous viewpoint, but I remember not so long ago, during the 1960s, hippies, like me, wore earrings made of feathers, fringed leather coats, vests and hats made of fur, and snakeskin belts. To us it was a fashion statement declaring our rejection of the older conservative establishment that wore polyester suits and nylon stockings, bras, and underwear. Wearing moccasins and dressed in our feathers and furs, we felt we were embracing a "back to nature" ideology, a nostalgia for a simpler tribal way of life. History proves how fickle cultural trends can be and how ignorant and callous the rationale that fuels them. The widespread commoditization of animal bodies, feathers, and furs fueled by the industrial age swept the world like a plague, resulting in the murder of millions of animals and even the extinction of many species.

Under Queen Victoria's rule, the British colonized many countries with abundant wild animal populations. Australia, Canada, India, New Zealand, the West Indies, as well as large areas of Africa and South America, provided bountiful places where defenseless animals could be found and massacred or easily captured. The decimation of wild animal populations resulted in compromised ecosystems because of the exodus of fairies, who could not survive where wanton slaughter bloodied the land. The trade in exotic animals was a huge and lucrative business. Millions of wild bird carcasses, feathers, and wings, as well as tons of fur pelts and whole animal carcasses destined for taxidermy, were being imported into Britain every year, where they fetched high prices. London was the world's principal feather and fur market during the second half of the nineteenth century.

In a few short years the wild bird and animal population all over the world began to rapidly decline because of exploitation by the fashion industry. The most repulsive and bizarre millinery trends of the Victorian Era employed not just the wings and feathers of birds but entire stuffed birds, as well as whole forest scenes that also included small animals like rabbits, squirrels, and mice arranged among twigs, moss, and silk flowers to convey a contrived "natural" habitat in miniature, worn on the head. The macabre "art" of taxidermy reached its commercial heyday during this time. Stuffed birds and small animals were a lucrative commodity in the fashion industry.

Victorian England may have been leading the Western world in the latest fashion at the cost of the demise of vulnerable animals, but it also gave birth to the first animal rights organizations. Budding activists, like the Plumage League, founded by Emily Williamson in Manchester, and the Fur and Feather Folk, founded by a group of women in Croydon, protested on the streets of London and other cities demanding the end of this cruelty. They combined their organizations to form the Royal Society for the Protection of Birds (RSPB). Queen Victoria's son Edward VII, having been swayed by the protestors, issued the RSPB the royal seal of approval in 1904.

The aim of the society was simply stated: "The members shall discourage the wanton destruction of birds and interest themselves in their protection and all members shall refrain from wearing the feathers of any bird, not killed for the purpose of food." It seems that whereas the society zealously championed the protection of wild animals, the members had no sympathy for the plight of domesticated birds and felt it was okay to wear chicken, duck, turkey, and goose feathers, because they came from animals raised to be eaten or exploited in other ways by human beings. A double standard, for sure, that continues to this day.

As an advocate for the RSPB, Edward VII was instrumental in petitioning Parliament to introduce laws banning the importation of bird plumage into Great Britain. A bill was finally passed in 1922, but by then fashion had moved on and feathers were no longer in vogue.

Conservation

When I read about some of the fashion trends of the past centuries that involved killing, stuffing, and displaying dead animals on one's person in the form of clothing and hats, or the home-decorating craze of displaying the heads of taxidermied animals on walls and stuffed bears standing full height to greet visitors in the hallway or wiping muddy boots on a tiger-skin rug, it's hard for me to believe that these trends were seen as contributing to the conservation of wild life. But zoos, circuses, and natural-history museums were being promoted as educational facilities, places where the rapidly vanishing wild could be preserved, displayed for the education and entertainment of city people. It seems to me like a perverse notion of caring, a weird idea about what love for animals and nature is. But this was the premise that motivated many people involved in conservation.

The first conservationists had interesting ideas about preserving wildlife, and taxidermy was the method of choice among most. William Temple Hornaday was an accomplished taxidermist who worked at the Smithsonian Institute in Washington, DC. When he learned that the American buffalo's vast populations had diminished in just a few short years to near extinction, he became distressed. The American buffalo, the largest of all grazing land animals in the world, whose population had numbered in the millions, by 1886 had declined to less than three hundred. In a mad rush to preserve them, so "that future generations would know what they looked like, after their expected extinction," he traveled out West and quickly killed twenty of the remaining three hundred and stuffed them. Sadly, while he was preparing them for display, he discovered that every one of the buffalo bodies already held bullets or bullet wounds. His buffalo display was a prominent feature of the museum for many years. I can't help thinking that Hornaday is an ironic name for a guy who killed and stuffed buffalo, proclaiming to "save" them.

Hornaday confessed that the decimation of the buffalo had had a profound effect upon him. It transformed him into a wildlife conservationist. Besides the dead buffalo that he brought back to the museum, he brought several live animals, "specimens," he called them, which were the beginning of the National Zoological Park in Washington, DC. To Hornaday, putting dead as well as live animals on display, stuffed and mounted in a museum or in a cage in a zoo, was a noble gesture. Hornaday went on to become the first director of the New York Zoological Society, officially known today as the Wildlife Conservation Society, and unofficially as the Bronx Zoo. He didn't limit his zoological collection to furred, feathered, or finned animals. In 1906, the Bronx Zoo, still under the direction of Hornaday, exhibited a human being: Ota Benga, a black African man from Congo, lived in an iron cage that he shared with chimpanzees.*

While society, at the time, may have applauded Hornaday's wildlife conservationist efforts, today his zoological exhibit of a human being would be viewed as criminal. Although most of us today, would not view the chimpanzee exhibit in the same light. But hopefully tomorrow, to exhibit any animal in a zoo, even the existence of zoos will be seen as cruel, perverse, and abominable; certainly not an acceptable form of conservation.

Music and Dance

Let us refocus on the industrial era of a bygone century and its yearning to embrace and conserve the natural world, and how that was expressed in music. The Romantic Era (1820-1910) of Western music was a break from the baroque and classical periods. Music was written not just for the sake of the music itself in an abstract, elegant, detached, mathematical way, but to tell a story, paint a picture, or evoke emotions. The highs and lows of real life, with all of its disappointments, yearnings, and joys, became important to the composer. The Romantics recognized the sacred in the secular and strove for emotional involvement in the music. They wanted you to not only hear the music but to see and feel it too.

Most Romantics believed that humans were born pure and good but that society corrupted them. Nature, therefore, became a symbol of the truly good life, a life not spoiled by mechanization. But the wild, natural world was slipping away, and sensitive people like artists deeply felt the loss. Romantics sought to restore a more balanced relationship with nature during a time when industrial progress was compromising it. They saw nature as something pure and uncorrupted, therefore spiritual. Romanticism was characterized by the awe of nature, with an emphasis on feeling and the ability of the imagination to pick up on nature's invisible subtle suggestions. Nature held the keys to the doorways of the world of spirit. Nature, with her elemental spirits, became the muse for artists working in all genres.

The Romantic composers blurred the boundaries that divided the arts. They were able to recite poems, tell stories, dance, and paint with music in unique, interpretive ways that glorified the sublime and spiritual aspects of nature. Franz Liszt called himself "a painter of sound." Composers became illustrators and narrators. Franz Schubert's songs were illustrations taken directly from stories and poems. Frederic Chopin wrote sketches. His short piano pieces, packed with color and emotion, were designed to be played in living rooms to small, informal gatherings rather than large concert halls. In such settings, people could hear and more freely respond emotionally to the music.

The most noteworthy of the Romantic composers were Beethoven, Chopin, Liszt, Felix Mendelssohn, Schubert, Clara Schumann, and Robert Schumann. All drew inspiration from nature and the supernatural realm that informed it. They sought to inspire a remembrance of nature's beauty in a world that was becoming increasingly mechanistic.

Liszt wrote *Deux légendes* (*Two Legends*), a pair of solo piano pieces, the first inspired by Saint Francis of Assisi preaching to the birds and the second inspired by Liszt's patron saint, Saint Francis of Paola, walking on water. The pieces unabashedly imitate and evoke the sounds of nature. In the first, Liszt ingeniously conjures ornithological effects, simulating, with multiple trills, the chirping and twittering of birds. In the second, when Saint Francis of Paola walks on the water, we hear the waves and feel the swell of the sea, as well as the serenity and faith of the saint as he is carried across the turbulent Straits of Messina using his threadbare cloak as a sail. Liszt wrote that the moral of these stories was to "show that the laws of faith govern the laws of nature and of man." Transmuting these sound effects into music predated Impressionists like Ravel and Debussy, whose works were to be full of references to nature.

Beethoven mimicked bird sounds. In his *Pastoral Symphony*, for example, the flute sings like a nightingale, the oboe sounds like a quail, and the clarinet is a cuckoo.

Mendelssohn's overture *The Hebrides,* or *Fingal's Cave*, presents the Romantic aesthetic of music being akin to painting. The aurality of *The Hebrides* not only creates a visual soundscape, but a landscape, or more precisely a seascape. It is a musical painting that suggests images of wide horizons, bleak Scottish cliffs, wind, and ocean waves. Shakespeare's fairy story, *A Midsummer Night's Dream*, inspired the seventeen-year-old Mendelssohn to compose his concert piece titled the same. It was not originally intended as a musical accompaniment to a performance of the play or to a ballet. He wrote it after he read the play and was inspired to create it as a stand-alone orchestral work, although it was so visual that, years later, George Balanchine choreographed his ballet *A Midsummer Night's Dream* using Mendelssohn's score.

Music and dance have always been artistic partners, and during the nineteenth century ballet experienced a heyday. Romantic composers, rather than focusing on abstract orchestral music were writing *program music*—music intended to tell a story. Ballets tell stories and so they were an obvious venue to express the deep emotional yearnings for a world that was slipping away. Fairies, those etheric beings who exist in both the real and unreal realms, became central figures in dance, as did birds, who were seen as sisters to fairies.

Ballet became very popular, as dancers were seen as ethereal, birdlike, fairylike creatures. Birds and fairies were seen as kindred spirits and portrayed as such in painting, theater, and dance. Both birds and fairies are difficult to catch, tame, and cage

—they have lightning reflexes and can fly away. They are wild and free. Fairies and birds frequent only places that are pure and good, and they subsist on nectar.

Maria Taglioni was the most famous and innovative dancer of the Romantic period. In 1832, she performed in the ballet *La Sylphide*, which means "the fairy" in Italian and was choreographed by her father, Filippo Taglioni. He also made special ballet slippers for her that enabled her to elevate beyond "half toe" so she could dance on her toes. It was the first time that a ballet dancer performed on pointe, which gave her the delicate, light, and airy appearance of a fairy. The ballet tells the tragic story of a man and a fairy who fall in love. When the man tries to possess the fairy by draping a magical scarf over her shoulders, her wings fall off and she dies. The moral is that wildness dies in captivity.

Cut Flowers and Potted Plants

Trying to keep or possess something wild by removing it from its natural habitat to preserve it became fashionable during the nineteenth century. To compensate for the destruction, and therefore loss, of nature, people started to bring nature into their homes. This trend instigated new business opportunities in the form of florists and nurseries opening in all the major cities. These places supplied the buyer with exotic plants and flowers all year round in the form of potted plants as well as cut flowers, corsages, and small handheld bouquets known as tussie-mussies. Cut flowers displayed in vases and potted plants became commonplace in most homes. Those in the growing middle class who could afford them constructed glass-walled botanical conservatories for their homes in order to exhibit exotic imported plants, flowers, and even trees all growing in pots. These greenhouses were inspired by the Crystal Palace, built by Prince Albert for the 1851 Great Exhibition, which took place in London's Hyde Park. This first of its kind structure was made from large sheets of glass framed with iron and wood.

Whether large or small, these glass structures for showcasing exotic plants and flowers could not have been possible without the invention of the Wardian case, a sort of terrarium, which English doctor and amateur botanist Nathaniel Ward designed around 1829. The simple wooden-framed glass box was essentially a protective container that allowed plants to survive for long periods of time without watering. The Wardian case revolutionized the world of botany and instigated new possibilities for international trade. The case made it possible for exotic plants from foreign lands, with warmer climates, to be shipped to places like England without having to be watered during the long ocean voyage. The container formed a closed environment that enabled moisture from the plants to collect on the glass and then drip back into the soil, creating a self-watering system. During Victorian times, it was quite a popular hobby among men and women alike to import wild jungle varieties such as orchids and strange carnivorous plants like the Venus flytrap to add to their collections.

The Egyptians were the first civilization to arrange cut flowers for decorative as well as symbolic and religious purposes, five thousand years before the Victorian Era, as evidenced in paintings, decorations, and sculptures unearthed from that time. Flowers were considered a link with the supernatural world and carried religious meaning. The deceased were adorned with flowers and herbs. The favorite flowers of the Egyptians were the iris, rose, and lotus (the symbol of the goddess Isis).

In Chinese culture, flower arranging dates from 200 AD. During the Han Dynasty (206 BC to AD 220), the art of flower arranging flourished, with innovations like the displaying of cut flowers in vases and bowls of water so they would last longer. Not just cut flowers, but branches from trees and shrubs with their leaves and flowers attached, were used in arrangements. The Chinese developed a symbolic flower language and paid close attention to the message they wanted the arrangement to convey. For example, bamboo symbolized long life, orchids and tiger lilies fertility. Peonies were the favored flower, signifying wealth, beauty, prosperity, and respect.

The ancient Greeks and Romans used flowers to represent victory in athletic and military events. The image of rose petals being thrown at the feet of a Roman warrior wearing a wreath of laurel on his head is a familiar one. The Greeks and Romans favored parsley, laurel, rosemary, and roses.

In Europe, flower arranging became an art around AD 1000. Flower arranging as we know it today began in Italy and blossomed during the Italian Renaissance. It then spread throughout Europe. Ornate vases were used and grasses, branches, and ribbons were added for accent. Many paintings from this period highlight detailed realistic renderings of cut flowers arranged in vases. The birth of the modern-day florist industry began in the Netherlands during the 1600s with the invention of greenhouses and the cultivation of tulip bulbs.

Although the Victorians were not the first flower arrangers, they were the most flower obsessed. Flowers were a sign of elegance and luxury. Open sewers ran through the congested streets of swarming cities with poor air quality. Carriage horses as well as homeless people relieved themselves openly. Butchers emptied buckets of offal outside their shop doors. All of it and more added to a cacophony of unpleasant smells. Both men and women who could afford it bought small bouquets from florists or street vendors known as tussie-mussies or nosegays. People would carry these tiny fragrant bouquets with them and frequently hold them to their noses throughout the day as a relief from unpleasant odors. It was a common gesture of friendship to give someone you cared for one of these small bouquets. No respectable lady or gentleman should venture out on the streets without one!

Besides these small must-have bouquets, necessary for braving the streets, ordering a large bouquet from the florist and having it delivered to someone's home also increased in popularity. Flowers became the preferred way to transmit coded messages. The reserved Victorians expressed their emotions through the language of flowers. Daisies stood for cheerfulness, geraniums innocence, gladiolas infatuation, daffodils chivalry, apple blossoms good fortune, honeysuckle and pansies affection, hyacinths forgiveness, lilies purity, and roses love.

Depending on their color, roses indicated the depth of that love. White for unconditional, selfless love; pink conveyed playful affection; yellow suggested elicit love; red passion and adoration. In the book *The Age of Innocence,* by Edith Wharton, set in New York during the late 1870s, the lawyer, Newland Archer, sends the countess, Ellen Olenska, with whom he has fallen in love, a large bouquet of yellow roses, meaning infidelity, but to his fiancée, May Welland, he sends a tussie-mussie of blue violets, signifying her virtues of humility, modesty, faithfulness, and simplicity.

I remember reading in a book about the Pre-Raphaelites a passage describing an incident in which the painter Dante Gabriel Rossetti was having dinner at William and Jane Morris's home. After dinner, as Rossetti was leaving, Jane discreetly pressed a pansy into his palm. He immediately and enthusiastically translated this to mean that she wanted to see him again soon, but in a more private setting.

Collecting Life and Death

Meanwhile, inspired by the Wardian case, there was a craze not only for flowers and plants inside the house, but also one for keeping small fish and other aquatic creatures in water-filled glass boxes. Aquariums became a way to bring the ocean right into the home. They dominated nineteenth-century parlors much like television sets did in twentieth-century living rooms and big screen monitors do today. But the technology was not sophisticated, and it proved difficult to keep sea creatures alive in captivity. The "Ocean at Home" gave way to the "Lake in a Glass," as freshwater fish were easier to keep alive in a tank.

England had colonies all over the world where exotic birds, reptiles, and other animals lived in forests and jungles and could be easily trapped and transported out of their native habitats to the wildlife markets in metropolitan cities. The trade in birds and both large and small mammals necessitated paraphernalia to go with the animals; ornate cages to display one's "exotics" became a very lucrative business. The wealthy expanded their collections into private zoos, menageries, and aviaries.

Collecting natural things both living and dead became an obsessive hobby. Homes were filled with plants growing in terrariums, fish swimming in aquariums, caged birds and monkeys, mounted butterfly and beetle collections, shells, stones, bones, and taxidermied animals—a conscious as well as unconscious attempt to get closer to nature. Capturing, caging, and preserving living beings and natural objects signified that you were a lover of nature, a naturalist, a protector of the wild. Taxidermy was taken seriously as a form of wildlife preservation.

One macabre hobby quite popular in Victorian times was to create vignettes using taxidermied animals. Anthropomorphic taxidermy, as it was known, was (and still is) the practice of taking the dead body of an animal, preserved through taxidermy, and displaying it in such a way as to endow it with human characteristics. Stuffed animals were dressed in appropriately scaled human clothing and placed in scenes arranged to depict human activity, often accented with miniature accessories: for example, a group of stuffed mice dressed in suits sitting on miniature chairs around a miniature table playing a game of cards. Or a stuffed fox wearing a dress and a pair of glasses holding a book as if reading. Or a group of cats wearing hats and drinking tea, holding miniature cups up to their mouths.

There was really no limit to the imagination when it came

to these morbid tableaus created to entertain. Painters often purchased taxidermied animals, which were readily available in shops and from street vendors, and used them as models, arranging them into a still life to be painted. The most famous cat painter of the period was Louis Wain (1860-1939). His realistic drawings and paintings of large-eyed cats depicted them doing humanlike activities, but unlike others, Wain never used taxidermied cats as models for his paintings.

The practice of arranging corpses so they look as if they were alive could be seen as similar to other forms of collecting in which a living entity is taken from its natural environment and brought inside to be displayed. Arranging flowers in a vase is a form of collecting, although most people would see it as a benign activity. But it is telling from a deeper psychological perspective how strong our yearning for a closer relationship with nature is. That yearning expressed itself as the desire to control, possess, and display someone or something who would most likely be happier and healthier if left to live out their life on their own terms.

I can't help thinking of the 1960 horror film *Psycho,* directed by Alfred Hitchcock, in which the main character, Norman Bates, murders and stuffs his dead mother and keeps her corpse around for company. Most of us would see Norman Bates as a creepy, severely mentally disturbed person, but not many of us would view possessing taxidermied animals or collecting butterflies in a similar light.

Painting

With the expansion of the British Empire, there was a surge of nationalism. Previously, those who could afford to bought paintings from French and Italian artists. But during the Romantic Era, more British artists were sought after. This gave rise to a revival of interest in some of the neglected areas of Britain's cultural heritage, including the druids, celts, fairies, and of course Shakespeare. The new Romanticism challenged the establishment and rebelled against reason and order, choosing instead to embrace emotion and all that was wild, exotic, and mysterious. The genre of fairy painting fell into this category.

When George III, the first British monarch in a while to have been born in England, came to the throne in 1760, themes with a British resonance assumed new significance. Britain stopped giving commissions to foreign painters and established its own national school of art under the direction of an enterprising mayor of London, John Boyle (1790). Boyle started to commission English painters to produce art that celebrated the cultural heritage of England. He started with England's most famous native son, William Shakespeare. Artists were asked to depict Shakespearean scenes, especially from *The Tempest* and *A Midsummer Night's Dream*. Fairies featured big in both these stories.

The opening scene of *A Midsummer Night's Dream* is a domestic squabble between Oberon, the fairy king, and Titania, his fairy queen, over a changeling—a beautiful little Indian boy with blue skin. The play predates Britain's colonization of India by centuries. The British raj period in India wasn't to start until 1853. But the inclusion by Shakespeare of the beautiful, Krishna-ish, blue-skinned boy reveals that the magic and mystery of exotic India had wafted its way into the British psyche of the sixteenth century. The fight over the blue boy shows that the seeds of infatuation with the riches of India had been planted in Elizabethan England. In the play, Queen Titania has taken the boy from "an Indian king" to live with her in fairyland. The boy has become her constant companion, and she is enraptured, spending all her time doting on him. Oberon is angry and wants the boy for himself, to raise him to become a soldier, a fairy knight. He does succeed in stealing the boy from her, by giving her a potion that makes her fall in love with the donkey-headed Bottom, and the story unfolds in funny and strange ways.

Scenes from Shakespeare's plays were depicted by many artists during the eighteenth and nineteenth and well into the twentieth century. Most noteworthy for incorporating fairies into their artworks were William Blake, Richard Dadd, Charles Doyle, John Anster Fitzgerald, Henry Fuseli, and Sir Joshua Reynolds, as well as many of the Pre-Raphaelite painters. Most painted the fairies as if they were human beings with wings. It was Fitzgerald who, in 1860, ushered in a new phase of fairy paintings. He showed the fairies scaled down, living in rustic settings with other woodland creatures. This was in contrast to previous artists, whose paintings resembled miniature stage sets in which the fairy subjects were drawn to human scale and appeared out of context to the landscape. His painting *The Wounded Squirrel* shows a concerned group of fairies nursing a squirrel who has been wounded by a thorn. The squirrel is about the size of an elephant next to the fairies and the squirrel looks very stiff and probably was. The artist most likely used a taxidermied squirrel.

Artificial World

The disappearance of the natural world and the demise of the wild animal populations in the nineteenth century were facts that could not be ignored. More humans were abandoning life in the country and living in urban settings. Within the isolated city worlds of close-packed living quarters, factories, shops, polluted air, and inadequate sewer systems, there were also great monuments to human achievement in the form of magnificent architecture. Large houses for the rich, exclusive hotels, theaters, concert halls, universities, churches, museums, and botanical gardens were part of the cityscape. There were also stone-walled government buildings for the law and its enforcers, essential for creating order and protecting the rich as well as the growing middle class. Within this rapidly increasing metropolitan population removed from nature, there was a desire to create an artificial world; a world reminiscent of connection to the wild world of untamed forests, the animals who lived there, and the spiritual beings, the fairies, who nurtured it.

We knew that these supernatural beings were the intermediaries between the natural and supernatural realms, and we wanted to invite them to live with us in our new emerging world. But it would prove not so easy to entice them. We would come to realize that ethereal creatures like fairies could not exist in our municipal environments, and neither could wild animals, unless, that is, we captured and contained them. And so we set out to do that. We created another world within ours for animals and plants. This was a confined world of terrariums, aquariums, bird cages, zoos, circuses, and taxidermy. A tight-laced, corseted, and pretentious world of fashion that incorporated the skin, fur, feathers, and dead bodies of animals. A theatrical world, of plays, opera, music, and dance romantically simulated on the stage, a rarefied world where humans artificially interacted with animals and supernatural beings.

Photography

Even though we might be able to cage a tiger and coerce it with a whip to stand on its hind legs, we couldn't seem to capture and display a fairy. But with the invention of the camera in the 1800s, photography provided a newfound hope for our quest. Since fairies are made of light and photographs capture and display light, this new technology was promising. The idea was to photograph a fairy and put the image in a frame under glass, like a collected item.

The most famous of the fairy photographs were the ones of the Cottingley Fairies, taken in 1917 by two young girls—Elsie Wright, sixteen, and Frances Griffiths, nine, cousins who lived in Cottingley, a village in West Yorkshire, England. In a 1983 article published in the magazine *The Unexplained*, the cousins admitted that the fairy photos had been faked, although both maintained that they had really seen fairies. They told the story of what really happened.

They related that at the time, they, like everyone else, were infatuated with fairies. Elsie had a children's book with drawings of dancing girls, and she made copies of some of them, adding wings so they looked like fairies, then mounting them on stiff cardboard, which they would play with. They then came up with a creative idea to take a photo of themselves with these fairies. Elsie borrowed her father's camera, and the girls went into the forest near a stream by the house. Later that afternoon, Elsie's father developed the plates. Over the next couple of weeks, they would take turns posing with the fairies and Elsie's dad would develop their photos. When Mr. Wright asked them about the subject matter of the photos, the girls would say, "We like to play with our fairies down by the stream and photograph them," which was true. He was proud of the creative artistry of the girls and began to share the photos with friends and neighbors.

It wasn't until Elsie's mother attended a lecture on fairies given at the Theosophical Society that the photos started to gain public interest. She casually told a woman sitting next to her about the fairy photos her daughter and niece had taken. This led to a leading Theosophist, Edward Gardner, taking a serious interest in the photographs. Gardner was a friend of Sir Arthur Conan Doyle, who, as I have already mentioned, was a staunch believer in fairies. Gardner knew that Doyle was writing an article for the popular British magazine *The Strand* about fairies and that he might be interested in using the photographs to illustrate it.

Doyle sent Gardner to Cottingley to check out the girls and determine if the photographs were authentic, and Gardner reported back that they were and would be essential to his article. When Doyle saw them, he agreed. So sure was Doyle that the photographs were of real fairies and that publishing them with his article would provide proof of their existence that he submitted them with his text. His article concluded with these words: "The recognition of their existence will jolt the material twentieth-century mind out of its heavy ruts in the mud and will make it admit that there is a glamour and mystery to life. Having discovered this, the world will not find it so difficult to accept that spiritual message supported by physical facts which have already been put before it."

In a 1985 television interview, Elsie said that at the time she and Frances were too embarrassed to admit the truth after fooling Sir Arthur Conan Doyle: "Two village kids and a brilliant man like Conan Doyle—well, we could only keep quiet." In the same interview, Frances said, "I never even thought of it as being a fraud—it was just Elsie and I having a bit of fun, and I can't understand to this day why they were all taken in—they wanted to be taken in."

This whole business about the Cottingley fairy photographs sadly shows that although we were desperate to capture a fairy, the best we seemed to be able to do was create another fake, lifeless world in the photographic emulsion to stir our curiosity and hope that the etheric world of fairies was not lost to us. We wanted to believe so much that we could clap our hands and bring the fairies back to life, to live with us in our new world. But that was not to happen.

Conclusion

As the twentieth century began to unfold, fairies disappeared, as pragmatism and science took the lead. We felt more and more isolated from the natural and supernatural worlds. Our isolation gave rise to arrogance fueled by ignorance. The life and richness of the natural world was created and maintained by an ensemble of forces all working together within the laws of harmony and compliance. But with the rise of technology, industry, and science, we became big-headed and paraded ourselves as a master species superior to nature and animals and on equal footing with God. We haughtily declared that we didn't need trees, animals, fairies, or God to create a world. We adopted a condescending attitude toward those who didn't share our views. To feel a kinship with nature, embrace such beings as animals and fairies with love and respect, and to believe in God was seen as childish or primitive.

In our ignorance we rejected our connection and

dependence upon nature and the Divine. Our folly was that we really knew nothing of the intricacy of life. Our shallow understanding led us to the conceited notion that we were the masters of life. We would capture majestic beings like whales, imprison them in aquariums, and make them do tricks for us. We would break the spirit of a wild mustang, strap a saddle on her back, force a bit into her mouth, and never notice the tears in her eyes. We boasted of being able to plant a tree but overlooked the fact that only God can make a tree. We had yet to realize that we can't plant a forest, although we will claim that we can. Attempts to reforest land after we have devastated it will fail. A forest, like life itself, is a complex web of interactions among countless beings and forces, material and spiritual, within and beyond the realms of space and time. In its wholeness, life is unmeasurable and unimaginable to our limited human intelligence. The unseen real will always elude us unless we can humble ourselves to its majesty and find joy in our dependence upon it.

Where have all the fairies gone, long time passing, where have all the fairies gone, long time ago? Where have all the fairies gone? These lines are adapted from Pete Seeger's famous song "Where Have All the Flowers Gone?"† I have obviously replaced flowers with fairies. The repeating refrain, "Oh, When will you ever learn / Oh, When will you ever learn?" stands as a question to ponder, much like the question the environmental writer Rachel Carson proposed in her 1962 book: Will our next spring be a *Silent Spring*? Whether it's the silencing of birds, or the fading of flowers, or fairies, in the past, present, or future, the disappearance of any creature, because of our callous disregard for life, can be seen as nothing less than a tragedy.

And yet, I am not convinced that we humans have won the war against Mother Nature, devastated our environment beyond salvation, and frightened all the fairies away. The image of a fairy, with mischief in her eyes, sitting atop a toadstool, pervades my mind these days. Yes, with our clumsy and greed-driven exploitation of nature, we have created wastelands, but nature is not so easily defeated. Nature is intelligent beyond our imagination. Life thrives in entanglement. Nature's organic worldwide web or the complex underground mycelium networks have enormous potential to heal the planet.

Mushroom mycelia act as a recycling mechanism to regenerate the soil, which in turn allows plants and animals to survive. Where there are mushrooms, there are mycelia.

Mushrooms and fairies are co-conspirators, noble entities, doing their best to impart to us, thick-headed humans, something of the reality of entanglement. If we could appreciate our interdependence with all species, rather than constantly trying to assert our independence by competing, we might be able to join in some delightful dances of cocreation and cooperation.

When Peter Pan asked his audience if they believed in fairies, he was asking if we believed in possibilities that were even beyond our wildest dreams. The choice is again put before us. Do we hold on to skepticism, pessimism, and cynicism, spiraling downward into an ever-increasing bleak and lonely materialistic world? Everyone seems to be looking for a magical solution to their problems, yet most refuse to believe in magic. Rather than succumbing to our old habit of seeing ourselves as standing apart from the natural world, could we shift our perceptions and find ways of feeling a part of the natural world? If we let go of insisting on our superiority, bent on conquering, subduing, and possessing nature, could we perhaps cultivate the renewal of a childlike curiosity and befriend nature? Could we find new ways to work and play with her and her creatures? Through cherishing our relationship with nature, we could discover that we, also, are a part of this enchanting world.

*Recommended Reading:
An Act of State: The Execution of Martin Luther King, by William F. Pepper.
Ota Benga, the Pygmy in the Zoo, by Phillips Verner Bradford and Harvey Blume

† "Where Have All the Flowers Gone" is an antiwar song written by Pete Seeger in 1955.

III

DEATH

Are you ready?

Sex, Death, Sleep, Love, Magic, and Pratyahara

Everything that is seen should be looked upon as the Self.
—Shandilya Upanishad

He is made of pure nectar, and when His elixir is tasted, the soul becomes full of bliss.
—Taittiriya Upanishad

"Guruji, what is *pratyahara*?" I asked my teacher. He came closer to me, turned my head to face a wall in his practice room, and said, "Look at that wall, what do you see?"

"A wall?" I asked timidly.

"If you see a wall, that means you have to practice pratyahara, then afterward you will see God, not a wall."

Yoga is a tantric practice in which the practitioner practices seeing all of life as alive, as the living manifestation of God. What is realized in the yogic state of *samadhi* is the Oneness of Being. A realized yogi does not see a world populated with others—living beings or inanimate objects—separate from themself. A realized yogi sees the eternal Self, sees God, in all of life. In the language of Sanskrit this realization is called *sarvatmabhava* and it is characterized by the rapture of *prema*—God's unconditional Love, which permeates and penetrates the fabric of life.

It is the illusionary appearances of others that must be overcome to break through the false separation between self and other, or between self and nature, or between self and God. Practically speaking, what that might mean is that you start by putting a face on the other, you relate to others that you encounter as persons, you even relate to the Earth as a person, to animals, trees, plants, even streams, rivers and oceans, rain and wind as persons. You don't see the living world as made up of inanimate objects or unfeeling, faceless animals, plants, minerals, and elemental forces, but as individuals, much like yourself. A newfound awareness is awakened when you take the time to look deeply and engage with others and the natural world respectfully. *Respect* comes from the Latin word *respectus*, which means "look and to look again." Disrespect implies a failure to look at—to really see or to consider the feelings and needs of another.

When you perceive the world as alive in this way, it is easier to interact with and relate to your environment; you don't feel so alone, or as if others or the world were coming at you and you were only a passive victim. Pratyahara is the practice of purifying your perception—not believing in only what you see with your physical eyes but looking deeper into the essence. When you can really relate to others as persons more like you than not, that provides a way, an access point, to get underneath or through the illusion of separateness.

You know how it feels when you fall in love with someone and at first they seem like a separate person, and you seem like a separate person, but then you become enthralled with the similarities rather than the differences between the two of you, which draws you even closer, and what seemed to separate you from them dissolves? You may even feel like the same person. It may dissolve for perhaps only a moment, but in that moment, you know that it's possible. They say that everyone experiences the true cosmic reality many times in their life. You don't have to be an enlightened being or a saint to have this experience of the Oneness of Being. It happens at the moment of sexual climax and at the time of death. And it also happens every night when you go to sleep, into deep sleep, when you lose your identification with your ego/personality, with your body and mind, and you no longer experience your own self as separate; you let it go. For most people the merger experiences of orgasm, death, and deep sleep are involuntary, beyond their conscious control.

A yogi wants the deep sleep experience while they are awake, a conscious experience of continuous ecstasy, like a perpetual orgasm. Well, we could use the metaphor of the orgasm, but we could also use the metaphor of death. Many tantric practitioners meditate on death, others on sex, and others on sleep. The word *tantra* means "to stretch across": *tan* means "stretch" and *tra* means "cross over." The tantric yogi stretches their perception of self and other so far that it magically encompasses all of existence, including, of course, the Divine. To the realized yogi there is nothing outside of, or separate from, God.

The word *sex* means "separation." Etymologically, the word *sex* is derived from the Latin roots *sexus* and *secare*, which mean "to divide, cut, or separate." The experience of orgasm is a resolving of sex, or separation, in which a person loses themself and feels the heightened experience of Oneness, if only for a moment. At the time of death, a person separates from their body and merges with the oceanic experience—no longer identifying as a separate being confined in a body of flesh and blood, but instead as one with the universe of potential. The experience of samadhi is akin to orgasm, death, and sleep, as it is a resolving of all forms of separation into the reality of Oneness.

Yoga means "to yoke, to connect, to dissolve disconnection." Yoga is the antithesis of sex, because sex means separation and *yoga* means "union"—to yoke or bring together. The state of Yoga is the state of Love, unconditional Love. To see yourself in others, to see so deeply into others that otherness disappears and only the Self—only God, only Love—remains is the yogic magical quest. Through the practice of pratyahara—looking deeply within—one refines the ability to go past the outer differences apparent in other beings and things to perceive what unites all beings and things: the universal solvent, prema, the divine force of eternal love, which is actually the essence of one's own self (the *atman*).

Patanjali describes Yoga as *nirodha: yogash chitta-vritti nirodhah* (PYS 1.2), a state where you cease (*nirodha*) to identify with the false reality of the fluctuations of mind (*chitta-vritti*). When you stop identifying with your thoughts, with your mind stuff, then there is Yoga, identity with Self, which is samadhi—happiness, bliss, and ecstasy. Nirodha occurs when your focus shifts away from the unreal—you drop all pretense of being separate—and what is left is what is real. Pratyahara is when the fluctuations of the mind are withdrawn from the outer illusionary objects of the senses. Nirodha and pratyahara are akin. The Hatha Yoga Pradipika describes the elation that results from the practice of pratyahara: "When the prana and the manas—the mind and heart—have been absorbed, an undefinable joy ensues" (HYP 4.30). The practice and results of the practice of pratyahara are described in many other yogic scriptures, including the Katha Upanishad, the Yogashiksha Upanishad, the Shandilya Upanishad, and the Bhagavad Gita.

Attempting to force nirodha or pratyahara through controlling efforts doesn't usually result in the sublime joy promised in the Hatha Yoga Pradipika. Shri Vallabhacharya gives many teachings about pratyahara from a devotional point of view of the Path of Grace*—how to control the senses by offering them to Lord Krishna and thus employing them in His *seva* (loving, caring service), which only elevates the sensual experience to a transcendental, ecstatic level. He describes the gopis of Vrindavan as the masters of pratyahara, of nirodha. They did not have to undergo severe yogic austerities to deny and control their senses; they simply lost interest in anything that wasn't related to their beloved Lord Hari. Their love for God elevated and transformed their material senses so that they could smell, taste, see, touch, and hear with exalted magical perception. You may want to investigate these *bhakti* teachings to gain a deeper understanding of the bhakti approach to pratyahara, which is anything but dry and austere.

*Shyamdas translated many of Vallabhacharya's teachings on this subject and are available in the books *Inner Goddess*, *The Path of Grace*, and *Loving Wisdom,* among others.

Closing the Gates:
The Practice of Dying

sarva-dvarani samyamya / mano hridi nirudhya cha
murdhny adhayatmanah pranam / asthito yoga-dharanam
Closing the gates of the body and drawing the mind into the heart,
then raise the prana into the head.
—Bhagavad Gita 8.12

The most important moment of our life will be the moment of our death. Don't expect that at that time you will automatically know what to do. If you believe in reincarnation, then you know that you have died many times already. The fact that you are here now in another life may be evidence that you haven't mastered the art of dying yet, even though you have most likely gone through it countless times. Life provides us with opportunities to learn, to resolve our past karmas and awaken to the knowledge of who we really are, and it even provides us with the possibility of enlightenment, along with liberation from the wheel of *samsara*—the continuous cycle of birth and death. We all die according to how we have lived, so the best way to prepare for a good death is to live a good life. No matter how long we live, life will be brief. Before you know it, your life will be over, and it will be time to die—again.

In the epic poem the Mahabharata, king Yudhishthira is asked, "Of all things in life, what is the most amazing?" He answers, "That a man, seeing others die all around him, never thinks that he will die." Death is an important topic for the yogi and often it is left unexamined in our modern approaches to yoga practice. But as the Dalai Lama says: "Awareness of death is the very bedrock of the path. Until you have developed this awareness, all other practices are useless."

If we as spiritual practitioners, of all people, don't try to understand death, then really, what are we doing with all the other practices we are involved in? Death is a serious subject, but it is a relevant subject to us all, because we will all have to die sooner or later. It's true that as yoga practitioners we are focused on discovering immortality. But immortality is only for the soul; all bodies die. We do our best to take care of our bodies—eat healthy food, exercise, sleep enough, use creams and lotions to help our skin retain a youthful glow—but no matter what we do, our bodies will get old and there will come a time when we will want to move out and get new ones. So, when the time comes for us to die, if we become afraid, freak out, and throw all of our spiritual practices out the window, then what good will they have been to us? It is imperative that we start now to develop the grace and know-how that will serve us when we transition from this present body to the next adventure.

As Michael Franti sings in the song "Yes I Will," "When you find you're at the end of the road / just lift your head up, spread your wings and fly away." So, if we want to be able to do that consciously and gracefully, we must start practicing long before it is time for us to die. Understanding what happens at the time of death, as well as some of the practices outlined in the ancient yogic scriptures, may help us achieve a graceful exit.

For many, dying is a time of great fear and resistance, for others a peaceful surrender, and for a rare few, a mindful intentional act. In all cases the separating process of the soul from the physical body occurs in a similar organized manner. The material of the physical body is composed of the elements of earth, water, fire, air, and ether. The five senses—smell, taste, sight, touch, and hearing—are related to the elements and are integrated with the *chakras*. The chakras correspond to doorways or levels of perception. Somehow their mysterious relationship is wrapped up in the very fabric of how we are put together as entities. The methodology of our physical experience as spiritual beings and how we perceive ourselves and others relates to the subtle anatomy of the chakras.

The dissolution of the elements always occurs in the same sequence at the time of death for every living being, human or animal. The Tibetan Book of the Dead stresses how important it is for the dying person to be able to recognize the signs that indicate that death is near and describes the eight elemental dissolutions like this:

Now this mirage you see is the sign of earth dissolving in water. This smoke is the sign of water dissolving into fire. These fireflies are the sign of fire dissolving into wind. This candle flame is the sign of wind dissolving into consciousness. This moonlit sky is the sign of consciousness dissolving into radiance. This dark sky is the sign of radiance dissolving into imminence. This predawn twilight sky is the sign of imminence dissolving into clear light.*

It may take days for the elements to dissolve, or the

dissolution may be accomplished in minutes or moments, but in every case, it happens in the same order, from the earth element in the root chakra upward. When the elements are still actively present in a living body, the soul experiences life through the bodily senses, which operate by means of the elements. The process of death involves the dissolution of the senses and elements, which is what the verse in the Bhagavad Gita refers to when it says "closing the gates." The gradual withdrawal of each element from each level, or chakra, in a sequential order starting from the earth element is what allows the body to fall away and the soul to move toward the top of the head, which is the best exit door. That is why it is advised to never touch the top of a person's head while they are dying.

There are certain signs that occur as the elements dissolve into each other and the senses fade. When the earth element and the sense of smell withdraw and dissolve into the water element, we have no appetite for food, our body feels unbearably heavy, we lose strength, and it is difficult to move. When the water element and the sense of taste dissolve into fire, we may become thirsty, but can't drink, and we lose control of our bodily fluids. When the fire element and the sense of sight withdraw into the air element, we feel cold. And when the air element and the sense of touch withdraw into ether, it becomes harder to breathe, the out-breaths become longer, and we feel a slipping away. It is at this point, when the *prana* is in the heart chakra, that we must consciously push our life-force upward and into our head. This final act of exertion necessary to eject ourselves out of the shell of the body takes all of our physical and spiritual strength. Some of us may not be able to do this without prior training.

The Gates

The verse from the Gita about closing all the gates of the body gives the instruction s*arvadvarani samyamya. Sarva* means "all," *dvarani* means "gates," and *samyamya* means "controlling" or "articulating." In the third chapter of the Yoga Sutra, Patanjali spends considerable time with the concept and practice of *samyama*. The term *samyama* refers to intense, one-pointed (*ekagraha*) focus—constraining the senses and directing them, in a simultaneous practice of concentration, meditative absorption, and ecstasy. The word *samyamya* is used in this Gita verse to describe the practice of doing intense, effortful, internally directed, controlled articulation of prana. At the time of death, one's consciousness in the form of *kundalini* will move into the central channel, the *sushumna*, drawing all of the impressions of one's current life into that channel. Consciousness will then depart the body through one of the ten gates.

Those gates are the: 1) anus, 2) urethra, 3) mouth, 4) right nostril, 5) left nostril, 6) right eye, 7) left eye, 8) right ear, 9) left ear, and 10) bregmatic fontanel, what is referred to in the ancient texts as the *brahmarandra*, at the top of the skull. These physical gates located in the body are the gates of the senses, which elementally lie in the chakras, and we are being instructed in this verse in the practice of pratyahara—sense withdrawal. I don't think the verse is saying to use our hands and fingers to literally close the mouth, the ears, and the nostrils, for instance, as in *shanmukhi mudra*. Instead, it refers to the dissolution of the elements that occurs at the time of death.

The verse is giving us a set of instructions that involve a very effortful, intentional pulling together of energy, using the closing of the gates as a *bandha* (energetic lock) practice to facilitate upward movement of prana toward the brahmarandra. The verse is advising us how to practice conscious dying: to draw the senses that are aligned with the elements into one another, starting from the root chakra (earth element), and moving prana into the central channel and upward to the heart chakra, holding it there, and then—by means of the element of air expressed as the exhaled breath—the soul takes wing and flies upward and exits out the brahmarandra, the hole in the skull at the top of the head.

It is a description of the dissolution of the elements from earth to air into ether, and this is how the soul, the *jiva*, disassociates itself from the physical body at the time of death to achieve the best release from the body. The element of air resides in the *anahata*, or heart chakra, where the sense of touch also resides. The verse describes how four senses—smell, taste, sight, and touch—leave the body with their corresponding elements. It is interesting to note that the verse specifically sites the heart as the launching pad and the air element as the fuel. The verse addresses yogis, those who want to obtain liberation at the time of death and know how to facilitate the soul's exit by means of upward-moving prana.

Many people are not able to achieve such an auspicious exit through the top of their head. Perhaps due to a lack of training, most people do not know that they have an option as to which gate to pass through at the time of death. The soul can exit through any of the ten gates, and without consciously closing the gates and directing the prana upward toward the brahmarandra, the soul may leave through one of the lower gates, accompanied by *apana*, the downward-moving prana. As I mentioned previously, we die according to how we have lived. Shri Shyamaji Bhatnagar describes this in his book, *Microchakras*:

The gate through which kundalini departs is determined by the level of spiritual development the person has attained and the quality of awareness when the last breath comes. In those who lead adharmic lives, kundalini usually leaves through the anus or urethra. This may occur literally while defecating or urinating. In most deaths, kundalini, accompanied by prana, leaves from the fourth gate and above. Udana is the carrier of kundalini and is summoned by her at the time of departure. Those who have worked intensively with the left hemisphere (such as intellectuals, scientists, and scholars) leave through the right nostril. Fine artists and those who have done selfless service leave from the left nostril. This includes those who have put their life on the line such as firemen, policemen, and soldiers. People who have done some deliberate (conscious) spiritual work go out of the right eye or left eye. Very advanced saints go out the right or left ear. The tenth gate is only for those who have reached the seventh chakra. Those who can leave from the tenth gate attain liberation from the cycle of birth, death and rebirth. Examination of a corpse may sometimes reveal the gate through which kundalini departed. Departure through the first two gates may be accompanied by signs of defecation or urination. When kundalini leaves from the third gate, the mouth is usually open. When departure is from the nostrils the face is pale with a pink area on the side of the nostril used. Departure from the eyes is indicated by a beam of light in either the right or left eye. When the ears provide the gate, there is a patch of pink on the earlobe of the gate used. Departure from the tenth gate is accompanied by an opening the size of a pinprick or tiny bulge in the area of the bregmatic fontanel.

When seen in the light of what the Bhagavad Gita suggests regarding how to achieve the most auspicious death—through a conscious closing of the gates and drawing the energy upward to assist the soul's exit through the top of the head—capital punishment, especially executions of a person by beheading, hanging, or electrocution, is horrific. To die from a violent death, whether by means of execution, murder, or a car crash, and not have the time or ability to exit gracefully is certainly not auspicious—although many people think that a quick and sudden death is preferred because it involves less pain than, for example, a lingering illness.

I don't know for sure if dying immediately from a heart attack or being hit by a bus is better than knowing you are going to die and having some months, weeks, or days to prepare yourself. Gandhi was hit by an assassin's bullet and instantly remembered to call out the name of God. Some might say he died a violent, sudden death with no time to prepare. While others might say he spent his whole life preparing and that was why he was able to remember to say the name of God at that opportune moment. Different people prepare in different ways, or not at all— they leave it to fate and are caught unaware, as Yudhishthira observed.

I was with someone very dear to me who knew they were going to die months before, but instead of utilizing that time to get her affairs in order, materially as well as psychologically and spiritually, she was in denial and spent her last few months watching television. When the final couple of days came, she was moved to hospice. It was then that her world seemed to come crashing down upon her.

Restless, filled with anxiety, frantic at feeling her organs failing, she finally started to realize that her time was running out. She was so besieged by nightmares and plagued by unresolved thoughts about the past that it was hard for me to watch her thrashing about on the bed and listen to her moan, her hands desperately clawing the air. Her pain was not physical but emotional. I conferred with one of the nurses on duty and asked: "What is going on? She seemed fairly peaceful before." The nurse replied: "She hasn't spent any time in reflection, coming to terms with these shadows of her past, and now it is all catching up to her, and with her body failing it is even more difficult for her to deal with. It is quite normal, though—most people die like this, fighting and grasping."

And what to say about the billions of nonhuman animals who die excruciating, violent deaths, routinely murdered by human beings to be eaten as food—beheaded, or hung upside down as their throats are cut and they bleed to death in slaughterhouses. Or the sad plight of a fox or other animal in a fur farm—killed through anal electrocution. Or the millions of dogs and cats who are euthanized ("put to sleep") at city shelters or by veterinarians by means of suffocating in a gas chamber or by a lethal injection of phenobarbital. These types of deaths seem even more horrible in that they severely deprive the dying animal of any chance to consciously eject their soul from their physical body.

Such a violent death may result in the person (human or animal) not knowing they are truly dead. Perhaps these people receive an additional death sentence—to be a ghost—and in this way their punishment is prolonged even after the physical body is severed from the soul. Of course, I do not know for sure—who really does? Death remains a mystery, but then again so does life.

Shastras

We know so little about how life works, and even less about death. Many people choose to avoid being with a dying person, feeling it would be too uncomfortable to deal with. Some people who might want to be by the bedside of a person dying are kept from the experience because of circumstances beyond their control—they couldn't book a flight in time, for example. Often parents will protect a child from seeing a dying relative, or pet, because they feel the child is not mature enough to understand what is going on—not considering that a child is closer to death, having had the experience of their own dying more recently than that of an adult.

Our Western culture does not provide us with much information about death. We are not taught how to die or be with the dying. We shield ourselves and others from even thinking about death. Death and dying are viewed as unpleasant and even morbid subjects that we will have to deal with later. But to the yogi, the seeker of enlightenment, the subject is of paramount importance and must be examined as part of the study of consciousness.

The Indian and Tibetan cultures have a more curious and practical approach to dying and death. Ancient yogis from these traditions have compiled their wisdom into written treatises—books referred to as *shastras*, or scriptures. Even lay people in India and Tibet are often well versed in these scriptures and how to apply them in the journey of life, death, and the in-between.

Robert A.F. Thurman, in his introduction to The Tibetan Book of the Dead, says: "No intelligent tourist would depart for a foreign land without a good guidebook, giving instructions on the basic preparations, necessary equipment, dangers, and obstacles. No intelligent Tibetan would depart the known territory of this life without a good guidebook for the between."

Patanjali, in his first yoga sutra, speaks about looking for the hidden meaning behind everything: *atha yoganushasanam* (PYS 1.1). The world, all the people, all of our experiences—actual, imagined, and dreamed, everything and everyone—communicate something important to us. There is nothing insignificant or meaningless in life or in death. If we want to realize the inner connections of life, then it is best to not dismiss anything or anyone as insignificant. When we start to listen, pay attention, and put things together, we begin to be able to solve mysteries— transforming theory into practice—and this is the great adventure of life, death, and the in-between. At least for the yogi, who is enthusiastic about living an examined life and asking the important questions, as well as looking for the answers. For instance: Who am I? How did I get here? Where did I come from? Where am I going? What is the purpose of my life? Am I more than my body, mind, and personality? Will I die? What happens after death? Can I survive death? Do I have a soul? What is enlightenment? Could I become enlightened? How do I know something for sure?

According to Patanjali, there are three means to acquire knowledge or *pramana* (proof): *pratyaksha* (experience; seeing for yourself firsthand), *anumana* (inference; reaching a conclusion through observation and reason—observing smoke and inferring fire, for example), and *shabda* (listening to reliable sources; trusting the words of an expert or having faith in scripture). *Shruti* literally means "that which is heard" and refers to revealed scripture of the most authoritative, ancient religious texts, like the Yoga Sutra and the Bhagavad Gita.

A yogi has a curious mind by nature and ventures into the yogic practices armed with a sense of adventure as well as the tools of critical thinking. Yogis question the relevance of all the prescribed practices and try to find answers through experience and reason, from teachers, and through the study of scripture. With a sincere and humble approach, insights may arise that will help put some of the pieces together. The yogic scriptures, and in particular the shastras, are instructional manuals for life and death. *Shastra* comes from the root word *shas*, which means "to instruct." The Yoga Sutra and Bhagavad Gita are considered shastras, yogic scriptures containing practical directions meant to be taken as instructions. They don't usually come right out and tell you something as fact. Instead, like cookbooks, they provide recipes and steps, formulas to follow, that will eventually lead to the creation of a dish.

Mystical teachings are often written, like cookbooks or musical scores, in code, the idea being that if you follow the instructions you will arrive at a transcendental experience that will go beyond what words could have described, even those in a holy text. In a similar fashion, when a composer writes music, the musical notation is meant to be instructional. Just because a musician can read the notation, the musical score, doesn't necessarily guarantee that they can play and manifest the sound as the composer intended it. That takes a special talent, which mysteriously comes from not only experience and practice but also intuitive wisdom, from being able to soulfully render into form what is essentially formless—the etheric sounds from the unseen world of spirit.

Like directions, formulas, riddles, or recipes, we, as spiritual practitioners, must be able to extract meaning according to what we need to learn at the moment. Sutras and verses are like tightly packed poetry. Scriptures are open to interpretation and have meaning only for the one looking to them to find meaning. Most of the yogic scriptures are written in Sanskrit, and Sanskrit words can have many meanings depending on where the word is placed in a sentence or a passage and which other words are nearby. But with patience, applied diligence, and faith, the practical application of ideas presented in the shastras will be revealed to those who desire to exit gracefully at the time of death.

The sense of hearing is associated with the fifth element of ether and with the *vishuddha*, or throat, chakra. The element of ether and the sense of hearing are not totally dependent on the physical body for their ability to operate. Many spiritual traditions say that the sense of hearing remains with the soul for some time after death. For this reason, you can still speak to a person who has died, as they will be able to hear you. This faith in the sense of hearing existing after the other senses have gone is expressed in The Tibetan Book of the Dead—an instructional manual, a shastra, intended to be read by the still living to the dying as well as to the deceased after they have died. It provides preparation to the dying, describing the signs they should expect. It also gives help to the deceased in how to navigate through the various bardos, or in-between states, that the soul encounters after death before reincarnating into their next birth. It is a guidebook for the traveler. Its original Tibetan title is the *Bardo Thodol,* which means "liberation through hearing in the in-between state."

Tears and words of lamentation are not helpful to the dying. When my brother was dying, I was sitting by his bedside and became overwhelmed with grief, crying uncontrollably. He said to me: "Please don't cry. Your tears feel like heavy boulders crashing into my heart—you are hurting me." If you have an opportunity to be present with a loved one at the time of their death, one of the most helpful things you can do is to clear your mind of negative thoughts and speak only sweet, loving, kind, and encouraging words to them as well as to other people who might be in the same room with you.

Leading up to their death, those words and your clear mind will help to calm their heart. The Tibetan Book of the Dead warns us that it is essential to be calm, kind, and encouraging while in the presence of a dying person. Becoming upset, thinking or saying harsh, unkind, or argumentative words to others who are also nearby could cause the soul of the dying person to be attracted to the negativity and pulled into a hell realm. After death, continuing to maintain a positive state of mind and speaking to the deceased in a loving, positive way will assist the journey of their soul, wherever it may be headed.

Shavasana

Delving into the yogic practice of *shavasana* provides an important key to understanding death and becoming better prepared for it. *Shava* means "corpse" and *asana* means "seat, connection, or relationship." The practice of shavasana helps us to connect to death, to develop a relationship with it while we are alive and well so that we are ready for the final moment of transition out of the body. I remember taking what was probably my first yoga class around 1973. Near the end of the class, the teacher instructed us to "lie down for the corpse pose," and then told us to "tense your body, make fists with your hands and toes, lift the legs, arms, and head off the floor, scrunch the face into a contorted 'prune' face, and ... hold ... hold ... hold ... then exhale and let go ... release ... relax." The instruction to tense the muscles of the body prior to letting go was done to facilitate deep relaxation.

A simple physiological exercise like this done after the exertion of a yoga asana class can bring about a deeper feeling of relaxation and be beneficial from a health point of view, but could it be far more significant if actually done as a preparatory practice for dying? If the tensing is done with the intention of facilitating the experience of drawing energy inward, closing the gates of the body so as to move prana specifically upward toward the heart and eventually out through the top of the head, then it could be regarded as important from a yogic perspective. I have, however, found that very few teachers instruct or practice shavasana with that yogic intention. After that initial class, I did take a few other classes where that same tensing of the body was instructed. But then I took other classes where it was not part of the practice and I gradually came to regard it as insignificant, and when I first started to teach yoga, I hardly ever asked students to do it, nor did I practice it myself.

It wasn't until many years later that I witnessed the deaths of three special beings. Those experiences helped me to gain insight about the possible purpose for tensing the body as part of the practice of shavasana and its relationship to the actual death experience. I have learned that through its practice we might be able to ready ourselves for our own deaths. While being with my brother, Marty, Grandma, and Thai Tea at the time of their deaths, I saw something similar. Right before death, all had done that same tensing/contracting of their muscles right before the final surge of the exhaled breath that propelled their soul out of their body. Let me now disclose some of the details of those three remarkable deaths.

Marty, My Brother

It is 1992, my brother is dying of AIDS and has been in a hospice for one week. During the first part of that week, he was quite active. He had many visitors and was always up and available for them—very upbeat, cheerful, communicative, and even entertaining. He would spend a lot of time making rounds, visiting other patients. Unlike Marty, these patients had become severely depressed, angry, and resentful. They were full of complaints and blame and were in denial of their pending death. He did his best to console and cheer them up. He even took several short walks with his family and friends outside in the park during those first few days. But during the last three days before his death, he started to slow down and spend more time in bed, with his eyes closed, "preparing," he would say.

The day he died, as well as the previous day, he had been pretty much unconscious. He appeared to us to be asleep. Then he woke up, and with some difficulty, sat up in bed. He was very weak at this stage, but even so, he called for me and my sister to sit close to him. He reached out his hands and held ours and looked into our eyes steadily for several moments—such a look of love, joy, and a mysterious sense of adventure! Then he said, very clearly, "Watch this," winked his left eye, tensed his body, his face all scrunched up, and then exhaled, released, and pulled his consciousness out of his body.

My sister, Ivy, who works for a hospital as a caregiver for dying people, has seen many people die and has said that the only time she witnessed that type of leaving the body was with the death of Marty. When my friend Prof. Robert Thurman, who is head of Tibetan Buddhist studies at Columbia University in New York, heard me describe how my brother died, he told me that his was indeed a rare death, and said: "Buddhist monks practice their whole lives to be able to do that at the time of their death, but few accomplish it. It is known in the Tibetan language as *phowa*, or 'conscious dying.' At the moment of death, the practitioner ejects their consciousness out of their body, through the crown of the head, and into the clear light of wisdom."

Grandma the Cat

We never knew exactly how old Grandma was. Our neighborhood veterinarian guessed that she might have been as old as twenty when she died. Julie, David's sister, had found her in a cardboard box in Tompkins Square Park on the Lower East Side of New York. She was emaciated, missing all her teeth, and almost blind. She lived with us for several years and was a happy cat during those times. A week before she died, she stopped eating and spent most of her time sleeping, intermittently drinking a little water or vomiting. She preferred to lie on the hardwood floor without any blanket or padding under or on top of her. She had been sleeping next to my bed when I awoke on the morning of the winter solstice in 2007, because I heard her get up. She was so thin, weak, and groggy, and yet she was trying to walk. I picked her up and put her on my bed and started to stroke and talk to her. She then meowed loudly and curled her body into a tight ball, held it, then relaxed. A moment later she curled her body into a tighter ball, this time with what seemed to be a lot more intensity, holding herself like this for a second, then she let out a soft meow, dramatically arched and lengthened her body, threw back her head, and exhaled. She was dead.

Looking at her, I realized that she was lying on her right side, and I wondered if that could be significant. In the time to come, when I seriously started to read and study The Tibetan Book of the Dead, I learned that lying on your right side, is considered to be the best position for dying, as it facilitates the exit through the top of your head. It is referred to as "the sleeping lion" and is thought to be how the Buddha positioned himself to die. Although it might be considered to be an opportune position, I don't think it is the only way that one can accomplish a graceful exit. My brother's death proved that.

Thai Tea the Cat

Thai Tea, or TT, as we called her, was my beloved companion for almost eighteen years. She was an elegant and very articulate Siamese cat. She died in bed in my arms on March 17, 2010. David and I had just returned from a very long world tour. When we got off the plane, Julie, who had been caring for her while we were away, called to say that TT was dying and that we had better get home as quickly as possible, as TT might not last much longer. We quickly drove to Woodstock. When I arrived, TT became very animated and excited to see me, expressing herself vocally and with physical affection, although she was very weak and had not eaten or drunk any water in four days.

I somehow did not think she was dying but that she was only dehydrated and that if we could get fluids into her she would revive. So I started, with a medicine dropper, to give her water, which she took gracefully. The next day we took her to the veterinarian, who put her on an IV drip to hydrate her. She took it all in stride. She spent all day at the hospital, and in the evening I brought her home to sleep with me. The next morning, I took her back again to the hospital for the same hydration procedure. When the doctor said that she wasn't responding, I suddenly realized that she was not just sick and would recover with proper care; I realized that she was dying.

In retrospect, I feel that I should have never taken her to

the hospital, that I should have kept her with me every moment of those last two days, but I was honestly blinded to the fact that she was dying and instead felt that she was ill and needed me to help her get well. Later, when I spoke to my sister, she told me that the reason a dying person stops drinking water is that it makes for an easier death. When the kidneys have shut down and there is too much fluid in the body, it can trigger the death rattle so often heard in the throat of people close to their last breath, which makes it uncomfortable for the person dying. Well, I didn't know this at the time. I also didn't put together what I know now about how drinking water will stimulate apana and inhibit the closing of the gates and drawing the prana upward toward the heart.

I took TT home from the hospital that afternoon and helped to prepare for her death. I burned incense and lit candles, played her favorite music—a CD by Jai Uttal called *Loveland*. She was very weak and quiet. We went to bed early that evening. I couldn't sleep and kept watch, her body lying close to mine as I witnessed her breathing begin to change, the inhalations short and the exhalations longer. I knew this to be a sign that death was close.

Sometime near dawn, her left back leg began to twitch, the twitching increased quickly in intensity, and I knew something was up, but even then, I ignorantly thought she might just be dreaming. Then she contracted all the muscles in her body, at which point I moved away to give her space. She held them tense for a moment and exhaled a soft murmur, as if to say, "I'm ready now." Then she appeared to take a deep breath—arching through her spine, expanding her chest, lifting her chin, stretching her front legs forward, spreading her toes—exhaled, and that was it: she left her body! It must have taken a tremendous amount of energy for her to accomplish what she did. But even with all the interruptions I had put her through with the trips to the veterinarian she managed it. She consciously ejected her soul out of her body at the end.

After Thai Tea's death, I spoke with my sister. I knew she had been with several of her cats when they died, so I asked her if they went through that tensing of the muscles before their last exhale. She replied very ponderously: "You know I have always taken them to the vet to be euthanized, so they are completely unconscious when they die. I realize now from what you are telling me that perhaps I didn't give them a chance to go as far as they could. But they seemed to be suffering so much, I just wanted to put an end to their pain."

After seeing the tensing of the body at the time of death three times, I couldn't write it off as insignificant, but what did it mean? Was it a normal way that most people died? Did only cats die like that, and was my brother a human exception? A veterinarian told me that it was common for animals to shudder right before death. He explained it to me as an involuntary nervous spasm that animals do. I am not so sure about that explanation. From my observations, I have concluded that in the three instances I witnessed, each person was able to perform the actions spoken of as "closing the gates," drawing prana upward to the heart and launching their soul out of the body, exiting through the tenth gate, accomplishing phowa, a conscious death.

Another idea that is presented in the scriptures concerns the importance of the dying person's final thought. It is said that what you are thinking at the time of death will take your soul into the next phase of its journey. To think of God at the time of death is advised and said to be the most auspicious thought to have. To say the name of God, out loud or silently, at the time of death brings with it the remembrance of God. So even if you aren't able to consciously close the nine gates, remembering God with loving devotion at the time of death will no doubt launch your soul into *ashraya*—the shelter of the Divine.

*Translation of The Tibetan Book of the Dead by Robert A. F. Thurman.

Say Om While Dying

om ity ekaksharam brahma / vyaharan mam anusmaran
yah prayati tyajan deham / sa yati paramam gatim
*If one can remember while dying to utter "Om,"
they will go to the supreme goal.*
—Bhagavad Gita 8.13

When I began to study the Bhagavad Gita, I was a bit baffled by this verse. I thought Krishna would have said, "Utter My name," but instead He says to utter Om while dying. I have often heard many of my friends who are Krishna devotees say, "Om is for yogis or Vedantists," not for Krishna *bhaktas*, and I have noticed that many of the Krishna mantras do not start with Om, as do many of the other deity mantras. But in the very next chapter of the Bhagavad Gita, in verse 17, Krishna says, "I am the sound Om." The sound of the Divine in its essential manifestation is found in Om. In other words, by saying Om, you *are* saying God's name. I think this verse is giving instruction for how to consciously pull your soul out of your physical body at the time of death with the magical potency of the sound of Om.

Krishna is known as the supreme yogi, and the best way to understand His teachings is to immerse yourself in the practices He suggests, as insight is more likely to dawn through experience.

My guru Shri Brahmananda taught me to chant the *bija*, or "seed," mantras in relationship to the *chakras*. Because of his guidance, I practice *shavasana* to prepare me for my own death. While lying on my back, I recite the bija mantras out loud, moving through the first six chakras, from the root (*muladhara*) to the third eye (*ajna*): *lam, vam, ram, yam, ham, Om*. When I come to the crown chakra (*sahasrara*), I silently chant *Om* as I am exhaling, and this silent chanting of *Om* acts as a profound launching of my awareness into an expanded reality. Here are the detailed instructions for the practice* as I do it while in shavasana:

1. Inhale while imagining you are drawing the breath into the body through the soles of the feet upward to the site of the **muladhara** chakra, pause, then exhale out through the soles of the feet while chanting outloud the bija mantra **Lam**. Repeat 3X extending the exhale and the "m" sound at the end of each bija mantra for as long as possible.
2. Inhale through the soles of the feet upward past muladhara to the site of the **svadhishthana** chakra, pause, then exhale out through the soles of the feet while chanting outloud the bija mantra **Vam**. Repeat 3X extending the exhale and the "m"

sound at the end of each bija mantra for as long as possible.

3. Inhale through the soles of the feet upward past muladhara, past svadhishthana to the site of the **manipura** chakra, pause, then exhale out through the soles of the feet while chanting outloud the bija mantra **Ram**. Repeat 3X extending the exhale and the "m" sound at the end of each bija mantra for as long as possible.

4. Inhale through the soles of the feet upward past muladhara, past svadhishthana, past manipura to the site of the **anahata** chakra, pause, then exhale out through the soles of the feet while chanting outloud the bija mantra **Yam**. Repeat 3X extending the exhale and the "m" sound at the end of each bija mantra for as long as possible.

5. Inhale through the soles of the feet upward past muladhara, past svadhishthana, past manipura, past anahata to the site of the **vishuddha** chakra, pause, then exhale out through the soles of the feet while chanting outloud the bija mantra **Ham**. Repeat 3X extending the exhale and the "m" sound at the end of each bija mantra for as long as possible.

6. Inhale through the soles of the feet upward past muladhara, past svadhishthana, past manipura, past anahata, past vishuddha, to the site of the **ajna** chakra, pause, then exhale out through the soles of the feet while chanting outloud the bija mantra **Om**. Repeat 3X extending the exhale and the "m" sound at the end of each bija mantra for as long as possible.

7. Inhale through the soles of the feet upward past muladhara, past svadhishthana, past manipura, past anahata, past vishuddha, past ajna to the **sahasrara** chakra, pause, then exhale out through the soles of the feet chanting, one silent **Om**.

After that final Om, there is a profound physical feeling of letting go. All the joints between the bones seem to unhinge, tension releases, and there is a mood of great spaciousness. Perhaps it is close to what I can only imagine and assume to be something like what a graceful death might be. My breath stops and along with it thought and sensation. I feel like I am floating bodiless—a freed spirit. This usually lasts for only a moment or so, but nonetheless it is quite extraordinary that the chanting of the bija mantras, culminating in that final silent Om, can facilitate an experience of *kevala kumbhaka*—a spontaneous suspension of the breath and thought, classified in the Hatha Yoga Pradipika as a preliminary level of *samadhi*.

For a short, almost timeless, moment, you can experience Yoga, free of all desire, feeling whole and complete, needing nothing. You don't stop breathing in the normal sense, but instead become integrated with the breath to such an extent that there is no need to breathe, no need to grasp the breath and bring it "into you." To be able to die with ease and a sense of direction is the definition of a good death.

Before that final silent Om, with each successive recitation of the bija mantras and focusing on the associated chakra and area of the body, I always feel like I am putting my life, via my body, in order. It is a "cleaning house" kind of feeling, where things that are no longer necessary are let go of and things that were out of place get put back and the "house" is more organized and spacious for it. It also prepares me for the silence of that final Om. I don't think you can take the shortcut by ignoring the other chakras and mantras and just lie down and silently chant one Om and facilitate the same kind of experience. If you don't believe me, just try it yourself. Lie down and inhale, then exhale with the sound of Om and see if the abbreviated experience is equal to the methodical process of moving up through the chakras, dropping each body part in successive order by means of the breath and mantra.

For many practitioners of yoga, the time spent in shavasana is taken as a time to rest from the exertion of the asanas. But when they begin to investigate the significance of shavasana, they will realize that it provides a tangible opportunity to consciously practice dying and even to experience samadhi, or something akin to it. Through the yogic practice of dying, the yogi can become liberated from the fear of dying (*abhinivesha*), which is an obstacle to Yoga, and move toward a good death and the ultimate attainment of the supreme goal, which is cosmic consciousness, liberation from *samsara*, the wheel of time, the cycle of repeated births. For the fully enlightened one, there is no need to take another birth.

During the death process, each element leaves the body in an organized progression, starting with the element of earth in the root chakra and moving upward into water, fire, air, and then followed by more subtle forms of ether. The shavasana practice I just described, the methodical process of successively moving *prana* upward consciously through means of the bija mantras, is a meditation on the dissolution of the elements that occurs naturally at the time of death to everyone, although it may occur more consciously to a yogi. This process is referred to in the previous verse in the Bhagavad Gita, in which Krishna gives instructions to "close all the gates of the body, draw the mind into the heart, then raise the prana into the head" (BG 8.12). If we utter Om when the prana is in the higher chakras, we might be able to guide our soul's flight out through the top of the head, the crown chakra, and reach our supreme goal—union with God. Shavasana, or corpse seat, can be a practice for that important moment, as the Mandukya Upanishad describes: "Om is the bow, the arrow is our own soul, Brahman is the target, the aim of the soul."

When I came upon the verses in chapter 8 of the Bhagavad Gita that deal with death and describe the best ways for a yogi to die, I was very intrigued and felt these passages were important and should be discussed with others. I remember the first time I started to do this was when I taught a regular meditation class once a week at the Lafayette Street location of the Jivamukti Yoga School in New York. A few minutes before the class started, I was looking for a passage to read. I pulled the Gita down from my shelf in the office and randomly opened to verse 13 in chapter 8, which talks about saying Om at the moment of death. So it was from this verse that the discussion originated that evening.

A few days later, I received a telephone call from the sister of a man who had been attending my meditation classes for the past several months. She called me to say that sadly her brother had died from a heart attack three days after they had both attended the meditation class. She felt she had to call me because, as she said: "I was with him, we were having dinner at my apartment when it happened. It was so sudden. The next thing I knew, he was on the floor, but still quite conscious. As I knelt next to him and cradled his head in my lap, he looked at me, closed his eyes, took a deep breath, opened his mouth, and said, 'Om.' Shortly after that he died. You know we had both been at your class when you talked about Om, and my brother was able to remember the lesson—isn't that extraordinary!"

Yes, it was indeed extraordinary. Teachings from holy scriptures are powerful; we should never doubt their potent magic, and we would do well to handle them with care, humility, and respect. When we recite passages from the yogic scriptures, our voices facilitate the bringing of these teachings into the atmosphere of the present time and are heard by those who are ready to hear them. That man was certainly ready to hear those teachings, and he had the good karma to remember them at the most important moment of his life—his death. The teachings from the Bhagavad Gita and other ancient texts are alive; they might have been written down thousands of years ago, but they are relevant to life and death now.

*Recommended viewing: *Chakra Balancing Yoga* DVD with Sharon Gannon available through acacialifestyle.com

To Bury or to Burn?
When I see a corpse, I want to bury it, not eat it.
–Ingrid Newkirk

Grandma the cat was twenty years old when she died on the morning of the winter solstice. We made an altar in the house and placed her body on it, surrounded by flowers, candles, and incense. We, along with the other cats, spent a day in front of her body, praying and remembering our love for her. On the second day we went outside to look for a suitable place to dig a grave. The ground was cold and frozen, and it was hard to make much of a dent with the shovel. David said, "Why don't we make a funeral pyre and cremate her body?" I envisioned myself sitting by that fire and watching her small black-and-white body burning in the flames, smelling like meat cooking, and said, "No, cremation is out of the question—we have to bury her!"

My emphatic response to David's suggestion led me to reflect: Why was I so appalled by the idea of cremating her body? Sitting with this, I came to realize something about how different cultures deal with their dead and how that was related to how those cultures viewed and treated animals. Members of the three religions founded by Abraham—Judaism, Christianity, and Islam —all adhere to the practice of burying their dead, unlike Hindus, who cremate the body shortly after death. Meat-eating, the eating of cooked corpses, is as central to Judaism, Christianity, and Islam as vegetarianism is to Hinduism.

I found that interesting. I was raised as a meat-eating Christian, and the smell of cooking flesh is ingrained in my consciousness as the smell of dinner, not as a smell I associate with the funeral of a friend or family member. The repulsion that I, as well as most of us in the West, would feel at the smell of burning human flesh stems from its similarity to the smell of cooked meat, animal flesh. In our culture, to eat a cooked animal without feeling any guilt, we must view that animal as devoid of a soul. Most people do, at least most humans who eat dead animals do.

In Western countries like the United States, cremation is, of course, an option for the disposing of a human body after death. But cremation entails a different process here than in countries like India, for example, where cremation is performed outside, in public view. In the United States, the body is taken away and put in a sealed, high-temperature oven at 1,500 degrees Fahrenheit for about four hours. To alleviate any risk of repugnance, the only thing that family and friends see or smell is the clean, odorless ashes that remain.

The story of Abraham is found both in the Old Testament of the Bible and the Quran, and it tells of how God asked Abraham to sacrifice his son Isaac. As Bob Dylan tells it, in "Highway 61 Revisited":

God said to Abraham, "Kill me a son."
Abe say, "Man, you must be puttin' me on."
God say, "No," Abe say, "What?"
God say, "You can do what you want Abe, but
Next time you see me comin', you better run."
Abe said, "Where do you want this killin' done?"
God said, "Out on Highway 61."

It may have been out somewhere on that mythical highway, but just as Abraham was about to slit his son's throat, light a fire, and cook up dinner, an angel appeared to say, "You have proved your faith and your fear of God; for that He is happy with you, so unbind your son and instead put a lamb on the fire." And so, the cannibalistic killing and eating of other human beings was replaced by killing, cooking, and eating animals, and this was deemed a progressive, evolutionary step for humankind.

The ritualized sacrifice of animals—killing them and cooking their bodies and then distributing the meat to others to eat, all in the name of God—formed the foundation of the three major Abrahamic religions. It also formed the political core and the establishment of urbanization—a sedentary way of life deeply rooted in the practice of enslaving animals—exploiting, buying, selling, and eating them—which demanded that they be viewed as soulless objects meant only to be used by human beings.

Prior to the great agricultural explosion, which gave birth to capitalism and urbanization and pretty much the world as we know it today, human beings lived wild with other wild animals in an untamed environment. At that time, human beings felt connected as kindred spirits with nature. But around ten thousand years ago, when we started to enslave (domesticate) other animal beings, we had to disconnect from them, as well as deny our connection to the whole of nature. Elaborate religious rituals were employed to accomplish this division, exonerate the executioners, and nullify guilt. Ritualized killing was part of this process. Domesticated animals were brought to temples to be offered to God, killed by priests while they recited incantations, put on a fire, cooked, and then the meat was either given back to the person for a fee or sold and distributed to others.

In time, as the human population increased, so did the herds of domesticated animals, and cities grew larger, as did temples and political power. Temples became more and more like commercial slaughterhouses. Two thousand years ago, Jerusalem was known as the "red city," not because of how the beautiful sunsets reflected on the walled fortress surrounding the city, but because of the crimson blood that overflowed the gutters running out of the main temple—the by-product of the many animal sacrifices performed there. All of the religions of Abraham uphold a speciesist view, which looks upon animals as inferior to humans, so cremation in those religions is not an acceptable way of treating the dead. Burning is for animals, not humans.

Before the story of Abraham and Isaac, there is the story of Cain and Abel, which describes the food offerings God likes best. Adam and Eve have two sons—Abel, who is a shepherd, a herder of goats and sheep, and Cain, a gardener who grows vegetables. Adam informs them that they must make a sacrifice to God to win His favor. Abel's sacrifice is a bloody one—one of his sheep, bound, its throat slit, and placed on a burning pyre to roast. Cain harvests an abundant variety of vegetables from his garden and places them on his outdoor altar as an offering. God speaks to Adam and tells him how delighted he is with Abel's offering of lamb chops and how unhappy he is with Cain's vegetarian platter. Cain feels rejected, becomes depressed, succumbs to a jealous rage, and kills his brother.

Many of us in the West remember being taught these stories as children, but how many of us reflect on their historical significance and question the practices they describe? Stories like these can provide insight into why animal sacrifice and meat-eating became so important to the beliefs of our ancestors. The stories in the Bible and the Quran formed the foundation of religions and evolved along with cultures—cultures that sanction and justify bloody sacrificial rites, meat-eating, and the exploitation and enslavement of defenseless animals.

Cremation is not acceptable to many Christians, Jews, and Muslims, because in those religions burning is for animals, not humans. So, putting an animal's body in or on a fire, whether as a religious sacrifice or to cook for dinner, is viewed as acceptable. But a human body should not be treated the same way. To many Jews, for example, there is a horrific reaction to the idea of cremation because of the holocaust, in which Jews were cremated in Nazi death camps. The Nazis viewed the Jews as no better than animals, and to burn an animal's body was certainly acceptable to them, so the Nazis used cremation as a means of desecration.

Christianity, Judaism, and Islam oppose cremation because of the belief that the body is sacred; cremation is considered an act of desecration. It is believed that the body and soul will eventually be reunited, and cremation ensures that no resurrection of the body can be possible. On the other hand, Hinduism, Jainism, Sikhism, and Buddhism mandate cremation. In these religions, the body is seen as a vehicle for the soul, and at the time of death the soul leaves the body; destroying the corpse induces detachment and helps to free the soul.

Vegetarianism was not always a central feature of Hinduism. The ritualized killing of animals played a big part in early Vedic culture. The Brahmin priests performed the animal sacrifices, and originally only Brahmins were allowed to eat meat. After the religious reforms brought about by Jainism and Buddhism, Hinduism began to uphold the virtue of *ahimsa* (nonharming) and extended it to include not harming animals. Thus, vegetarianism became part of the practice of ahimsa. In turn, cremation became the popular method used to dispose of human corpses among the vegetarian Hindus, Jains, and Buddhists.

When we begin to look deeply into the rituals of our culture, including funeral ceremonies, we may uncover the roots of many violent practices that have been ingrained and unquestioned in our way of life, and we may come to realize that many of these practices have been learned. The good news is that when we recognize the origins of certain behaviors, we realize that they aren't necessarily natural or hard-wired in us, and that when something is learned it can be unlearned. We can dismantle the old ways of our present animal-slave-based culture and create a new way of living. We can create a peaceful, kinder world for all beings. We can rise like the phoenix from the ashes of the sacrificial fire and fly to greater heights than have even yet been imagined.

Recommended Reading:

An Unnatural Order, by Jim Mason.

Yoga and Veganism, by Sharon Gannon.

The World Peace Diet, by Will Tuttle.

Gods of Love and Ecstasy: The Traditions of Shiva and Dionysus, by Alain Daniélou.

Presence

gate gate paragate parasangate bodhi swaha
*Gone, gone, real gone, beyond even the most gone,
only in going that gone is there awakening.*
—Heart Sutra

Our beloved teacher Swami Nirmalananda would often remind us to "practice dying every day of your life, and when the time for your death arrives you will be ready for the great samadhi." Yoga is eternal. It exists in the infinity of the present; there is no future for yoga, nor can it be imprisoned in the past. What does it mean to be a yogi? To be a yogi is to live in timelessness, to be free, absolutely wild, and completely at ease. To step into the *atha*, where eternity is happening—now. To be able to die to the past and give up the illusion of a future is to be born into the present. This demands an understanding of *karma*, action. Our time-bound reality comes from our karmas, from identifying with our actions.

Engaging in the various practices of yoga can help purify your karmas by revealing them to you. You will come up against obstacles that will distract you from the present moment. These obstacles may arise in the form of competitive projections, for example, which will tempt you to focus on achieving specific goals, to feel that you are accomplishing something; others will arise from the past, tempting you to run away to avoid pain. Both habits arise from identifying with karmas.

We believe it is possible to escape from the present because we are caught in the illusion that things, people, or circumstances are separate from us and are coming "at" us. This illusion is due to ignorance, or *avidya*, which is actually a case of mistaken identity. The truth is that there is no one else really "out there," to come at us. In fact, there is no "out there" out there at all! All that we experience, whether actual or virtual, appears the way it is as a result of our own past actions, our karmas. When unpleasant things appear in our reality, instead of avoiding them, we can investigate our discomfort by simply witnessing. To witness our feelings is to watch without judgment. Through witnessing rather than identifying, we will begin to develop *chitta-prasadanam*, or serenity of mind. With this serenity of mind established, we may be able to fearlessly delve deeper into our own beings, allowing all negative emotions and habits to be illuminated by the light of awareness and be dissolved: going, going, gone. What will remain is the unchanging, blissful reality of the soul, the *atman*.

The practice of yoga is the practice of dying—of dying to who you thought you were. The process involves the meditative practice of witnessing. With detached observation, you watch who you think you are, and you continue to pierce the layers of illusion, going, going, right through each one. Through investigation, through keen and consistent impartial observation of the self, through self-inquiry, you walk through one doorway after another. These doorways are constructs, ideas of who you are. If you can keep going, continue to walk through doorway after doorway, concept after concept, you will come to the realization that "you" don't exist. Yourself, who you think you are —the ego, the body, the mind, the personality—doesn't really exist. It is only an abstract concept, a mental construct composed of your karmas, designed by *maya* (illusion), the agent of the Supreme Divine Self.

As Alan Watts says, "You, who you think you are, like the equator, you can't really find it, you can't trip over it, because it doesn't really exist." If you truly observe something, anything really, the thing will disappear. You will disappear. You as a separate entity will dissolve once you enter the presence of the present moment, which is a space outside time, and therefore devoid of thought. Thinking, by its very nature, is designed to separate the pulsating interconnected reality into the illusion of separate beings, things, and moments in time.

At the so-called time of death, it is said that we will see our entire lives pass before us. If we have some training, we can allow it to pass right *through* us. During the death process, all the ghosts of our past will come knocking on the door. We must be able to let them in and allow them to pass right through and exit through the back door. In this way we will see them for what they are: phantoms from our past. We will see our small selves, our personalities, and our separateness for what they are: empty.

Love is the only power that can invite this kind of apocalypse, where all is relinquished and no-thing exists; a supreme love, *prema*, love for God. *Bhakti*, loving devotion to that, which is eternally blissful, is the key that opens the door of our hearts wide enough to allow everything and everyone that needs to pass through to pass through. We will see the everlastingness in everything that's passing, and we will become that everlastingness through everything that's passing.

IV

PRACTICE

What to do?

I Me Mine

saktah karmany avidvamso / yatha kurvanti bharata
kuryad vidvams tathasaktash / chikirshur loka-sangraham
The unwise are attached to their actions,
while the wise are unattached and act selflessly to benefit the world.
—Bhagavad Gita 3.25

All through the day / I me mine / All I can hear
I me mine, I me mine, I me mine
Even those tears / I me mine, I me mine, I me mine.
—From "I Me Mine," by The Beatles

A few months after the September 11 tragedy, I was having dinner with a highly respected Indian spiritual teacher. We were talking about how our lives had changed because of 9/11. He was quite candid and told the following story:

After I heard that the second plane that hit the towers had taken off from Boston, I freaked out and was in a panic. You see, my son was scheduled to fly out of Boston that morning, and I thought my son was on that plane and was now dead. As you know, it was impossible to get any information for a long time. The city was at a standstill. There was no phone service, transportation was halted. Everyone was in the dark. I had never experienced such fear and distress. All my so-called, calm, yogic detachment was thrown out the window. Then, after two days, I received word that he was okay. He was not on the plane that crashed into the south tower. The happiness and relief I felt were indescribable. I was euphoric. I cried, laughed, screamed, danced, rolled on the floor, and jumped up and down.

Then it hit me. The realization that there were passengers on that plane who were dead and many of them were the sons of somebody. From a state of elation, I plummeted into anguish, and it wasn't because I was sad about those who had died. I was in a state of despair about myself. I realized how selfish I was. I only cared about my own son. I was faced head-on with the truth of my self-centered I-me-mine-ness. My reaction had shaken me and caused me to see that I was a fraud. All my years of study, practice, and teaching yoga had been a sham. I knew nothing about yoga. I had no equanimity of mind. I only cared about "my" son. I was an unenlightened, selfish, normal jerk. But I am grateful for it all, because having been brought to my knees, now the real work begins.

Although we may do our best to be kind, caring people and think of ourselves as good, when a crisis challenges us, falls on our heads, out of the blue, we may not always react in an enlightened manner. There are many potential obstacles on the path to enlightenment, but there is one that is particularly challenging to deal with and underlies many, if not most, of the other obstacles: selfishness. Negative emotions sustain a self-centered attitude that pits us against others and reinforces selfish tendencies.

There are basically three kinds of people: selfish, less selfish, and selfless. The first is the most numerous, the second is in the minority, and the third is very rare. The only difference among them is the intention underlying their actions.

Very selfish people feel that the world and everyone in it owes them a good life. They work to fulfill their own desires. They serve none but themselves. They cannot even serve their own families. They are so self-absorbed that they usually live in a constant state of fear. They fear losing—property, time, or life itself. They worry about being robbed or violated in some way. Death is the ultimate outrage to these people, and they fear it above all else.

People who are a little less selfish are able, once they've provided for themselves, to care for their families. They may work very hard and believe that they are sacrificing everything for their children, but this is actually a selfish act. They have produced their children, and their genes will survive through them. These people may put money into a trust for their children or spouse, but they wouldn't think of sharing with others who aren't related. Their vision is not wide enough to extend their circle of compassion beyond a narrow perimeter. As Ingrid Newkirk points out: "You care for and look out for your baby or your friend, of course. That's easy. You love them. The test of moral fiber is to stick up for those you relate to least, understand minimally, and do not think are that much like you."

You may find selfish people practicing yoga. Their intention, though, is typically limited to using yoga practices to become more physically attractive, less injury-prone, or to boost their careers. Dancers or actors who practice yoga asanas to become better performers are an example. Such practitioners are hoping to improve their own lives, but not necessarily the lives of others.

Rarer are the less-selfish, charitable people, who work to improve the lives of others unrelated to themselves. They may not be without selfish motives, however, as they expect credit for their service. They first care for themselves and their loved ones, and then, if there is money or things they no longer use left over, they may give to others in need. They try to help, but only approach the situation on the symptomatic level. Rarely do they help to stamp out the cause of suffering. Receiving a tax write-off or seeing their name in a program or on a plaque gives them considerable satisfaction.

Scientists and religious leaders who are absorbed in investigating the workings of the cosmos can make useful contributions to the world. Often, however, pride contaminates their contributions. A lack of humility can diminish the positive karmic results that could be incurred by such valuable contributions.

Selfless people, on the other hand, are in service to the cosmic will and may help shift the consciousness of an entire age. The truly selfless person works for the sake of the work, knowing that the Divine is the real doer at the core of every being and thing. All work, all effort is without struggle or expectation of reward. These people offer themselves as instruments for divine will.

These selfless, humble people work joyfully and remind us of our true nature. Usually, their effect upon others lasts long after their death. They don't see themselves as separate from others. By serving others they feel they are serving themselves and God. These truly caring individuals see themselves as part of a greater whole and devote their lives to uplifting the lives of others, not as martyrs forsaking their own happiness but as embodiments of happiness. The great saint Ramana Maharshi was asked, "How should we treat others?" He replied, "There are no others."

To awaken the ability to see ourselves in another, we have to address our own negative emotions. They come in many forms, but all derive from self-cherishing—seeing ourselves as separate from others, holding on to that sense of separateness, and wanting things our way. This is the "I, me, mine" syndrome. I want—what's in it for me? This is mine—this belongs to me, I own it, it is not yours, etc. This self-centered focus on I, me, and mine feeds the ego while contributing to our disconnection from others and from our eternal soul.

To free ourselves from the grip of negative emotions, we must first learn to recognize them. Negative emotions are feelings that disrupt our *bhava*—our good mood. A truly good mood comes from feeling the presence of goodness and divine love in our heart and allowing that expansive feeling to permeate throughout our being and spill over into the world around us. Negativity is constrictive rather than expansive. Negative emotions are feelings of denigration aimed toward others, the world, God, or even ourself. Generally, they fall under three main headings: anger, jealousy, and fear.

Negative emotions are often triggered by the "fight-or-flight" reflex that arises as a reaction to a life-threatening situation. For example, if someone is attacking us, we will react by fighting them or running away. Our instinct for self-preservation and the fear of losing our life will dictate our actions. Most of us do not encounter an adversary intent on killing us in our daily lives, and yet we still operate from fight-or-flight nonetheless and allow fear to motivate us.

Here's an example: A new person is hired at work and is given a lot of the responsibilities you once had. Although your life isn't threatened, you feel that your job, your livelihood, is. You are afraid and angry. Should you storm into your boss's office and fight or angrily react by quitting your job? If you could recognize that the situation has triggered your fight-or-flight instinct, but that the situation is not really life-threatening, you could see that you have a third option—and that option does not have to involve negative emotions. Instead of feeling resentful, you could be grateful that your workload has been lightened. You could decide to be kind to everyone involved and make the new person feel welcomed.

We often do not get what we think we deserve. People don't always behave the way we think they should. Negative emotions can arise when we don't get what we want. Here's an example: You have been dating someone you feel you are falling in love with. You arrive at a party and see your girlfriend making out on a couch with somebody else. You become infused with jealousy, anger, anxiety, and competitiveness mixed with embarrassment, sadness, and self-loathing. These negative feelings are devastating to your mental and physical health as well as to your spiritual well-being.

Negative emotions, if left unchecked, could trigger other debilitating reactions, such as seeing yourself as a victim of unfair treatment. The resentfulness you then feel grows into feelings of superiority that manifest into complaining and blaming. This negativity could snowball into wishing ill toward others and feeling good when others experience misfortune—feeling they deserved it. Negative emotions are also expressed verbally in the form of lying, cursing, gossiping, boasting, exaggerating about our accomplishments, and finding fault with others, degrading them, talking about their shortcomings, etc. Negative emotions can be expressed physically in the form of stealing from others, abusing others, and being greedy. Also by harming or killing others or causing them to be harmed or killed, such as when we eat meat, fish, milk, or eggs, or wear leather, fur, wool, or silk. Negative emotions pollute our minds, hearts, and bodies, clouding our perception of beauty and truth and separating ourselves from others as well as from God.

If we want to realize enlightenment so that we can truly be of service to others and experience lasting peace and happiness, we must free ourselves from self-cherishing and the negative emotions that feed upon it. Three yogic practices can be very effective for opening the heart to love: *japa*, *maitri*, and *karuna*. These practices shift the focus away from our small self, or ego, and toward others and to God.

Japa is the repetition of a mantra, it is a form of meditation. Such mantras as *Let go* or *lokah samastah sukhino bhavantu*, when said daily with sincerity over a long period of time, will work on a subtle vibrational level and result in the purification and rearrangement of the cells and tissues of our physical, energetic, emotional, mental, and spiritual bodies.

Mantras composed of the name of God—like *Shri Krishna sharanam mama* or *Hare Krishna Hare Krishna Krishna Krishna Hare Hare Hare Rama Hare Rama Rama Rama Hare Hare* or *Om namo Narayanaya*—are the most powerful agents of transformation. By repeating God's name, *bhakti*, love for God, is cultivated. God's name has the power to build a divine body in the form of the deity whose name we are repeating. Gradually, over time, we begin to feel the divine presence of love (*prem*) and let go of our identification with our material, temporary body and mind, which is the source of negative emotions. Patanjali says, "By the study and repetition of a mantra, one establishes identity with the mantra, and the transcendental knowledge and form of the mantra is revealed" (PYS 2.44).

Practice japa every day for as long as you can, chanting mantra over and over silently to yourself. And throughout the day, silently chant mantra whenever you remember to do so, but especially when you notice that you are having a negative thought or feeling, or you are starting to gossip or speak unkind words or are finding fault with others or being sarcastic or cynical. In this way you will train yourself to substitute a higher intention or a more elevated spiritual longing for habitual negative thoughts and words. As the bhakti poet Rasakhan says, "The tongue that does not delight in the nectar of Your name utters constant blame."

Maitri means "friendliness." To be someone's friend and sincerely wish them well washes away envy, jealousy, and the tendency to find fault. Through maitri you develop appreciation and respect for others.

Karuna means "compassion." *Compassion* literally means to "feel together," but the term goes beyond empathy. Compassion encompasses the motivation to relieve suffering, understanding that when you relieve the suffering of another, your own suffering will be relieved too. Maitri and karuna are given by Patanjali in the Yoga Sutra as two practices for maintaining one's innate serenity of mind. A serene mind contributes to a good mood. A good mood leads to equanimity of mind, which enables a person to have equal regard for everyone— enemies, friends, relatives, and even those of a different religion, ideology, nationality, or species.

Essentially, the practice is to put others first, to avoid dwelling on what we think is good for us and instead devote ourselves to uplifting the lives of others. That is a foreign concept for most of us; we are usually taught to take care of our own needs first and to stand up for our "rights." But that approach only reinforces the sense of separateness that is the source of negative emotions and suffering. Consider the question, Would I rather be right, or would I rather be free? Egos can be right, but they can never be free, because the nature of the ego is to hold oneself separate from others and even from God. The *atman*, the divine soul within, loves what is and is not concerned with self-righteousness.

To shift your identity away from your ego and toward the Divine, you must train yourself to overcome negative emotions. Let go of resentment when you see others succeeding, or satisfaction when you see others failing, or self-righteousness when you see others behaving badly, and instead recognize that happiness and compassion for others, even when it feels unjustified, will ultimately lead to lasting happiness for yourself. Be a well-wisher. Cultivate compassion by being kind to others and finding ways to joyfully serve them; devote your life to making them happy. It may not be possible to directly serve every single being in the world, but when you offer your actions to God and sincerely desire to feel God's presence in your heart and all around you, then you may be able to enhance the lives of others and, most importantly, increase the awareness of God's bliss in the world. When the bliss of the Supreme Atman, the *Paramatman* is increased, negativity is decreased.

There is no negativity in the enlightened state. But to get there, we must become acutely aware of our negativity in all its forms and do our best to let it go, using japa, maitri, karuna, and other selfless devotional practices. Only true love can rescue us from the prison of I, me, and mine. May we all be released from the bondage of our insatiable small selves and dwell forever in the loving presence of the Divine Self.

Compassion During Crisis

yam hi na vyathayanty ete / purusham purusharshabha
sama-duhkha-sukham dhiram / so 'mritatvaya kalpate

*The person who is not disturbed by happiness and distress
and is steady in both is certainly eligible for liberation.*
—Bhagavad Gita 2.15

Everything in this material world changes. It doesn't always change according to how we would like it to, but as yogis we learn how to be steady and even joyful amid upheaval. Remembering who we really are during times of crisis is essential. Happiness is our true nature—to be unhappy is to deny our true nature and instead choose to dwell in ignorance. *Avidya* is ignorance and means "to be ignorant of who we really are." Avidya causes us to identify with our body and mind, a misperception of our true nature. The body and mind experience suffering, so when we identity with the body and mind we experience suffering. The true Self knows that suffering is temporary and that happiness is eternal. From this point of view there is never a good enough reason to be unhappy, because unhappiness is contrary to our true nature. As Shyamdas said, "Our greatest wealth is the remembrance of who we really are." To discover our connection to the eternal Self, to God, will bring happiness. To seek this discovery is the purpose of our lives.

Many years ago, I was invited to teach yoga for a few days to a Buddhist teacher who was doing a three-year retreat in the Arizona desert. Every six months he would come out of retreat for three days to give public teachings. I met many people there who had come to listen to his teachings. Several of them I recognized, having seen them attending classes at the Jivamukti Yoga School in New York. When they encountered me, they seemed amazed to see me there and would say somewhat apologetically, "I love yoga, but feel I need a spiritual practice to help me cope with the real issues of life, and that's why I'm a Buddhist now." I was surprised that these people felt yoga was not a spiritual practice applicable to their daily struggles and challenges.

Recently in response to the current events in the world, most especially the Covid-19 pandemic and racism in the US, a Jivamukti Yoga teacher said despairingly, "Yoga is not the answer to everything; now is not the time for introspection but to act." I have heard similar responses from yoga teachers and students over the years at other times of crisis—be they a personal crisis (for example when a loved one dies), a national crisis (like the 9/11 attacks), or a global one (the devastation of our environment).

When overwhelmed by circumstances that appear to be out of one's control, it seems to be an all-too-common response by yoga practitioners to throw yoga out the window and adopt an attitude of anger, sadness, and blame, as if these emotions could bring clarity or practical solutions to the issues at hand. The crisis we are all facing is a spiritual crisis. If one feels that yoga doesn't have anything to contribute during a time of crisis, then they must have a limited conception of what yoga is and how the practice works.

Yoga comes from *yuj*—"to yoke, unite, or reconnect to or remember God," the eternal Self. There are many yogic practices that help to bring about this reconnection to the eternal source. Chanting God's name, prayer, meditation, and asana are just a few. Any action if done with the intention to remember God can be a yogic practice, including marching in the streets, providing food for the hungry, and comforting the sick. If, however, the action is motivated by anger and blame, it will not bring about a reconnection to God, but only reinforce the domination of the ego within a person. The ego by its nature is selfish and incapable of compassion. Yoga practices help us to bypass the relentless demands of the ego, expanding our perception of self.

The presence of God can be felt through compassion. We come to know God through compassion. Compassion is a yogic practice that leads to Yoga—to enlightenment—to the reconnection with the eternal Self. This process of transformation is spiritual activism. By relinquishing one's own petty agenda, the individual becomes a spiritually activated instrument for God's will (*not mine but Thine be done*). In the space of meditation or contemplation, one can have *darshan*—see beyond judgment, be able to shut up and listen to that still voice within—and find out "how" to respond compassionately to situations that arise.

Devdutt Pattanaik, in his commentary on the first chapter of the Bhagavad Gita, speaks of the yogic development of darshan —clear perception that arises through compassion:

A world based on judgment evokes rage, life becomes a battleground where both sides feel like victims, where everyone wants to win at all costs, where someone will always lose. In judgment, the world is divided: good and bad, innocent and guilty, polluted and pure, oppressor and oppressed, privileged and powerless. In darshan, one sees a fluid world of cause and consequence, where there are no such divisions. A world created by observation evokes insight, hence affection, for we see the hunger and fear of all beings. Life becomes a performance on a stage. If you can empathize with the fears that make people heroes, villains, and victims, then you are doing darshan. For then with compassion, you can look beyond the boundaries that separate you from the rest.

Negative emotions like anger, sadness, confusion, despair, and blame cloud one's perception of reality and disable one from acting from a place of serenity. It is from this place of calm clarity that solutions will be found and a new direction perceived. It is a normal reaction to feel angry and sad when thousands of people are dying from the viral pandemic, others have lost their jobs, and many are being violently abused, even murdered, because of their skin color. Yes, these reactions are normal, but a yogi must resist the seduction of negative emotions, which only heighten the polarity observed. A yogi is not a normal person, easily satisfied with *samsaric* existence. A yogi is interested in living liberated, becoming a *jivanmukta.*

Then, what to do? What action is appropriate during times of crisis? Can you still take to the streets and protest? Can you still wish for a kinder world? Yes, if you are willing to be motivated by a power beyond anger, blame, and preference. Patanjali suggests that when you encounter suffering, *duhkha,* you should meet it with compassion, *karuna* (PYS 1.33).

Compassion brings about the arising of enlightenment—seeing beyond the limits of one's ego-encapsulated small self. But what is compassion? Is it the same as sympathy or empathy? No. Sympathy is to recognize that someone is in pain; empathy is not only to recognize the pain of another but also to feel it as if it is happening to you. Compassion includes sympathy and empathy, but it raises the bar a few notches. A compassionate person recognizes that someone else is in pain and feels that pain but is committed to finding a way to alleviate it, understanding that relieving the suffering of another will alleviate their own suffering as well. Yoga practices are designed to help one develop compassion and by means of compassion dissolve the illusion of otherness and all the prejudices that arise from that polarity.

As a person exercises compassion as a practice, they get better at it, and the result is that they grow into humility—a direction away from selfish ego concerns. To be humble is to be close to the earth, unpretentious, to bend like a blade of grass, to serve rather than expect to be served or acknowledged. It is possible to let go of the demands of the ego, but it does take practice. The yogic nature is to be a servant—to others and to God —rather than be self-serving. As a servant you do your best while not being concerned with controlling the outcome of your actions. You do your best and let God do the rest—meaning that you act without selfish motives, trying to manipulate the outcome. This involves *vairagya*, the yogic virtue of nonattachment. The Bhagavad Gita speaks of Yoga as the perfection of action. If we want to act perfectly in a time of crisis, we cannot allow negative emotions like anger, sadness, or blame to motivate our actions, because if we do our actions will be imperfect and result in future suffering.

At this time of crisis, all those who are acting selflessly, responding to the suffering of others with compassion and humility, are coming closer to Yoga—to the remembrance of who they really are—to the reconnection with the *atman* (the eternal divine presence within). Through service we understand that we cannot "help" anyone—we can only serve. As we become a channel for service, the understanding of the yogic teachings that mysteriously speak of God as the doer begins to dawn. Through compassionate service the presence of God is revealed. When this occurs, it is felt as joy and with it comes the realization of grace, and the only response is gratitude—to the crisis for providing the opportunity to serve.

This awakening to the joy of serving is what my friend, the Catholic priest Father Anthony Randazzo, calls "radical servant-hood," in which you become a channel and are serving from the core, from the root of your being, from your soul, rather than your ego. The more you serve in this radical way, the more fulfilled you become and the more able to serve you become. When you tap into the well of compassion, you discover it is limitless—as it is the loving nature of God. As God spiritually activates you with compassion, your activism becomes *for* rather than *against*, and you become clear, steady, and joyful in the midst of crisis, able to uplift the lives of others.

Do Your Best and Let God Do the Rest

tyaktva karma-phalasangam / nitya-tripto nirashrayah
karmany abhipravritto 'pi / naiva kinchit karoti sah

*The one who has let go of the results of their actions is content
and free of dependency knowing that,
although they appear to be acting,
they are actually not the doer.*
—Bhagavad Gita 4.20

We cannot do everything at once but we can do something at once.
—Calvin Coolidge

Time is a wonderful gift that keeps everything from happening at once. Many of us struggle with time. We curse it, we fight against it. We try to fit everything in, and we worry that we may have missed windows of perfect timing. *If I had just been ready, the timing would have worked out. If I had just had more time, I could have done it better. There's not enough time to get everything done.* And on and on.

There are many books and workshops on the topic of time management and organization, and they may provide some helpful tips. But as yogis, we look to the root causes of our dissatisfaction, and in this case, the underlying issue is disappointment and self-loathing—thinking that we're not good enough, that there's something missing, that we should be able to accomplish more. We all suffer from these self-doubts to some extent; none of us is alone in this.

How can we resolve this struggle? By doing our best to make the most of our time, but at the same time knowing when to ease up and acknowledge that *I did my best, and guess what? I'm going to get up tomorrow morning and try again to do my best.* That is the practice—to renew our commitment to doing our best while simultaneously not holding ourselves to any particular outcome. If we color our efforts with a constant feeling that we didn't do our best, that we're disappointed in ourselves, that there was some better way, and if we could only find it or someone could help us, then everything would be okay, then we experience the suffering of time. In fact, we have found the solution already. What we are doing now in this very moment, how we are doing it, is exactly what we should be doing—there is no other thing to do or other way to do it! And if we could just get inside one moment of that, instead of doubting and thinking, *This probably is not ... I don't know ... it might not ... it's the only thing I ... it's what's happening ... well, I don't ...,* you just inhale and exhale and step one foot in front of the other.

If we give our energy over to our problems, they grow larger and maintain their prominence in our experience. The major problems in our life are usually never solved through thinking. When we can elevate our mind beyond our thoughts, a solution will be evident.

The practice of *shavasana* (corpse seat) is very useful in this work. It helps us not quite to overcome, but at least to begin to understand, this struggle more deeply, because it brings us to an awareness of the impermanence of life and the nearness of death. Shavasana is the practice of dying. We lie down and tell ourselves: *This is it; I can't do anything else, there are no more projects I can do, there's nobody else to call, there are no more emails, there's nothing else. ... All there is is just to let go into this.* And as yogis we practice that every day. Through that practice, we prepare ourselves for death, not in the way we have been conditioned by our culture to operate—by getting as much done as quickly as possible, frantically, against all odds—but by actually, consciously participating in the doing of everything we do.

Dhyana, or meditation, is another profound yogic practice that can help us connect to the eternal, unchanging reality within and come to see that our struggles and self-doubts are not who we really are. That's the art of yoga: exploring how to participate by asking questions like: What is this *me* who's doing these things? Who is this *ahamkara*—this sense of self, or ego? Who is the real doer here? A yogi strives to relinquish doership through surrender to God, by praying, asking to be made an instrument for God's will.

What can we really do but do our best and let God do the rest? We must find some way that works for us every morning, or at least some time during the day, to offer ourselves as a conduit for the Divine Will, because if we, meaning our limited personality self, think we must do the whole thing, it gets overwhelming, and we will never feel we have enough time and we will be doomed to fail. But if we can surrender to limitless potential, if we let go and let God, if we can make ourselves into a conduit, then we *can do it.* Then we will realize that we have just the right amount of time.

Three Steps

tad viddhi pranipatena / pariprashnena sevaya
upadekshyanti te jnanam / jnaninas tattva-darshinah
*If you seek enlightenment, find a teacher, prostrate before them,
question them, serve them, listen to them,
and be open to their knowledge.*
—Bhagavad Gita 4.34

*You can teach a person all you know,
but only experience will convince them that what you say is true.*
—Richelle E. Goodrich

My first real spiritual teacher was an alchemist named Randy Hall. By "real spiritual teacher," I mean that he consciously gave me teachings and practices to help me understand the spiritual principles underling all of existence. By "alchemist," I mean he practiced the ancient art of alchemy, of transforming the ordinary into the extraordinary. My teacher was a photographer by profession, and his knowledge of chemistry was not only practical but metaphysical as well. I initially came to him because I wanted to know the cause of physical matter. I asked him, "What makes form, form?" We started with chemistry.

Under his tutelage I studied the basic building blocks that constitute matter—the twelve cell salts. These salts, being crystalline in form, provide a mathematical or geometrical grid that attracts subtle vibrations and organizes them into what eventually becomes manifest form. I also learned how to grow crystals in test tubes in a laboratory setting and assisted him in classical long-term alchemical projects that dealt with elemental properties of minerals, especially mercury and gold. He taught me the value of meditation and how to look deeply into ordinary things to discover their essence, which included the investigation of words and their etymological meanings. He infused our lessons with practical science, providing what he promised was an experiential connection to truth.

During this time, because of his guidance, I was drawn to the Theosophical Library, an occult library in Seattle, Washington, where I spent many hours reading books about yoga, saints, Eastern religions, and enlightenment. Several books stand out in my memory—all biographies: *The Autobiography of a Yogi*, by Paramahansa Yogananda, and two books by W. Y. Evans-Wentz, *Tibet's Great Yogi Milarepa* and *The Tibetan Book of the Great Liberation*, a biography of Padmasambhava. After I read these, I professed to my teacher that above all else I wanted to become enlightened and asked if he could help me. He raised his already very arched eyebrows and slowly, with a kind smile, said: "First you must master three things, which by the way, are basic to alchemy: 1) Cooking—you have to learn how to become a good cook; 2) Cleaning—you have to learn how to keep the place you live clean and organized; and 3) Gardening—you must learn how to grow, nurture, and care for plants."

I was incredulous at his response. It disappointed me, and I couldn't embrace his advice seriously as it didn't seem "spiritual enough" for me. Cooking? I was an impatient, skinny girl who disdained eating and was trying to reduce my food intake to a minimum and eventually live on air. How did he think I could get into cooking, what possibly could be the point? Cleaning? Oh, come on, that's for housewives—I was a liberated woman! Gardening? How old-fashioned—in the modern world we all live in cities; farmers grow crops, and landscapers deal with flowers and such. I thought I was too intellectual and spiritual for those types of pursuits. Besides, I didn't want to waste my life in such ordinary activities; I wanted God-/Self-realization right then.

My teacher was patient. He taught by example and was often in the kitchen mindfully preparing a vegetarian meal, focusing on each moment of preparation—scrubbing carrots, slicing cucumbers, or measuring out rice as if he were in deep meditation. There would be no small talk in the kitchen—all his focus was on the meal preparation. It was, after all, an alchemical experiment, and he didn't want to miss one moment.

His living space was immaculate, sparse, Zenlike, with every item carefully placed and cared for. His clothes were always folded, and he didn't keep extra clothes he never wore. He had a minimum of possessions—"More time to meditate!" he would say. His altar was simple but beautiful. He would always remind me how important it was not to allow clutter or dust to settle on one's altar, as it was the mirror for one's mind. On most of his windowsills, there were vibrant potted plants, and in the summer, he grew organic tomatoes, cucumbers, and herbs in window boxes.

Observing him, I came to understand how work could be transformed into worship. He knew how to see the extraordinary in the ordinary, and he tried to teach me how to do it too. He would say encouragingly: "Whatever it is you are doing, do it wholeheartedly, be completely involved. Don't stop doing your spiritual work to take a break to do your other work; do you really have time for *other work*?" I came to realize that he saw everything he did as part of his spiritual work. I remember watching how he washed dishes, handling each dish as if he were bathing a newborn baby. When he scrubbed the floor, he would get down on his hands and knees with a cloth to wash it by hand. I still find that this is the best way to clean floors. He would comment that it enabled him to be fully present in the task and that it then became a ritual that resulted in not just a cleansing of the dirt from the floor but also a purification of the subtle atmosphere of the room.

I'm sure he was reciting prayers or mantras to himself as he scrubbed; for him, housework was a spiritual practice—a form of purification. When he was cleaning, sweeping, or scrubbing floors he was concentrated on what he was doing. He was careful not to distract himself by chatting or listening to the radio or music through headphones. And he also never did anything that he didn't want to do; for instance, he never took a job just for the money. "How could I spend time in something I didn't enjoy? This is my life!" he would say. He often had to take dishwashing jobs in restaurants to earn money, but he never perceived the job as mundane; he was somehow able to elevate it in his own mind. He was certainly the most dignified dishwasher I had ever seen!

It took me many years to realize the wisdom of my teacher's advice, but I have come to see it as essential to a spiritually fulfilling life. These three steps have universal application to your relationship with the basics of your life: what and how you eat, where and how you live, and who the other living beings around you are. Are you relating in a way that enhances the lives of others and your own life, or not? Are you getting so far out and overextended that you are forgetting to go far in and pay attention to what is happening in front of you?

Spiritual aspirants often become so focused on what they perceive as their spiritual practice that they not only neglect, but even become estranged from, physical things. When this happens, it pulls them further away from the goal of spiritual enlightenment—the realization of the Oneness of Being. It also draws them back into the negative viewpoint of our culture, which has conditioned us to think of the physical as mundane and vapid and the intellectual as superior.

For example, we generally give the jobs of cleaning, cooking, and farming to lower-class people, mostly women, and leave the jobs that are considered more important and more lucrative, like those in finance, law, and medicine, to those we deem higher-class professionals. But this overlooks the great value in attending to the physical and the basic, which are the foundation for the spiritual. As John Lennon discovered when he became a "house husband" and spent his days cooking, cleaning, and caring for his baby, "Life is what happens to you while you're busy making other plans."*

The third step—gardening—can encompass taking care of anything or anybody: feeling joy in contributing to nourishing another and seeing them blossom, becoming happy and healthy. You don't have to have a plot of land in your backyard and grow lots of vegetables, particularly if you live in a city. You could have one rosemary plant in a small pot on your kitchen windowsill, or you may have a cat or a dog you take the time to feed well and provide for, thus improving their life. That animal may or may not live with you, might be a feral street cat or a dog who lives at the local shelter whom you visit regularly, volunteering to take them for a walk or bring them some special food. Through your caring they feel nourished and can blossom.

When I lived with my alchemy teacher, I also had a cat. Her name was Eva. I did not know enough at that time to feed her well. Basically, I would buy the cheapest box of kibble and sprinkle it in a bowl a couple of times a day. My teacher would say, "She is your cat, she is totally dependent upon you, you say you love her, so why not at least provide her with the best food possible?" I pooh-poohed him, as I felt I was doing my best. I wasn't conscious enough to see his wisdom, but nonetheless he took it upon himself to cook for her. I laughed at him the first time I saw him kindly present her with a home-cooked meal, which she graciously and enthusiastically accepted. But within a few weeks I saw her change and become much more beautiful, healthy, happy, and vivacious.

The idea of gardening, which is in essence the caring for or nurturing of life, can also be extended to taking care of wild animals. You could feed the wild birds and/or squirrels who might live near your apartment, home, or workplace. You could hang a bird feeder out your window. Or if you live in an apartment in the city and your building doesn't allow that, feed the birds on the streets, always remembering to bring a bag of organic seeds and nuts with you as you leave your apartment and distribute that food generously to the hungry birds and squirrels trying to stay alive in the midst of a city dominated by human beings. Ultimately, gardening is about taking care of something or someone and deriving pleasure by contributing to their well-being and seeing them thrive.

The three steps can also be a guide to yoga asana practice. Asana is often relegated to the status of menial labor—something one does merely to get in shape, as if that were less valuable than any other activity one might engage in. By paying attention to the basics—maintaining the seat of the asana (the connection to the Earth), proper alignment, breath, and intention—the practitioner can delve more deeply into the subtler aspects of the asana, which will make the practice much more powerful and yield more profound results.

Without mastering the seemingly ordinary basics of living, no spiritual maturity, much less real spiritual evolution, is possible. One must first grasp the magic in the ordinary before the extraordinary dawns, and once it does the everyday is never the same as it was before. It will take on a vibrant richness that was always there, but that you are now able to perceive and feel the joy of.

*Lyrics from "Beautiful Boy (Darling Boy)," by John Lennon, from the album *Double Fantasy.*

Prayer for Universal Peace

Om dyauh shantir antarikshagum shantih
prithvi shantir apah shantir oshadhayah shantih
vanaspatayah shantir vishve devah shantir brahma shantih
sarvagum shantih shantir eva shanthi sa ma shantir edhi
Om shantih shantih shantih

May the heavens—the sun, moon, stars, galaxies, and all zodiac signs—
be in peace and harmony. May the space between the earth and the
sun, moon, and stars be peaceful and without pollution. May our mother
earth be happy and peaceful and free from all pollution. May all the
waters be peaceful and free from pollution—the oceans, rivers, drinking
water, and rain, with no acid rain. May all the medicinal herbs and
plants be in their natural state and be free from pollution. May the
whole vegetable kingdom, especially all the trees and forests, be in a
natural state, healthy and free from disease due to pollution. May all the
elements—earth, water, fire, air, and ether—and all the cosmic forces be
in peace and harmony, without pollution. May our body, mind, and soul
and all of existence be in peace and harmony, free from pollution. May
everything, in and out, be peaceful and in natural harmony, without
pollution. May peace itself be real peace, not artificially maintained by
military and police forces or balance of nuclear power. And last but not
least, may that natural peace, harmony, and unity blossom and flourish
through us.

Om shanti shanti shanti: peace—physically, mentally, and spiritually.

—From the Yajur Veda,
interpretative translation by Shri Brahmananda Sarasvati

Yoga provides the means to reintegrate all aspects of one's
being. If your heart is filled with sincere, pure, and selfless
intention, then you will experience a deep internal healing and a
deep inner peace in your own body, mind, and soul. But more
than that, yoga will provide the means to reintegrate the
individual with life itself, so that you may experience the
unchanging eternal cosmic reality, the blissful source of all beings
and things.

The practices of yoga can transform us into spiritually
activated beings, free from fear, fueled by the power of peace,
compassion, and love. The practices will help us heal the dis-ease
of disconnection in ourselves. A state of disconnection leads us to
pollute our inner and outer environment. That pollution comes in
the form of our thoughts, words, and actions.

You will be able to tell if you are making progress in your
yoga practice and causing less pollution to the environment by
the words you choose, and by the sound of your own voice. When
you can say what you mean and mean what you say—with your

whole being—then you know you are moving closer to your highest potential, which includes the ability to truly serve others. You enlarge your circle of compassion to include all others—not just those few human beings you know and like, but even those you find difficult to relate to, perhaps even those who speak a different language or belong to another species. You begin to understand who you are and who "they" are. You begin to see through the differences and into the sacred truth of Oneness.

This practice of living and expressing yourself peacefully will naturally evolve into mindfulness regarding your actions, including your diet. A plant-based vegan diet will contribute more to reducing the pollution of fear and violence in your own body, in the bodies of others, and in the world around you than any other action you could take.

The practices of yoga create peace in ourselves, and that peace will be reflected in the world around us. If we truly want world peace, we must begin by embodying that peace ourselves. The practice of yoga will end war, even wars of which we often are not aware. Unfortunately, there are many human wars being fought on this planet at this time, but the ongoing war is the war against Mother Nature, human beings versus all other animals as well as the planet.

Traditionally, the yogi has been that member of society who strives to live harmoniously with Mother Nature. The true test of moral fiber during these violent times is not to stand against war but to stand *for* peace. Speak out for peace, live peacefully, think well of others, do what you can to uplift the lives of others. Find a way to live so that your own life enhances the lives of others. Give up the love of power for the power of love. Peace will come when we have given up hateful thoughts, cruel words, and violent actions in our own daily lives. Cultivate hopeful thoughts, sweet speech, and kind actions. Don't wait for a better world. Start now to create a universe of harmony and peace. It is up to you. It always has been!

Breathing

God is breath. All that breathes resides in the Only Being.
From my breath to the air we share
to the wind that blows around the planet: Sacred Unity inspires all
—John 4.24
interpretive translation from the Aramaic by Neil Douglas-Klotz

All living beings are spiritual beings, because in one manner or another, all of life breathes. Breath is an indication that spirit is present. In the ancient languages of Aramaic and Hebrew, the word for spirit (*ruha* and *ruach*, respectively) also means breath. Even in English, breath is defined as the vital spirit that animates living beings. Our breath is connected to the air that every being breathes. By breathing consciously, we acknowledge our communion with all of life. There are atoms of air in our lungs that were once in the lungs of everyone who has ever lived and is living now. In essence, we are intimately touching and connecting with one another with every breath we give and take.

To be alive is to breathe. To live and breathe with an exclusive focus on our small self, disconnected from the whole, is the definition of egotism. The enemy to the spirit is the selfish ego, who thinks that happiness can be gained through causing unhappiness and disharmony to others, through possessing and labeling. In many ancient languages, the word for enemy means one who falls out of rhythm, one who is not working in harmony with the larger group. Freedom from this enemy can begin by letting go of the breath as "my" breath. As we let go of the tendency to possess the breath, we enter into the shared life force, into a sense of harmony, which connects us all: the breath of life, the Holy Spirit.

If you want to know if someone is a "spiritual being," ask yourself, "Are they breathing?" If the answer is yes, then you know that you are in the presence of a spiritual being. May we have the good sense to bow to one another in celebration of this universal tribal community of sacred, holy beings. Perhaps this is what Patanjali was suggesting when he said *sthira-sukham asanam* (PYS 2.46), "May our relationships with others be based in steadiness and joy and be mutually beneficial."

The Hopi Elders tell us that we have passed the Eleventh Hour, the time of reckoning, and that *now* is the hour. Because of this, we should deeply consider all of our relationships, including whom we are breathing with, what or whom we are eating, where we are living, and with whom we are living. The Hopi wisely tell us: "At this time in history, we are to take nothing personally, least of all ourselves. For the moment that we do, our spiritual growth and journey comes to a halt."

What could it mean to take oneself personally in such a way that it would impede one's spiritual growth or cause it to stop? Our culture is essentially a domineering, herding culture. It is founded upon the enslavement of others, primarily other animal nations. We consider it our right to rob these others of their life breath. We stop their breath by slitting their throats by the billions every day in abattoirs. The mores of our culture encourage us to seek self-gratification at the expense of others, even at the expense of the greater Earth community, assuming, mistakenly, that we can exist outside that community. The separation of spirit and body and of humanity and nature is the result of the notion that the Earth belongs only to human beings. This ignorance (*avidya*) and egotism (*asmita*) lead to low self-esteem and to our feeling that what we do as individuals has little bearing overall, and as a result we can feel inadequate and insignificant. This feeling of insignificance represents the "personal' delusion that the Hopi Elders describe as the ultimate hindrance to our spiritual advancement.

Through communal yoga practice, self-confidence arises as we experience the wonder of breathing together in a variety of ways. Through chanting mantras and prayers, a greater sense of well-being is revealed by adding our voices to the choir. When we rhythmically move together, in tune with breath and intention, we overcome debilitating estrangement, as we feel a part of a greater community. This unifying experience comes from a deep-rooted space of expansive, yet inclusive, consciousness, where all of existence is connected and pulsating with the joy of this wholeness, or holiness. That realization of unity is joyful and cannot be attained through hard struggle, working against something, but only through holy celebration.

Holy celebration is inclusive, as it embraces the whole community. Not one of us is an isolated case. Every action has tremendous impact upon all of creation. The key that unlocks the door to unlimited possibilities, providing us with hope for a future life on Earth, is to actually take responsibility for our individual actions. Could we investigate the possible outcome of each exhaled breath, each word spoken, each action taken, and ask ourselves, "Are my actions contributing to the happiness and well-being of the greater community?" If not, then could we have the courage to recognize that our actions are not being done in holy celebration, because they don't include the whole? Could we bring more sacred awareness to how we breathe and interact with the world?

Through the act of breathing, we intimately interact with the world: we give and take with life by means of the molecules of air we exchange with each other. We are breathing one another! So, stop holding your breath and get yourself in tune. Let us breathe with one another, and together dismantle our present master-slave culture by finding a new way of living, based in the universal or unifying pulsating, musical language of harmony and partnership.

The Hopi Elders inspire us to pulsate with the global community when they encourage: "The time of the lone wolf is over, gather yourselves! Banish the word *struggle* from your attitude and your vocabulary. All that you do now must be done in a sacred manner and in celebration. We are the ones we have been waiting for."

Taking Yoga to the Next Level

The question is not, "Can you make a difference?"
You already do make a difference.
It's just a matter of what kind of difference you want to make
during your life on this planet.
For an activist to make positive change in the world
they must be spiritually activated.
—Julia Butterfly Hill

To be a true anarchist is to be ruled by the true Self.
—Swami Nirmalananda

All of life is sacred. The manifest world is a divine creation, an extension of God. God dwells in all beings and things. God can be found in the world, but one must seek to find the presence of God. One must desire to know the truth and beauty that underlies all things. The highest purpose of life is to seek enlightenment, the remembrance of God. Yoga is the enlightened state. The enlightened yogi feels the presence of the *atman* as their eternal blissful soul. The enlightened one realizes the Oneness of Being and perceives the interconnected and interdependent nature of all forms of life on Earth.

The yoga practices emphasize our relationships to all of life, because only when these relationships are mutually beneficial will there be an opportunity for the healing of the dis-ease of disconnection that plagues us. When the disconnection is healed, then the presence of God is revealed. The yogi recognizes the divine presence in others. Yoga is a peaceful, practical philosophy leading to the perfection of relationship and mutually enhancing connection to all creatures and things. Compassion is the means to perfect our relationships with others, bringing about the realization of the interconnectedness of all of life. Compassion makes enlightenment possible; this is what it means to live liberated, to live as a *jivanmukta*.

Our inner life creates our outer environment. When our inner state is refined, we become spiritually activated and we see the vibrant calmness of our soul reflected in the lives of others in the world around us. Yoga teaches us how interdependent we are. How we treat the world will determine how the world treats us. As yoga practitioners we cannot be content to live in our own little "I, me, mine" yoga bubble while the rest of the world deteriorates. We are amid a global crisis; we human beings are causing it, and most of us are totally unaware that we are causing it and/or that we are in a crisis. Only a small fraction of human beings are aware of this crisis.

Yoga provides us with tools to transform our perception; the change we wish to see in the world, must start within each of us. We must reinvent ourselves and find a way to think, live, breath, speak, eat, create, as well as shelter, clothe, entertain, educate, and transport ourselves so that our entire presence enhances the world and all of its creatures, as opposed to degrading and destroying it and them. To do this demands that we see all of life as sacred, not disposable, and not existing for our exploitation. This is what spiritual activism is.

Our teacher Swami Nirmalananda considered himself an activist and an anarchist. He defined anarchism as Self-rule, and he made the important distinction between Self and self. Enlightenment is the only type of anarchism that would benefit everyone in the world and is the only type of activism to pursue. To be ruled by the eternal Self, the atman, is to be free of hate, jealousy, fear, greed, and anger. The Self dwells in joy and, with equal vision, devoid of prejudice, beholds all.

Jivamukti Yoga is a path to enlightenment through compassion for all beings. The fundamental premise of the Jivamukti method is to act in such a manner as to be fully aware of the existing conditions, and, rather than complain, blame, and find fault, to instead create a new, joyous, and harmonious way of living that will enhance the environment as well as the lives of all other beings. Drawing inspiration from the desire to reconnect with the divine Self, this method supports physical, energetic, and spiritual activism that promotes environmental health, human rights, animal rights, veganism, and peaceful coexistence with Mother Nature.

Now, while we still have some choices left, let us choose to be kind to others, let us look to the happiness, well-being, and liberation of others, and in so doing we will find our own happiness, well-being, and liberation.

Political Activism
and Spiritual Activation

We live in a world that is full of problems,
and we are the solutions to those problems.
—Julia Butterfly Hill

The activation of an ethically based and philosophically sound spiritual practice means the integration of those precepts into the body politic, meaning the environmental, social, and political realms. We are members of various communities. Some of these communities are based on geography and others on genealogy; both are profoundly affected when selfish viewpoints are replaced with compassionate wisdom. The larger world community is thus positively affected by the political activism resulting from the critique of a truly activated spiritual being—the *jivanmukta*. Each action, every choice we make as individuals and as members of communities, affects the world in which we live. *Politic* refers to the tribe, the people, the other folk we live and thus interact with on all levels. We live under the same sun, we breathe the same air, we drink the same water. Our individual actions affect the communal sun, air, and water. If we reflect upon that, it becomes apparent that all actions are political.

In fact, we determine our shared future by our actions and choices in the immediate present, today, right now, wherever we are. Our karmas are intricately intertwined, and it is of the utmost importance to make conscious, kind, educated choices that will inevitably shape our communities far and near. Yoga practice is about cleaning up our actions. *Karma Yoga* translates as the "perfection" (*yoga*) of "action" (*karma*). A perfect act, from a yogic point of view, is a selfless act. The yogi acts perfectly, through their *satsang,* or community of truth-seekers, because what is best for the individual can be determined only by considering what is best for the whole. To be politically active, in truth, means to actively look after the safety and welfare of the others with whom we live. Caring for others will bring us closer to enlightenment quicker than any other action.

To vote means to care, to vow, to wish, to express an opinion, to choose, endorse, or authorize. Voting is a verb. We vote with every action we take. Certainly, we cast our vote every time we purchase something. We may complain about the greed of "big business." We may point our fingers and accuse our government of selling out to corporate seduction. But *we the people* must realize that it is we—you and I—who fill the coffers of the corporations. In our desire for happiness, we consume the products they provide and then demand more. We expect our politicians to maintain our high standard of living, with the military forces of the police and army if necessary. Our standard of living is based on personal wealth, not on the quality of life for all beings. Through these selfish actions, we deaden our senses and widen the gap of disconnect between ourselves and this Earth and all other beings who share it with us. There is no end to our insatiable appetites, however, because material objects can never satisfy the desire for happiness. Things or other people cannot give us happiness. We already have happiness, it is our very nature, it dwells within our souls regardless of external material conditions. To discover it, we must look within ourselves. When we look outside ourselves for happiness it will always elude us.

It is we the people, whether rich or poor, who seem to want more and more. More shopping malls, more gasoline, more oil, more clothes, more cars, more shoes, more entertainment, more pharmaceuticals, more theme parks—we want it all. The conditioned mind desires unceasingly and mostly unconsciously.

We must look beyond our conditioned minds and deeply into our own souls to find what is really valuable. Love is the hidden wealth within our own souls. When we delve into the infinite well of love within us and share it with the communities to which we belong, we start to free ourselves from the chains of complacency. Project positive thoughts, words, and actions. Always vote *for*, never vote *against*. Like Gandhi, "Be the change you wish to see." Yoga teachings reveal that when we can take responsibility for the discord we see in our world and not blame others, then we are at a very important step in our path to enlightenment. When we recognize that others do not hold the key to our happiness, that we hold it within ourselves, a true sense of confidence arises.

See yourself as part of the problem, but most importantly as part of the solution. Stay positive, refrain from anger, divisive speech, and gossip. Reduce the amount of stuff you buy. Reduce the amount of gas and oil you use; don't drive if you can walk or bike. Clear out the clutter in your home. Try to live even more simply than you do now. Do your part to reduce the amount of garbage in the world. Go vegan.

Swami Nirmalananda said: "We do not seem to realize that

each of us is responsible for the present condition of the world and society. Therefore, each one of us has to cease contributing to the problems so that we may have a better world and society." We will see an end to war and hunger when we can find a way within ourselves to live simply so that others may simply live. We will see peace on Earth when we ourselves can dare to have the courage to create that peace within ourselves and embody it.

Don't be silent, but use your words to uplift, speak sweetly, kindly, and respectfully. Dare to care: Devote yourself to the global community enough to vote for Love with every action you do.

What Is Yoga?

yogash chitta-vritti-nirodhah
When you stop identifying with your thoughts, fluctuations of mind,
then there is Yoga, identity with Self,
which is samadhi, happiness, bliss, and ecstasy
— wow, what a concept!
—Patanjali's Yoga Sutra 1.2

sada santushta-manasah / sarvah shivamaya dishah
sharkara-kantakadibhyo / yathopanat-padah shivam
Feet that wear shoes walk in comfort over stones and thorns;
so, too, the person encased in the peace of the Atman,
finds joy wherever they are.
—Shrimad Bhagavatam 7.15.17,
interpretive translation by Ramesh Menon

Sutra 1.2 is how Patanjali defines Yoga. It can be translated as, "When you cease to identify with your thoughts, fluctuations of mind, then there is Yoga—identity with Self, which is samadhi, happiness, bliss, and ecstasy."

Wow, what a concept! And it is from this simply stated concept, this simply stated idea, that the philosophy, paths, methods, and practices of yoga have emerged and developed. But if we take into consideration the thousands, maybe millions, of books written about yoga since Patanjali made this statement, we must conclude that the question What is Yoga? has continued to challenge and confound scholars, practitioners, and devotees alike, even though Patanjali gave us the answer in four straightforward words. But can words alone ever answer our deepest questions?

Well, we can at least look at the words and contemplate what they might mean: *yogash*, "then there is Yoga—the realization of the connection to the supreme Self, ecstasy"; *chitta*, "the content of the mind"; *vritti*, "the fluctuations, whirling, or movement of the chitta"; *nirodhah*, "the cessation or letting go of identification with the movements of the mind." By means of nirodha, the revelation, the remembrance as well as reconnection to the eternal Self arises. Yoga is that reconnection, that remembrance. This magical occurrence is a shift in one's perception of reality.

Nirodha makes Yoga possible. Nirodha means to stop or to cease. Nirodha, in this sutra, means ceasing to identify with your personality, or limited self, which is composed of thoughts— worldly thoughts that mire you deeper into *samsara*. Nirodha, from a yogic viewpoint, is the renunciation of suffering. It is not a renunciation that can be forced. Shyamdas described it like this: "Nirodha, true renunciation, is when you simply forget about samsara, because you are so filled with bliss." Nirodha is the state of one's consciousness being absorbed into the Supreme Self.

Yoga means "union with the Self": not the self in the limited sense of mortal self, the body/mind/ego/personality, but the higher Self, the divine, eternal, Supreme Self—God. The practices of yoga are concerned with shifting one's identity away from the unreal to the real. To dwell in the eternal reality of the *atman*, the Sanskrit term for the manifestation of the Supreme Self that dwells within each being, is Yoga. Yoga is synonymous with *samadhi*, enlightenment, and *moksha* (liberation). When the individual soul, the *jiva*, is liberated from *avidya*, or misidentification, it is liberated from samsara, the world of suffering, the wheel of time.

The unenlightened identify with the self not the Self. Nirodha causes you to remember who you really are—you remember your connection to God, the atman, the Self, the divine soul within, beyond your body and mind—and this is Yoga. The practices of yoga can help you to develop nirodha—to stop associating with ideas, things, and activities that don't bring you closer to God. Swami Satchidananda said: "The cause of bondage and liberation is our own minds. If we think we are bound, we are bound. If we think we are liberated, we are liberated. It is only when we transcend the mind that we are free from all these troubles." Yoga practices help to purify your mind and direct it toward that which is transcendental, that which is real. But yoga practices alone cannot bring you to that goal. Your own efforts can only prepare you to receive God's grace.

Yoga arises magically. It is a gift of grace from the Divine. You can't make it happen and you can't go and get it—you can't *do* Yoga. All you can do is to let go, and *it* will reveal itself because *it* was always there. Your connection to God was and is always with you. As many religious scriptures have said, including the Christian Bible: "Be still, stop striving, let go, and know that I am God and am with you always" (Psalm 46.10). And the Bhagavad Gita: "I am seated in the heart of all living being" (BG 10.20).

When you cease to identify with your thoughts—to see yourself as defined by your thoughts, to mistake yourself for your thoughts, or to see yourself as the sum total of your thoughts— then Yoga will come. Your remembrance of your eternal, blissful connection to God, your identity with the atman, will be the result, because there is nothing left after you have dropped everything that is unrelated and surrendered to God. Therefore, Patanjali's answer to the question What is Yoga? is paradoxical. He does not give the answer, because the answer cannot be adequately explained, it must be experienced, and so it is with continuous practice, continuous dedication, and loving devotion that the revelation arises ... and arises ... and arises. Divine ecstasy is like that—it continuously unfolds, blooming beyond mental comprehension.

In the Yoga Sutra, Patanjali provides us with many practices to facilitate an expansion of awareness, to pull us out of stuckness, including asana, that can facilitate the realization of who we really are, our connection to that which is eternal, and with it resolve all our questions. The radical psychologist Carl Jung recognized Yoga as the union of the individual self with the transcendental Self and that the practices could lead to a "natural process of introversion." He felt that psychological healing could arise through the contemplative practices of yoga and take us out of our preoccupations with our personal problems and connect us to something larger than our individual psyches.

All the greatest and most important questions and problems are fundamentally unsolvable. They can never be solved, but only outgrown. This out growing proves on further investigation to be a new level of consciousness. Some higher or wider interest appears on the horizon, and the unsolvable problem loses its urgency, fades out when confronted with a new and stronger life urge.—Carl Jung

The yoga mat is a good place to cultivate this experience of introspection. When your body is in an asana, what thoughts go through your mind? *This is too hard? This is too long? This is not for me?* Or are you able to simply sit with the asana, be present, and witness what is happening, rather than identify with it, allowing thoughts and feelings to arise without providing mental commentary or judgment? Most of us are obsessed with our body and its physical comfort and with what we think we want or don't want. The yogi, who gets a glimpse of happiness beyond the temporary wants of the body and mind, simply shifts their interest toward that which was always there—the eternal, blissful soul, the atman. The yogi finds joy everywhere they go, because it is the nature of their own soul.

This shift happens by means of nirodha, by letting go. Nirodha doesn't mean to force yourself to stop doing or thinking something; it is a more organic process. To cease to do something because you have lost your interest in it is very different from forcing yourself not to do it. To restrict yourself forcefully can cultivate negativity. Nirodha is a state of renunciation that occurs through *vairagya*. *Vairagya* means "dispassion or lack of interest." It happens when you lose your passion for things unrelated to Yoga, for things that don't increase your *bhava*. You don't have to force yourself, you just lose interest in what used to obsess you; it just drops away. You grow out of it. "A yogi," Shyamdas would say, "is someone who has lost their taste for things that don't taste good."

Practice and Nonattachment

abhyasa-vairagyabhyam tan-nirodhah
*Identification with the fluctuations of mind
is stopped by practice and nonattachment.*
—Patanjali's Yoga Sutra 1.12

In sutra 1.2 of his Yoga Sutra, Patanjali defines the state of Yoga as the cessation of identification with the fluctuations of mind. He is describing meditation—connecting to the eternal unchanging reality within. Then, in sutra 1.12, he offers a two-step method for how to meditate—how to stop identifying with the fluctuations of the mind and thus how to attain Yoga. He tells us that through practice (*abhyasa*) and nonattachment (*vairagya*), Yoga will arise. When we stop identifying with our thoughts, we will see the true reality of who we are. We will feel the presence of the *atman*, the eternal soul, within. At that point, we will have reached enlightenment—the remembrance of God and the realization of eternal bliss.

So, all we need to do is practice and not be attached. All very good as concepts. But how to implement them? What do those concepts really mean? *Abhyasa* means "practice," and to practice something implies that you stay with it for a while. You sit with it, with the thoughts in your mind, and every time you have a reaction to those thoughts—for example, *Why do I have to work at this job? Why doesn't my spouse listen to me? Wow, why do we have to hold this shoulder stand for five minutes?* Or, *Why should I just sit here and try to meditate when I have important things I need to be doing?*—you note your reaction and you let it go. Then you note your next reaction, and you let that go too. And on and on. You keep witnessing your thoughts and your reactions to them. You let it all pass through your mind.

Through practice, what will happen eventually is that what is disturbing and not useful to you anymore will just fall away, and what is pleasant and useful will keep arising more and more. And in time you will be able to feel your soul—the presence of the blissful atman. But it won't necessarily mean that thoughts stop running unceasingly through your mind. The nature of the mind is to think. Annoying thoughts become amplified when you attempt to deny and push them away. As Sanskrit teacher Manorama D'Alvia says, "We need to sit with our chatter, our confusion, in order to find clarity, understanding, and stillness."

So why don't we all just do that and leave behind the

suffering of human life? One of my teachers once told me that anyone can experience *samadhi* if they lock themself in a room alone with no books or TV or phones and meditate sixteen hours a day for three weeks. But almost no one can do that, because after a short time of just sitting we feel we must get up and do something. Our past unresolved karmas and hankerings come to the surface and do their best to distract us, to pull us away; they make it too uncomfortable, too intense to just sit with ourselves and our thoughts. When something disturbing arises, most often our reaction is to run away from it. We "change the channel" so we never get to sit with it long enough to experience it fully. And when we do that habitually, we reinforce the difficult thing, we make it into something that can't be faced. It becomes buried deep within our psyche and stops us from moving forward and evolving spiritually.

To sit with something and not be disturbed by it, you must sit long enough to experience the disturbing thoughts without labeling them disturbing. Abhyasa allows you to witness the fluctuations of the mind and recognize that whatever feelings are triggered by those thoughts, whatever the experience is, it is just that: a feeling, an experience, and nothing more; it is not you.

Besides abhyasa, being able to sit with something, Patanjali gives equal importance to vairagya, detachment, as a necessary virtue to cultivate to enable Yoga to arise. Vairagya is needed to be able to sit with something. Vairagya allows us to face our thoughts and feelings without identifying with them, without thinking they are who we are.

Vairagya means "renunciation." But the yogic sense of renunciation isn't a puritanical type of forced ascetic self-denial; rather, it is a dropping away of interests that no longer increase your *bhava* for the Divine, a drying up, a disinterest in the material world of change and impermanence. To cease to do something because you have lost your interest in it is very different from forcing yourself to abstain from it because you think it is a bad thing to do.

Enlightenment is inclusive; judging things or others as bad is a negative projection, and negativity is a hinderance to enlightenment. You can't force vairagya. Of course, people try to, but it never turns out to be beneficial. Restricting yourself is when you tell yourself that you will not indulge in something you still really want because you are trying to be good, and you think that by abstaining from it you will develop the willpower to become a more spiritual person. But this kind of renunciation usually results in anxiety and suppressed emotions rather than enlightenment, because it is motivated by an egoic sense of willpower not a love for God.

True vairagya cannot be forced, but must be allowed to ripen naturally. When it does, the individual simply loses interest in things unrelated to their supreme goal. The following example is meant to shed light on vairagya as a natural development rather than a virtue to be forced—it's a bit worldly, but will, I think, nonetheless convey the point.

Did you have a favorite toy or game as a child, something you cherished dearly and couldn't bear to be separated from? For me it was the board game Clue. I was mad about it. Besides playing detective and wanting to solve the "Who done it?" mystery, I loved the little figurines of Colonel Mustard, Miss Scarlet, Professor Plum, and the rest, as well as the miniature murder weapons, the candlestick being my favorite. My mind was filled with thoughts about Clue. I dreamed about it. I would spend all day and into the night playing it obsessively with anyone I could get to play with me. But now, many decades later, I have no interest in playing Clue, although I still have the box with the game in it, stored in the closet with my old Barbie doll, whom I also lost my passion for. I don't have a negative view of Clue or of Barbie, it is just that my passionate interest in them has dried up, I have moved on to other interests and passions.

There is only one asana, and that is the relationship with yourself. Being comfortable with yourself—with your body and your mind—is the goal of asana practice. The English word *ass*, which means "seat," is related to the Sanskrit words *asana* and *abhyasa*. All relate to sitting as connecting—staying with something for a duration of time to understand its connection to you and being comfortable with it. The body and mind are composed of past karmas, unresolved issues. Allowing your relationship with yourself (your body and mind and all of its issues) to be steady and joyful will reveal the true Self, the atman inside of all the whirlings and changes. The true Self is eternal and unchanging, not dependent on any material condition for happiness; it is composed of bliss. Asana and meditation are the same practice—both are about being able to sit with whatever may be happening and trusting that inside it all is that eternal joy that is the actual true reality, and that is your own Self, the atman.

Every feeling, every emotion, positive or negative, has a starting point, an origin. According to ancient wisdom—not just yogic tradition, but all spiritual traditions—the source of everything is *ananda*, joy. The source of the entire universe is joy: boundless, limitless joy. The nature of our soul is joy. So, if we want to resolve a negative emotion like anger, we must allow it to go full circle. To resolve means to bring something back to its origin, to go full circle. That's the process involved in yoga. Whether it's asana or meditation, a disturbing emotion, or a feeling, you sit with it long enough and let it run its course; you feel it deeply and let it come out the other end, let it go back to where it came from, which is actually joy.

The paradox is that for practice to be effective, we need detachment; but to develop detachment (vairagya), we need to practice (abhyasa). So we go through a yoga class, a day at work, an evening at home, or a dinner with friends, and no matter what comes up, we sit with it. Sitting with it doesn't have to always mean sitting down on a meditation cushion. Sitting with something is being present with it, welcoming it—that is, not running away from it or resorting to blame or arrogance or other externalizing mental reactions, or if we do, then we note that and try not to be attached to it.

We try to avoid criticizing ourselves by, for example, saying, "Oh, I'm no good at this, all I ever do is lash out!" Little by little, we find that we can sit with it a little longer and remain unruffled. We embrace what is happening, but we don't hold on to the negativity that might be arising; we watch the passing and as we do, we begin to feel more serene, more detached from suffering. We realize that happiness is a choice. Joy, which is the nature of our soul, begins to arise, and that is the beginning of understanding the two-step method of abhyasa and vairagya that Patanjali offers as a means to Yoga.

Partner Exercise to Help Develop Abhyasa and Vairagya

• Partners 1 and 2 sit facing each other in comfortable positions, close but not touching.

• Partner 2 tells partner 1 a story about something painful, frightening, terrifying, worrisome, and/or upsetting that happened to them. Instructions for partner 1: Sit still and be completely attentive, listening to everything partner 2 shares, without reacting. Practice restraint by sitting with what you are hearing, not allowing your face to reveal what you might be thinking or feeling. Don't reach out to try to comfort your partner. Sit as if you were the impartial witness—the *sakshi*. This will allow your partner the freedom to express their feelings without being prompted by you.

• Set a timer for five minutes. When the timer goes off, partner 2 will have one minute to finish their story. After the conclusion, allow a minute or so of silence.

• Change roles, with partner 1 sharing a story and partner 2 listening.

This exercise shows how difficult it is to practice meditation, which is really the practice of sitting with the thoughts and feelings that make up your body and mind and not getting involved with identifying with those thoughts and feelings. The difference, of course, is that when you are sitting and practicing meditation both partners are inside you.

Sadhana Pada

*Chapter two [of Patanjali's Yoga Sutra] describes
the means of attainment of a concentrated state of mind
for one whose mind is restless and distracted.
Union and identity with Cosmic Consciousness cannot be obtained
by one whose mind is not self-disciplined and purified.*
—Shri Brahmananda Sarasvati

Yoga means "union with the Divine." This union with Bhagavan cannot be attained through effort alone—it occurs only through God's grace. All that exists is God, and all exists because of God. In an absolute sense, nothing is separate from Bhagavan. All is God's divine play. If one is to attain liberation from *samsara*, that would only happen as a gift from Bhagavan. All is God's to give or not to give.

There are two yogic paths (*margas*): *maryada marga*, "the lawful way," in which the yogi applies discipline and self-effort to bring them to the goal, and *pushti marga*, "the graceful way," in which the yogi surrenders to God's will. Both paths can bring the practitioner only to the doorway of liberation; it is Bhagavan who ultimately and gracefully carries the devotee across the final threshold. You cannot "do" Yoga. Yoga is who you really are. Yoga cannot be attained through effort alone—it arises gracefully. Grace, however, can arise only after the mind has been purified through much disciplined effort. You do your best and let God do the rest.

Patanjali opens his discourse on Yoga by stating in the first chapter of the Yoga Sutra, the Samadhi Pada, that Yoga occurs effortlessly when the mind has become purified and concentrated: *yogash chitta-vritti-nirodhah* (PYS 1.2)—when you stop identifying with your thoughts, the fluctuations of mind, then there is Yoga, identity with Self, Bhagavan, which is *samadhi*. According to Patanjali, the most direct method of bringing about *nirodha*, or Yoga, is by surrendering completely to God. *Nirodha* means "to be absorbed in God." Patanjali gives his one-step method to attain Yoga in the first chapter as *Ishvara-pranidhanad va* (PYS 1.23)—by giving your life and identity to God, you attain the identity of God, meaning, you come to know God. Some souls, because of past karmas, may be able to follow a path of total surrender as suggested in the Samadhi Pada. By "letting go and letting God" through graceful *sadhanas* like *satsang, kirtan, japa,* or *seva,* one can live a life of devotion—

cultivating *bhava*, the intoxicated mood of love for the Divine.

But the graceful path is not for everyone. In the second chapter, the Sadhana Pada, the chapter on practice, Patanjali describes a three-step method: *tapah-svadhyaya-Ishvara-pranidhanani kriya-yogah* (PYS 2.1). Here he provides the practical means of purifying and concentrating the mind so that nirodha is possible for those who cannot surrender everything to the Lord, yet. Some feel that they must "do" something, and some minds are restless, doubtful, and easily distracted. These aspirants can find solace in the Sadhana Pada. Patanjali has compassion for souls who are unable to surrender themselves to divine grace alone and provides a whole chapter describing more detailed sadhana.

The chapter begins by suggesting to the aspiring yogi that, not only is effort essential, but it must be the unrelenting kind of effort. *Tapas* means "to burn." We must have a passionate, burning desire to undergo whatever discipline is necessary in order to purify our thoughts, words, and deeds. When we let go of all self-cherishing, ego-driven, or selfish desires, then we can concentrate on *svadhyaya*, the study of the Self. *Svadhyaya* means "to focus upon the Supreme Self in all circumstances without any distraction." To study something means to give it our unwavering attention. These two *kriyas* (tapas and svadhyaya) will purify and render us able to surrender to God, expressed as *Ishvara-pranidhana*, the third part of the three-step system.

Then Patanjali notes the hindrances that may cause the practitioner difficulty in adhering to the three-step plan. He lists and describes these *kleshas*, along with the underlying karmas that allow obstacles to arise. Even though he has already provided us with a one-step as well as a three-step plan, from a place of seemingly tireless patience, Patanjali provides an eight-step plan (ashtanga yoga) for those of us who still need more "how to" direction in order to untangle ourselves from the *duhkha* (suffering) that binds us. Since many of us feel that our unhappiness is caused by the actions of others, the eight-step plan begins with the *yamas* (the Don'ts). The five yamas address our relationships with others. The first yama suggests that as long as we perceive others and not God, then whenever we interact with another we should not cause them harm, that we should treat others with kindness. The other yamas tell us not to lie to others, not to steal from others, not to abuse others sexually, not to hoard (to share what we have with others).

The *niyamas* (the Dos) are the second step of the eight-limbed system. The niyamas are five practices directed toward our personal world. They are composed of *shaucha* (cleanliness), *santosha* (contentment), *tapas* (discipline), *svadhyaya* (study of the Self), and *Ishvara-pranidhana* (devotion to God). The third limb, *asana*, addresses our physical presence in the world. Patanjali suggests that our relationship to the Earth should be mutually beneficial—it should be steady and joyful. The fourth limb focuses on the life force, *prana*—that invisible force that permeates all of life. To learn how to direct the flow of prana in our own body is to learn how to control our own mind and thus begin to free our mind of whatever may be restricting it from divine ecstasy. The fifth limb, *pratyahara*, deals with the discipline involved in drawing the senses away from outward hankering and redirecting our attention inward, toward independence, toward being dependent on the divine Self. Through these practices the content of our mind becomes more and more purified preparing us for the more inward oriented, subtle, esoteric, meditative practices that comprise the final three steps.

Sadhana Pada, the second chapter, lists all the eight limbs, but only describes the first five. Sadhana Pada concludes with the practice of pratyahara. Patanjali then begins the third chapter (Vibhuti Pada) with descriptions of the final three steps: *dharana* (concentration), *dhyana* (meditation), and *samadhi* (ecstasy). When the various practices described in Sadhana Pada have been mastered, the aspirant has achieved a mind capable of resisting distractions and is then able to probe into and gain knowledge of reality. They are ready to embark upon the final three steps and eventually embrace the practice of *samyama* (the combination of the three), and this is what the third pada will deal with.

The fourth and final chapter (Kaivalya Pada) will conclude with descriptions of the exalted state of Yoga and how the effortful practices described in Sadhana Pada, as well as ideas of doership, and all that seemed to keep the aspirant separate from Bhagavan is eventually dissolved into grace.

Ahimsa: The Foundation
of the Yoga Practice

Nonviolence is absolute commitment to the way of love.
Love is not emotional bash; it is not empty sentimentalism.
It is the active outpouring of one's whole being into the being of another.
—Dr. Martin Luther King, Jr.

Yoga is becoming popular all over the world, while meanwhile we are experiencing a global crisis. Human beings have caused this crisis, but yoga may hold the key to saving the planet, because yoga teaches us how to live harmoniously with the world, and with all other beings and things. As a species, we have forgotten how to do that, and yoga is waking us up and reminding us how to live. When we rediscover our connectedness to the whole, the shackles of culture will fall away, and we will find ourselves in the land of freedom. Yoga teaches us that every action we take matters, and that everything we experience in our life is a direct result of how we have treated others in our past. Kindness is the only action worth pursuing, and the best way to uplift our own lives is to do all we can to uplift the lives of others. *Ahimsa* is the foundational practice for these realizations and is vitally important for the understanding of yoga and how it works.

Ahimsa allows compassion to arise within us. This compassion provides us with the means to let go of "otherness" in order to see our self in the other, our true Self. The biggest obstacle to that realization is seeing others as separate from ourselves. What is realized in the enlightened state is Oneness: the interconnectedness of all beings. Ahimsa is a key practice in facilitating this awareness. Patanjali gives us the very practical practice of ahimsa as a means to this yogic realization of the interconnectedness of all beings. As the first *yama*, or restraint, ahimsa provides guidance for how to direct our behavior toward others: as long as we see others, don't harm them. Patanjali also tells us that if we continue to practice ahimsa, nonharming, we change and so do the people around us, and eventually the whole world changes for the better. He says that when we become established, *pratishthayam*, in this practice of not harming others, then others will stop harming us, not just physically, but through their thoughts and words too.

Wow! Imagine living your life with that kind of security and ease, never worrying that someone is thinking or dreaming something negative about you. You always appear as a benevolent presence in their waking, as well as in their nightly, dreams. No one speaks harshly to you or gossips about you. No one looks to hit you or bang you over the head. No one will ever wish to terrorize, exploit, or harm you in any way. You will live amid a society of peace.

To create that society of peace, we must understand how karma works. According to the laws of karma, everything has a root cause, and so whatever we want, we can have, if we are willing to provide it for others first. If we want happiness, then we must make others happy. If we want to be free, then we shouldn't enslave anyone. If we want enlightenment for ourselves, then we must begin to see others as holy, enlightened beings. Through such purification of perception, we become enlightened, because ultimately, it will take an enlightened being to see another enlightened being, because "it takes one to know one." The practice of ahimsa helps us to further understand the laws of karma in order to alter our perception of ourselves and others.

To live in a way in which our own life enhances the lives of others is a radical concept, as it gets to the very root of how happiness arises. If we want to be happy, we do what we can to bring others happiness, not suffering. Yogis by nature are radical; not content to live superficial lives, but instead, they enjoy diving into root causes. Patanjali opens his Yoga Sutra with *atha yoganushasanam* (PYS 1.1), which translates as, "Now this is Yoga as I have observed it in the natural world," implying that any of us could come to these yogic realizations if we were willing to look deeply into causes, and not just skim the surface by identifying with symptoms.

We live in a culture that tells us that the Earth belongs to us, and that it is our right to exploit others for our own needs and desires. A yogi, on the other hand, realizes that violence brings only more violence. Violence can never bring peace. Ahimsa is the practice of nonviolence. By understanding how things come about, yogis then consciously attempt to choose their actions wisely, doing their best to plant only the seeds they want to reap.

The Five Tenets

Om saha navavatu saha nau bhunaktu saha viryam karavavahi
tejasvi navadhitam astu ma vidvishavahai
Accept us both together. Protect us both together.
May our knowledge, wisdom, and strength increase together.
May we not resent one another.
—Kena Upanishad

Jivamukti Yoga is a path to enlightenment through compassion for all beings. *Ahimsa, bhakti, dhyana, nada,* and *shastra* are the Five Tenets that form the foundation of the method. The tenets provide a structure and through their exploration enable a practitioner to find ways to awaken compassion in their own hearts. Each of the tenets is a practice on its own, but when linked together and applied to *asana* make the ancient teachings of yoga profoundly relevant in our own lives and in the lives of others.

Asana practice gives us a starting place. Our bodies provide us with a wealth of hidden potential. When the threads of the Five Tenets are woven through an asana practice, the weave gives substance. We are aroused from the sleep of mundane existence and see with wonder the vast resources inherent in our lives. We grasp the connection between the physical and the spiritual and realize that we are much more than a body, a skin-encapsulated ego. We come to perceive how our actions affect the lives of others as well as reality itself. How gratitude awakens humility and in turn will awaken the love within us for God and all beings and things.

By taking the time to be still with deep reflection, we come to understand our bodies as instruments for love. As the incessant chatter in our minds begins to subside, we hear the music of the spheres and tune ourselves to those harmonious frequencies. As we delve into the study of the ancient teachings and hear the messages from the yogis who have gone before us, we feel an affinity. Our quest for truth is kindled with the fire of determination, tempered with respect and kindness. Our lives take on profound meaning as we feel a part of a greater whole.

The Five Tenets inform everything a Jivamukti Yoga teacher does, whether in classes, workshops, at home, or in other community interactions. In a Jivamukti open-level class, they have a special role, helping students learn not to see asana as separate from the practice of nonviolence, devotion to God, meditation, chanting, or scriptural study. The tenets integrate all the elements that make up Jivamukti Yoga into one unified practice. This provides a well-rounded approach to the goal—enlightenment through compassion for all beings.

When I first started teaching yoga, there was no Jivamukti Yoga School, nor had the Five Tenets been assembled as the foundation of what became our method. I taught in health clubs. Although the managers of these clubs appreciated my skills, they made it clear that I was hired to teach "yoga" and should not teach meditation, speak about God or spirituality, chant Sanskrit mantras, and certainly not say the word *vegan* or speak about diet, but yes, I could play music. I was grateful to have a job, and so I respected their wishes.

After some time, David and I opened the first Jivamukti Yoga School. We were then able to teach yoga in a way we felt most aligned with, as a path to enlightenment, to increase devotion to God, and as a means to dismantle our present culture, in which cruelty and exploitation of animals and the environment is normalized.

At the time yoga was mostly viewed as nothing more than a physical-fitness regime. Yoga teachers did not teach asana as a means to delve deeply into unresolved karmic issues with others that are held in the body. There were a few yoga centers that offered meditation, chanting, and bhakti-related subjects, but no yoga center offered all of that in an asana class setting, and no one played music in class or discussed veganism, animal rights, environmentalism, or activism on any level. Yoga was perceived as apolitical. We were criticized by other more established yoga teachers, who told us that our way of presenting yoga was too provocative, not commercially viable, and we would not stay open for long.

The almost instant popularity of Jivamukti Yoga in New York City proved them wrong. Students flocked to our classes *because* they were unabashedly God-centered, infused with Sanskrit chanting, scriptural teachings, and a radical pro-vegan message—and great music too. When some of those first students became teachers, we encouraged them to not be afraid of being radical. We urged them to teach yoga as a spiritual practice relevant to today's world, and the school gave us all a place to do that. The Five Tenets were developed to provide guidelines to us as teachers; to foster a way to continuously deepen our understanding of the practices of yoga and their far-reaching capacity for individual and global transformation.

I want to share some thoughts about how those tenets can be incorporated into a yoga class. The list is alphabetical and does not reflect a hierarchy of importance; they are each integral to the whole.

1.   **Ahimsa:** A nonviolent, compassionate lifestyle extending to other animals, the environment, and all living beings, emphasizing veganism and animal rights.

Ahimsa is the primary ethic of yoga, and we model that ethic through the practice of veganism and/or animal rights in some way in every open-level class. Usually there is a way to share the message through teachings found in the Focus of the Month essay. But even when the Focus of the Month does not seem to create an opening for this moral point, it is always possible to include it by telling a personal story or sharing an anecdote or even just by a short phrase inserted somewhere in the class. At the end of class, the teacher might say, "Have a nice vegan lunch!" or, "Don't forget to feed the birds!"

Not all the students who come to a class will be vegan or have even considered becoming vegan. Judging and positioning yourself as superior to others has no place in a yoga class. Humility and respect are important virtues to cultivate as a teacher. The amount of respect we receive is in accordance with how much we respect others. If we want to be instrumental in awakening compassion in another person, we must also show compassion to that person. If we feel compassion only toward animals and are not able to feel it toward the students who come to us to learn, then we have no moral grounding with them. Without affinity, communication will be difficult.

That is one reason that it is important for us to always remember that when we give teachings, about ahimsa or anything else, we should consider in advance how we want the students to feel about themselves and then craft our message to achieve that result. Wanting them to feel guilty will only instill defensiveness, fear, and self-loathing in them. We must strive to empower. To this aim, the first step is for us to cleanse our perception of the students we are teaching. The most effective way to do this is to drop the notion that they are ignorant and that we are there to enlighten them. Instead, we must try to see them as God in disguise, giving us an opportunity to express with our whole being the very thing we are teaching. As educators, our job is not to cram information into students' heads, but to bring out the wisdom that is already there within them. That demands that we first bring it out in ourselves. If we can do this effectively, then even those students who seem not to be interested in veganism will have the experience of what it could be like to practice ahimsa, and with that seed planted, the possibilities are infinite.

Ahimsa is essential to a yoga practice, because the biggest obstacle to the realization of the Oneness of Being is otherness. Yoga helps us to expand our definition of self to include the larger Self, beyond our body and mind. The ego is self-centered and incapable of compassion. Through the practice of ahimsa, we become more other-centered and challenge the ego's assumption of what is possible. Compassion leads to humility and the realization of how we are a part of everything and everyone. With that realization comes the understanding that what we do matters and that everything we do will come back to us. Ahimsa is the key to peace. When we stop harming others, others will cease to harm us.

2. **Bhakti:** Acknowledging that God-realization is the goal of all yoga practices.

Bhakti means "loving devotion to God." The practice of bhakti nurtures faith and the acknowledgment of a higher power beyond our individual egos. Each person must discover the particular form of God that is most meaningful and relatable to them. Patanjali, in his Yoga Sutra, uses the term *Ishvara* to describe one's personal choice of deity. The Yoga Sutra emphasizes the importance of devotion to God and suggests that the aspiring yogi surrender completely and offer their very life to God, to attain the goal of Yoga—God-realization. The danger of practicing yoga without bhakti is that the person may easily get caught up in their own accomplishments, miring themselves deeper into *avidya* and identification with their body, mind, and ego. Devotion promotes humility, and humility is the key to enlightenment. The enlightened one realizes the *jiva* (individual self) as part of the greater Supreme Self. The practices of yoga are designed to help us develop humility. Humility releases us from obsessive self-concerns.

One way to incorporate bhakti into a yoga class is by setting a high intention at the onset. This can be done by the whole class reciting a prayer out loud together or silently. That intention should in some way reflect the aim of the practice—

enlightenment, God-realization. Since the intention behind an action will determine the outcome of the action, to practice with a selfish intention will not help us realize Yoga, while offering our actions to God would help. Some of us may not be comfortable with having God as the focus of our intention and may instead find it more comfortable to focus our devotion on a saint or spiritual teacher who represents the realization we are working toward. Another way to bring a devotional mood into the class would be to set aside a few minutes for the practice of *kirtan*, chanting God's name, or *japa*, repeating a mantra. However we choose to do it, infusing our class time with bhakti will help us step outside our ego-driven material desires and explore what it feels like to connect our hearts with the higher, universal Oneness. There is no doubt that any practice, asana included, that is infused with bhakti can lead to enlightenment.

3.   **Dhyana:** Connecting to that eternal unchanging reality within.

Dhyana means "meditation." Meditation is a part of every Jivamukti open class, both as one of the Five Tenets and as one of the Fourteen Points that must be covered. Meditation is integral to the practice of yoga because through its steady and consistent practice, you become more at ease with your thoughts and ultimately come to realize that you are not your thoughts. Meditation develops your ability to sit as a witness to your thoughts. When you can watch something, for example, your thoughts in meditation, you come to know that you are *not* that something (you are not your thoughts). Patanjali speaks of this process, *yogash chitta-vritti-nirodhah* (PYS 1.2): when you let go of identifying with your thoughts—the fluctuations of the mind—then there is Yoga, which is happiness, bliss, and ecstasy. This sutra implies that Yoga, or your connection to God, the unchanging reality, is your true nature.

Meditation facilitates this remembrance or realization that who you are is beyond your body and mind. You realize your eternal soul, the *atman*. Therefore, Yoga is not something you can attain or go out and get. You can't "do" Yoga or "do" meditation; *nirodha* is a process of letting go so that Yoga is revealed. There are many approaches to meditation. Some traditions suggest following the breath, others focus on gazing at a candle or an image. The Jivamukti style utilizes mantra as the focus. There are two mantras embraced by the Jivamukti Yoga method: the

183

mantra *Let go* and the Sanskrit mantra *Shri Krishna sharanam mama.*

Here are the basic instructions for the Jivamukti meditation method:*

1. Choose your seat.
2. Be still.
3. Focus.

To practice, you must sit down and be still for some duration of time. Figuring out how to sit can take some trial and error. It is best when you are beginning not to choose a seated position that is too difficult to maintain. Beginners need not aspire to imitate the image of a yogi sitting in *padmasana* (full lotus seat) to meditate. Any position, even sitting in a chair, can be used if it is comfortable. Choose a position that is comfortable at least at the onset, because it will most likely become uncomfortable as the minutes of your practice tick on. When physical distractions arise, like a throbbing pain in your hip or an annoying itch, try your best to let go of the discomfort and concentrate on your mantra.

To develop concentration, become aware of your breathing: feel each time there is breathing in and breathing out. Don't try to manipulate the breath; don't breathe in any special way. Don't even breathe; instead, allow the breath to breathe your body while *you* watch from the place of the nonjudgmental witness, the *sakshi.* Focus the mind by using the mantra *Let go.* Silently say the words *Let go* with the passing of each breath: breathe in *Let*, breath out *go.* Allow there to be a continuous movement of breath through the body and thoughts through the mind while you let go of identifying with your body and mind by letting go of each breath and each thought. If you feel comfortable with a more traditional mantra, then instead of saying *Let go*, recite *Shri Krishna sharanam mama*, which translates into English as, "My shelter is Krishna, the beautiful Lord of Love."

4. **Nada:** The development of a sound body and mind through deep listening.

The scriptures speak of *nada* as the primal sound vibration that is realized through hearing. Listening is an essential skill in yoga practice. When we develop our ability to listen, we become more receptive. Receptivity quiets the mind, along with the ego's incessant urge to do something. The Hatha Yoga Pradipika teaches that as we approach the enlightened state, we will be able to hear the *anahata nada*, the unstruck sound that reverberates in our hearts and throughout the entire universe. Incorporating sound into our classes is a way to help students develop the faculty of listening, which will help them on the path to enlightenment. Speaking, singing, playing live as well as recorded music and spoken word are some of the ways that a teacher can facilitate the development of listening in a classroom situation.

The visual sense speaks directly to the intellect, while the sense of hearing encompasses the heart and emotions. By using our voices effectively, we help the students shift away from reliance on their eyes to guide them and toward reliance on their ears, which have a more direct connection to their hearts. We might be able to deceive the eyes, but the voice never lies. It's not just the words we say, but how we say them. Others can pick up a lot of information from the tone, pitch, and inflection of our voice, which can reveal subtle meaning and intention. A student can hear in the teacher's voice how the teacher feels about them; in turn, this can encourage or discourage their openness to learning. Even when we aren't saying something out loud, our thoughts can be heard. Therefore, as teachers we must spend a lot of time purifying ourselves from negative thinking before we enter a classroom.

As a teacher, you may also wish to rely on the voice of another. Playing spoken-word recordings of great teachers infuses another dynamic into the classroom and is an effective way to develop listening. You might have given the same teaching, but when that teaching is spoken by someone else, in a somewhat different way, it can validate it and increase the chances of its being heard.

Because of the power of music and the names of God, leading the class in kirtan, or group singing, can purify everyone's mind. As a teacher you may not feel comfortable singing. It is appropriate to play recordings of other people and invite everyone to sing along. Listening to instrumental recorded music is another way to improve listening skills. Carefully chosen music can uplift and support the teachings you want to convey.

Even though the live voice of the teacher as well as the addition of recordings can be very effective, don't underestimate the power of silence, which can be a valuable way to teach students about listening. The ultimate listening experience is not to hear external sounds but to hear the inner *nadam*, which is, in essence, the sound of Om.

5. **Shastra:** The study of the ancient yogic teachings, including Sanskrit chanting.

Shastra means "scripture." Yoga is a practice that leads to enlightenment. A yoga teacher teaches how to navigate the spiritual path. The most qualified teacher to teach you Yoga, how to be enlightened, would naturally be an enlightened teacher. But it might be difficult to find one, since to recognize an enlightened being you also must be enlightened. You can't fake enlightenment, so what to do? Can you still be a yoga teacher, even though you may not consider yourself enlightened? Yes. The alternative would be to immerse yourself in the study of the enlightened teachings known as shastras, or scriptures. The words of *rishis*, holy beings, and yogis who have walked the path before us have been written down and are available to us.

Many of the scriptures are in poetic form, in the language of Sanskrit, which makes understanding Sanskrit valuable for a yoga teacher. Although it is not necessary to become fluent in Sanskrit, learning the basics of the alphabet and a bit of grammar will enable you to pronounce words correctly. The main texts that have been embraced by the Jivamukti Yoga method are Patanjali's Yoga Sutra, the Bhagavad Gita, and the Hatha Yoga Pradipika, which have been translated into many languages by many commentators. Becoming familiar with, and comparing different translations of, the same scripture will help you deepen your understanding of the verses and spark your own insights as to their meaning and application.

The study of scripture is a yogic practice described by Patanjali as *svadhyaya* and is thought to be an essential component of the eight-limbed system. *Satsang* is also regarded as a key element in yoga practice. *Satsang* means "being in the company of truth" or "keeping the company of others who are seeking truth." To commune with others who believe that enlightenment is possible and who feel the benefit of elevated discussion provides opportunities for the expansion of our own concepts and beliefs.

To this aim, the Jivamukti Yoga global satsang is supported primarily by the Focus of the Month (FOM), an essay that deals with a particular aspect of the yoga practice. Every month an essay written by a Jivamukti Yoga teacher is offered to our community to provide a focus for our practice and teaching. Teachers and students in many countries around the world read, study, and discuss the same FOM essay each month. Orienting our classes around the ideas presented, conveying those ideas to students, and discussing them among ourselves gives us a way to stay on point. Through the discipline of staying on the same point together for the month, we learn through our mutual study and research of the ideas presented in the essay.

The FOM essays usually begin with a succinct verse from a scripture that is then elucidated in the essay. One direct way to introduce the tenet of shastra in a class is to chant that verse in a call-and-response way in every class during the month. Focusing on one verse for a month, chanting it, and discussing it every day helps everyone learn that verse, pronounce it correctly, and contemplate its meaning. Over many months, we add to our repertoire as we immerse ourselves each day. By the end of the month most teachers and students find they have a pretty good grasp of how to pronounce the scripture correctly and have a good understanding of its meaning. Even more importantly, though, we come to grasp the relevance of the scripture to the asana practice we are engaged in, as well as the relevance of the scriptural teaching to our lives both on and off the mat.

Integrating the Five Tenets—ahimsa, bhakti, dhyana, nada, and shastra—into our practice and teaching of yoga helps our satsang strengthen as we grow together in spiritual wisdom. As a global community of individuals, we find common ground that supports each of us, enabling us to contribute in our own unique ways. Our roots entwine, broadening our understanding and increasing our capacity for compassion. We become *jivanmuktas*, spokespersons revealing that the ancient system of yoga is a living practice of spiritual activation with far-ranging implications for the individual as well as the world.

---

*You can find more detailed information about each of the Five Tenets in *The Jivamukti Yoga Chant Book, Yoga and Veganism,* and *The Magic Ten and Beyond*, all by Sharon Gannon; and in *Jivamukti Yoga,* by Sharon Gannon and David Life.

The Sound of Yoga

*Sound is the force of creation, the true whole. Music then,
becomes the voice of the great cosmic oneness
and therefore the optimal way to reach this final state of healing.*
—Hazrat Inayat Khan

When a goal is established, all faculties can then begin to align themselves toward the realization of that goal. All of the practices of yoga train the faculty of attention, harnessing and directing it toward the goal of Yoga. *Yoga* means "union with God," the unchanging, eternal ultimate reality.

Patanjali declares in the Yoga Sutra that God manifests as Om, as the *nadam*, supreme music. According to the Hatha Yoga Pradipika, the supreme yogic state is achieved when the nadam, or cosmic sound, can be heard. The aim of the hatha yoga practices is to render the practitioner able to hear this sound. The practices of yoga result in a sound body and a sound mind. The true meaning of this goes far beyond the usual understanding of physical and mental health. A truly sound body and mind is tuned to the cosmic vibration. In the final chapter of the Hatha Yoga Pradipika, we find this sutra: "When one hears the nadam, the quintessence of which is the supreme, the mind then becomes one with that supreme object and is dissolved in it (HYP 4.100).

The ability to listen is essential for God-realization. We can develop our ability to disengage from the *chitta-vrittis* (chatter of the mind) and listen beyond thought by developing the meditative method of witnessing. By observing the mental chatter, but not listening to it, the witness allows a deeper listening to occur. The development of refined listening results in an evolution of hearing. What does it mean to really hear? The Sanskrit word *shravana* means "hearing," but it has a fuller meaning than our English word *hearing*. *Shravana* is hearing in which the listener has not merely heard but has fully comprehended what they have heard, so that complete learning or knowing is the result. It is like when using the phrase "I hear you!" to mean "I really know what you mean, I got it, I fully understand."

The refinement of hearing is essential for the attainment of Yoga. One important method for refining your ability to listen, and thus to hear, is to listen to elevating music. Good music defies the thinking mind by going beyond it. Good music has no literal meaning at all. The music itself is its meaning. The spiritual experience, as well, defies the thinking mind and cannot be described in words. The best music to listen to is music that turns the mind and senses inward toward the Divine, allowing you to feel through hearing the cosmic vibration.

The Hatha Yoga Pradipika further informs us that audible sound frequencies influence the mind and body; even subtle frequencies affect underlying layers. When you listen to music it arouses different emotions and states of mind and affects different areas and centers of the body. Sound is the most powerful tool in pacifying the restless mind: "The mind, under the sway of the senses, is likened to a raging elephant confined within a garden. Nadam is likened to a goad, because it draws and directs the mind toward internal absorption and union with its source. Just as music can calm and relax the mind, making one completely forget problems and worries, so absorption in the subtle nadam brings forgetfulness of the external world" (HYP 4.91-93).

The Sufi mystic musician Hazrat Inayat Khan has declared, "The knower of the mystery of sound knows the mystery of the whole universe." The popular interest in Eastern philosophy and yoga entered Western culture via music during the 1960s. The Beatles spearheaded this interest. Swami Satchidananda gave the opening talk in 1969 at the Woodstock festival, where the theme was "Peace, Love, and Music." "Music is the celestial sound, and it is sound that controls the entire universe," he said. "So let all our actions and all our arts express yoga. Through the sound of music let us find peace."

With the contribution of The Beatles, especially George Harrison, Indian music became hip and Sanskrit lyrics along with Indian ragas entered Western popular consciousness. The Beatles were instrumental in turning us all on to things magical and mystical. They became vegetarians; practiced yoga, meditation, and chanting; and shared their experiences in song with us. George Harrison developed a lifelong association with his teacher, the Indian sitar master Ravi Shankar. Indian music is profoundly spiritual. As Ravi Shankar puts it: "Our Indian tradition teaches us that sound is God—*Nada Brahma*. Musical sound and the musical experience are steps to the realization of the Self. We view music as a kind of spiritual discipline that raises one's inner being to divine peacefulness and bliss."

A hatha yoga practice should incorporate methods that develop one's ability to listen. These methods include listening to spiritually uplifting music as well as the recorded voices of saints and insightful teachers during an asana practice. They include listening to the teacher's voice for direction and guidance, chanting holy words and sacred mantras, devoting time to the practice of *mauna* (silent listening), and perhaps the most important practice of all: listening for the sacred Om in all sounds.

Where Does She Go at Night?

Up on the rooftop top click, click, click,
down through the chimney comes old Saint Nick.
—From a Christmas song by Benjamin Hanby

There are three states of consciousness that a normal person goes through during every twenty-four-hour cycle: waking (*jagrat*), dreaming (*swapna*), and deep sleep (*sushupti*). There is also a fourth state known only to advanced yogis called *turiya*: it is a state of *samadhi*, or super consciousness. Each of us is conscious when we are awake, but it is said that when we go to sleep at night we "lose" consciousness. When we awake, often we do remember our dreams, but we never remember deep sleep, and yet if we are not able to enjoy a deep sleep, we will not feel rested upon awaking. Sleep-deprivation studies show that a person will become severely ill and could even die if they are not allowed to experience deep sleep. It is interesting that spending time every night in deep sleep, a state we don't even remember, could be that essential. The experience of deep sleep and its profound effects on us can be likened to Santa Claus coming down the chimney: no one sees him come, no one sees him go, but the gifts he leaves and the glee they evoke on Christmas morning are evidence of his visit the night before.

The Sanskrit word *kundalini* means "a coiled serpent." Kundalini is our consciousness or awareness, our ability to know, to understand, to perceive ourselves and others, to make sense of things and put things together. In a normal person, she is said to lie dormant in the lowest *chakra* most of the time. That place becomes her whole world—the world of mundane survival—eating, sleeping, working, etc. But secretly, there is nothing that kundalini wants more than to be reunited with her beloved Shiva, who resides in the crown chakra (the rooftop) at the top of the head. However, that reunion is difficult because of her imprisonment by her jailer, known to all as the mighty ego. Kundalini is beautiful, intelligent, and capable; she is *satyam, shivam, sundaram*—truth, bliss, beauty. But like many women, she will often cloak her true form, awareness, and capabilities and appear dumb in order not to appear *too* intelligent, lest she alienate or challenge the all-powerful ego.

Even though ego's attributes pale next to the serene beauty of the bliss-filled, immortal Shiva, for kundalini, ego does have a few qualities that Shiva could never boast of: a thinking mind, a heart filled with an almost infinite variety of emotions, and a firm commitment to time in the form of past, present, and future possibilities. To be married to ego ensures you of a mortal trip: the promise of the adventure is enough to seduce most souls to put aside immortality and climb on board the ship, the train, the bus, or the shiny motorcycle revved up and ready to go—the custom-made helmet even has your name on it, as if that is going to really protect you on the dangerous roads of life.

Succumbing to ego and allowing ego to run your life is addictive. Most ego addicts remain enthralled by ego's promises for millions, maybe billions, of lifetimes. But thank God, there are moments of respite from the constant demands of ego, and kundalini surely secretly looks forward to these breathers. Fortunately, these breathers usually come daily. Every night when ego goes to sleep, kundalini quietly uncoils from her resting place, unfolds her wings, and stealthily moves through the central channel to unite with her beloved on the rooftop. She may ascend and descend several times during the night. Characteristic of her gracious nature, as she moves up and down, she may stop and whisper or sprinkle magical dust in the form of a dream to gently feed the unfulfilled yearnings that live in each lotus chakra. But as day breaks, she faithfully returns, unnoticed, to her abode in the first chakra, and ego never knows of her nighttime rendezvous with her lover.

As normal people, we hide from our true Self, pretending that we are ignorant, mortal, and unenlightened. Identifying with ego, we spend our lives insisting that this is all there is to life. The spiritual aspirant, however, is not normal; the spiritual aspirant wants to wake up. Yoga practices stimulate that awakening. Yoga practices stimulate the awakening of kundalini. Meditation has been described as sleeping while awake. Instead of losing connection with consciousness, which is what happens when we fall asleep, in meditation the yogi sits and stays awake, trying to catch kundalini as she rises from her coiled resting place and ascends to the rooftop—Shiva's abode of joy in the highest chakra.

Much like children who attempt to stay awake on Christmas Eve to catch a glimpse of Santa, yogis attempt through rigorous *sadhana* to be able to see and unite with God. Some may view this as the extinguishing of ego, but to the yogi, when kundalini opens her wings and flies to her final destination, it is also freedom for the ego as well. Samadhi is yoga through meditation; the yogi yokes their ego to kundalini and rides the snake to the ultimate wish-fulfilling, immortal, blissful, stillness of the *sahasrara* chakra—the ultimate movement into stillness, turiya. Liberation is accomplished—all are freed from *avidya*. Kundalini is no longer imprisoned by a time-bound, mortal ego. Ego dissolves into the radiance of a fully conscious kundalini, who is now known as her true Self: the atman, cosmic consciousness. This final transformation is into *prema*—true and eternal cosmic love.

Karmic Loopholes

Blame keeps the sad game going.
It keeps stealing all your wealth—
giving it to an imbecile with no financial skills.
Dear one, wise up.
—Hafiz

The Bhagavad Gita opens with a chapter entitled "The Despondency of Arjuna." The scene is a battlefield. A great war is about to start. Arjuna, a champion warrior for one side in the conflict, asks Krishna, his friend and chariot driver, to draw the chariot between the two armies so he can see his opponents. Arjuna recognizes, in both of the assembled armies, people he knows. He sees his teachers and kinsmen: uncles, grandfathers, cousins, sons, grandsons, brothers, and friends. On seeing his friends and relatives positioned on both sides, all of them eager for the slaughter that is about to begin, the horror of the sight overwhelms him, and he freaks out, which is described in detail.

His arms and legs become weak, his knees buckle, his mouth becomes dry, his body trembles, his hair stands on end: *sidanti mama gatrani / mukham cha parishushyati / vepathush cha sharire me / romaharshash cha jayate* (BG 1.29). His bow falls from his hand, his skin burns, and his mind becomes agitated—whirling with confusion: *gandivam sramsate hastat / tvak chaiva paridahyate / na cha shaknomy avasthatum / bhramativa cha me manah* (BG 1.30). Furthermore, he has premonitions and sees that the outcome of this war will bring only sadness, grief, and fear: *nimittani cha pashyami / viparitani keshava / na cha shreyo 'nupashyami / hatva svajanam ahave* (BG 1.31).

Filled with dread, he collapses in despair and tells Krishna that he absolutely cannot fight the battle—that nothing good will come of it. Krishna responds by saying that he must fight and reminds him that to fight is his duty, his dharma—in other words, his job. This is the first great lesson in the Bhagavad Gita. It is Krishna's insisting that Arjuna fight that is most upsetting and confusing to many students of yoga, as it is hard to reconcile the teaching of *ahimsa* (nonviolence) and *shanti* (peace) found in Patanjali's Yoga Sutra with this directive to engage in battle, fight a war. It is unfortunate that a lot of people dismiss the study of the Gita right here, close the book and go no further.

But looking deeper can yield insight. The question of why

the Bhagavad Gita seems to condone violence when Patanjali suggests the opposite can be answered in this simple way: Patanjali is addressing yogis, or at least wannabe yogis, while Krishna is speaking to Arjuna, a prince and a soldier. Arjuna is not a yogi, yet.

We should also take into consideration that the Bhagavad Gita, being an Indian scripture, reflects the Indian caste system, under which society is divided into four groups: *brahmins* are the priests and scholars dealing with religion and philosophy; *kshatriyas* are the aristocrats and warriors; *vaishyas* are farmers and merchants; and the *shudras* are the artisans and workers. Arjuna is a kshatriya, a warrior prince, a politician. In his society it is his job to fight wars. Through his karmas, he was born into a royal family, in which his brothers, uncles, father, grandfathers, great-grandfathers, etc. have all been soldiers, involved in guarding and protecting kingdoms. It is in his blood. You could say that the *samskaras* (psychological imprints in the subconscious) of his previous karmas have dictated his present birth and profession. His dharma is to guard and protect his people. The fact that he is on the battlefield dressed for war is evidence of that.

But as we have seen, Arjuna is not acting like his usual self: up at dawn, dressed, weapon in hand, ready to ride bravely into battle. No. He is upset. His body trembles, his mind reels, he is unable to focus, and his heart is filled with fear and loathing for what he is about to do. He doesn't want to fight; he doesn't want to do his job. He wants to renounce war and be a peaceful yogi. His friend Krishna is there, by his side, to advise him.

Krishna, acknowledging Arjuna's anxiety, hopelessness, despair, and despondency, compassionately tries to convey to his friend that because his mind is unstable, overwhelmed by negative emotions, and not in a state of peacefulness, he is in no position to change the direction of his destiny. Krishna uses this opportunity to teach Arjuna about yoga and how to bring the mind to a place of equanimity.

When you want to change the course of your destiny, when you want to stop going one way, perhaps a way you have been going unquestioningly for some time, and instead shift and move in another direction, you must always make that change from a place of steady, calm clarity, if, that is, you want to stay on your new course and achieve positive results. Otherwise, it is just a matter of time before you will find yourself seemingly victimized in a similar situation, faced with the same problematic issues.

Arjuna's situation is not uncommon. There are times many of us find ourselves in a state of anxiety and want to alter our circumstances. We feel that our present circumstances are not providing us with the peace and happiness we want. Since we long for peace and happiness and think we can find it by changing our situation, most of us, like Arjuna, don't think the solution is in our own minds. So, instead we search outside ourselves for what we want. The path of the yogi is the path that reveals the secret to peace and happiness and how to realize it. We must change our minds from a state of anxiety into one of peacefulness. It starts with understanding that negative thoughts and projections are not helpful in bringing about a positive change in the direction of one's karmic trajectory. Anger, sadness, blame, etc. just keep the sad game going.

For instance, if you find yourself unhappy at work, in a job you hate, where there is constant tension between you and your boss, and you really would like to quit and get another job, then you must not stay at the job and build up resentment day after day until one day you explode, yell, "I quit!" and walk out. Why not? Because it will just be a matter of time before you find yourself similarly agitated in your new job. If you want to get out of *samsara* (same agitation), then you must be very careful not to make a life-changing shift while in a state of turmoil, with your mind filled with negative emotions, your body trembling, and your skin burning.

Here is another example: You feel that you are in a bad marriage and are very unhappy with your husband. Every day you find more and more evidence of how uncaring he is and how unfair and unfulfilling the relationship is. Over time you become more and more depressed and angry, until one day you blow up and scream that you can't take it anymore and want a divorce. You get your divorce, but then guess what? You soon find yourself in another relationship in which the situation repeats itself and you are once again very unhappy and disappointed. "All men are alike," you say with resentful resignation, and on and on it goes.

Yet another example: You are driving down the freeway at 80 mph and you suddenly realize you are going the wrong way. "Oh, no!" you say and slam on the brakes. The result will most likely land you in the hospital or the morgue—not necessarily where you were hoping to go. A better approach would have been to slowly take your foot off the gas pedal, shift gears, pull over, consult a map, and calmly plot a new course for your journey or keep going until you find the next exit so you can turn around.

This is an important lesson. Whenever you want to make a significant, potentially life-altering decision, you must do so from a place of mental equanimity. You must be calm and serene. You cannot redirect your karma successfully if you come from a mental state riddled with negative emotions. If a person is worried, has anxiety about the future, and acts from that place, he or she is not acting as a yogi.

The Bhagavad Gita offers an important lesson about karma. Arjuna is upset and wants to make a career change, but Krishna tells him: "No, this is not the right time. Now you must fight, because it is your duty. But if you are serious about changing your karma, I *can* help you with that. I can teach you yoga—the methods that can help bring about equanimity of mind and enable you to become the master of your destiny." And thus, as the rest of the Gita unfolds, Krishna teaches Arjuna what yoga is and how to become a true yogi—one who has joy in his heart and equanimity of mind. A true yogi is able to perceive a lump of clay, a stone or a nugget of gold as the same: *jnanavijnanatriptatma / kutastho vijitendriyah / yukta ityuchyate yogi / samaloshtashmakanchanah* (BG 6.8); and has equal regard for friends, companions, enemies, neutral arbiters, hateful people, relatives, saints and sinners: *suhrinmitraryudasina- / madhyasthadveshyabandhushu / sadhushv api cha papeshu / samabuddhir vishishyate* (BG 6.9).

Krishna mirrors what Patanjali says about Yoga being revealed through renunciation (*nirodha*), or the letting go of negative thoughts (*chitta-vrittis*) that disrupt the mind, taking one away from peace and happiness. Patanjali says that when you stop identifying with your thoughts, the fluctuations of mind, then there is Yoga, which is samadhi—happiness, bliss, and ecstasy: *yogash chitta-vritti-nirodhah* (PYS 1.2). Krishna suggests that the most direct means to Yoga—to God-realization, the release from suffering and turmoil—is to remember God in everything you do and surrender your actions to God. Renouncing the fruits of your actions will bring about peace of mind immediately—liberation from suffering. Renunciation is better than practice, knowledge and even meditation: *shreyo hi jnanam abhyasaj / jnanad dhyanam vishishyate / dhyanat karmaphalatyagas / tyagach chantir anantaram* (BG 12.12).

Our past karmas determine the path, the dharma, of our

present lives. Does this mean we have no free will? The Sanskrit word *dharma* means "to fix in place." Seen in that context, our past actions fix in place our future. The law of karma says that our past determines our future. We cannot change what we have already done, but we can change what we do now ... to a certain extent. This is where free will comes into play.

Every action—every thought, word, or deed—plants a karmic seed, which, under the right conditions, will sprout, grow, and bear fruit. The law of karma says that you reap what you sow. For example, if you hurt others in your past, you are destined to be hurt in your future. Violence brings violence, anxiety brings anxiety, etc.

But the yogic scriptures speak about loopholes that allow someone to free themselves from such results. The trick is to find a way not to water or fertilize negative karmic seeds, so that eventually but inevitably, they dry up and are never allowed to sprout, grow, and bear fruit in the future.

One loophole I know of is *bhakti*, which Patanjali mentions in the Yoga Sutra: *Ishvara-pranidhanad va* (PYS 1.23), which means that when we completely surrender our lives (*pranidhanad*) and offer our love to God (*Ishvara*), then Yoga is positively assured (*va*). He also says later that the karmas of a normal person are black, white, or mixed, but that the karmas of a yogi, one who has realized their connection to the Divine, are clear: *karmashuklakrishnam yoginas tri-vidham itaresham* (PYS 4.7). In other words, God frees His devotees from having to suffer their past karmic misdeeds.

Another loophole is described in the teaching of the Bhagavad Gita, as I described earlier: When you find yourself in a situation that triggers a negative response like despondency, anger, jealousy, revenge, or sadness, instead of indulging those negative emotions, you can use your free will to embrace the situation with calm discernment. In other words, you don't have to react with negativity. Although Arjuna was born a kshatriya, a warrior, when faced with the idea of killing his own relatives and friends, he became depressed and despondent and wanted to change his career and become a yogi. But because he was in a "bad place" emotionally, Krishna tells him that he is not in the right frame of mind to make a decision that would alter the direction of his karma. So he has no choice and must go through with it and fight. The outcome of the battle of Kurukshetra might have been different if Arjuna had approached his situation with *vairagya*, calm yogic discernment, and was evolved enough at that time to walk away from the battlefield into the forest to live the peaceful life of a yogi. But he wasn't.

The message for us all is to do our best to be free from negative emotions, not allowing them to determine our actions. We can start by not resorting to blaming and complaining and seeing ourselves as victims of others or of circumstances and instead embrace each moment with love—being able to love what is, seeing everything that happens as God's way of drawing us closer to Him. Seeing everything that happens as an opportunity for love allows us to truly exercise free will and move toward enlightenment.

The Seven Bhumikas

I shall now describe to you, O Rama, the seven states or planes of wisdom. Knowing them you will not be caught in delusion. Pure wish or intention is the first, inquiry the second, the third is when the mind becomes subtle, establishment in truth is the fourth, total freedom from attachment to bondage is the fifth, the sixth is cessation of objectivity, and the seventh is beyond all these. The highest state of consciousness can be obtained by all souls, including animals and illiterate persons, by those who have a body and even by disembodied beings, for it involves only the rise of wisdom.

—Yoga Vasishtha 3.118, translation by Swami Venkatesananda

Once upon a time, a long, long time ago, thousands of years, way back in another yuga, Rama, an avatar of Lord Vishnu, descended to Earth. He was born into a royal family as a prince. While a teenager, he embarked with his brothers on a tour of his country. When he returned home to the capital, he was changed, no longer a happy, enthusiastic youth. His view of life had been shattered by the reality he had encountered. He was devastated and haunted by the images that were replaying in his mind. His mind was consumed by the visions of poverty, sickness, cruelty, strife, pain, depravity, and suffering he had witnessed during his travels. Apathy had overtaken him; he found no joy in anything. He stayed in his room, with the drapes closed to the sun and his heart closed to his family and friends; he stopped eating. The boy became depressed and questioned the purpose of doing anything. He knew he was destined to rule the kingdom, but an ominous cloud of pessimism and hopelessness hovered over his heart, as he felt he could do nothing to change the miserable situation of the world and the pitiable fate of all living beings.

His father, King Dasharatha, was worried and asked Rama's teacher, Vasishtha, to intervene. Vasishtha meets with Rama, who reveals his anxiety, sadness, and feelings of ineptness regarding the overwhelming injustice and suffering he has seen. Rama concludes his speech by asking his teacher to help him understand:

I am filled with grief. My mind is confused, I shudder, and at every step I am afraid. What is the condition or state in which one does not experience grief? How can one who is involved in the world and its activities, as I am, reach the supreme state of peace and bliss? What is that attitude that enables one not to be influenced by various activities and experiences? Pray tell me: How do you people who are enlightened live in this world? Holy sir, instruct me in that wisdom which will enable my otherwise restless mind to be steady like a mountain. You are an enlightened being, please instruct me so that I may never again be sunk in grief. Obviously, this world is full of pain and death; how does it become a source of joy, without befuddling one's heart?—Yoga Vasishtha 1.30-31*

Vasishtha hears him out, and then they engage in a dialogue about the nature of reality, God, devotion, and the means to liberation, which has become known as the Yoga Vasishtha or Vasishtha's Yoga and contains 29,000 verses. Most scholars agree that the sage Valmiki was the author. The Seven Bhumikas compose a small part of this vast scripture. *Bhumi* is a Sanskrit word that means "stage, level, or place."

When Rama asks Vasishtha if there is a way out of ignorance, sadness, and suffering, Vasishtha assures him that there is. The great sage discloses to Rama that there are seven stages a soul goes through on the path to enlightenment. These stages, known as the Seven Bhumikas, the unfolding process of the aspirant's evolution toward Self-realization, are also discussed in another ancient yogic scripture, the Varaha Upanishad. The fourth chapter of that text relates a conversation between the sage Ribhu and his student Nidagha. Nidagha asks Ribhu to describe enlightenment and the characteristics of an enlightened being (a *jivanmukta*). Ribhu replies that there are seven stages of development.

The first stage, or bhumika, is *shubheccha* (good desire); the second is *vicharana* (right inquiry); the third is *tanumanasi* (thinning of the mind); the fourth is *sattvapati* (the attainment of *sattva*, or truth); the fifth is *asamshakti* (nonattachment); the sixth is *padartha-bhavana* (the disappearance of visible forms); and the seventh is *turiya* (the final stage of liberation). The text also describes in many verses what a jivanmukta is like, for example: "He is said to be a jivanmukta (an emancipated person), the light of whose mind never sets or rises in misery or happiness and who does not seek to change what happens to him, either to diminish his misery or increase his happiness" (VU 4.22).

Not everyone is ready to embark on the journey and enter the first stage; to travel the path to liberation one must be inclined to take the *nivritti marg*, the spiritual path that leads away from the world of changeable forms. Yoga is not for everyone. Many souls seek happiness in the material world, and so they follow the *pravritti marg*, the path that leads toward the temporary. Through both paths you acquire knowledge. If you follow the pravritti path, you get *jnana-vritti*—knowledge of the vrittis, of the material, changeable world of duality, with all of its fluctuating ups and downs. If you follow the path of nivritti, you get *atma-jnana*, knowledge of the *atman*, the eternal soul, the connection to the source, to God.

There really is no *good* or *bad* path to take, and you can't take the *wrong* path. The fact is, we don't choose our path; our past *karmas* (actions) do. Our repeated actions over many lifetimes create *samskaras*, which have established tendencies called *vasanas*. Vasanas determine our interests and which path we are inclined to follow. But what happens is, after thousands of lifetimes of wandering in the world, seeking lasting happiness, only to be disappointed again and again, the *jiva* comes to a point of realization that the material world is not going to satisfy their search for lasting happiness. It is then that they begin to look inward to discover what is eternal.

The Yoga Vasishtha states that you can embark on the first stage of the bhumikas only if you are on the nivritti path, if you have more of an interest in what is spiritual rather than material. The ancient Vedic system outlines the four pursuits of life as *dharma* (work), *artha* (wealth), *kama* (sensual pleasure), and *moksha* (liberation). Vasishtha says that the bhumikas are for those who are done with pursuing work, wealth, and sensual enjoyment and are ready for liberation. Moksha is their priority. Ultimately, when enlightenment dawns, the aspirant perceives the world not as a worldly place that must be negated but as God's manifestation.

Embracing faith is an important prerequisite before the path to enlightenment is revealed. The soul must believe that enlightenment is possible. They must sincerely want liberation more than they want *samsara*. Until then they will remain shrouded in ignorance. This ignorance, or *avidya*, will cause forgetfulness and blindness. The soul will forget their true nature, their eternal connection to God. They will be blind and not be able to see the eternal, blissful nature of reality. But if the desire for truth is sparked within and that spark is not ignored, but kindled by goodwill, then the first step is taken on the path. Goodness is the nature of the atman, the eternal soul.

The awakening of goodness can seemingly come out of

nowhere. It can be sensed when someone is kind to you. Its presence is often experienced as grace. It is felt as a good feeling. When you experience goodness, you want more of it, and that's good wanting. If you realize that the good came from within you and not from outside you, you want to discover the goodness of your soul. It is then that the first step on the path is revealed. That first step is *shubheccha*. It means good wanting.

1. SHUBHECCHA

The first bhumika, *shubheccha*, implies that you have a desire for good, that your preference is goodness. You have good intentions, which inclines your will toward what is good. Shubheccha is often translated as "goodwill." The Sanskrit word *shubheccha* is a combination of two words, *shubha* and *iccha*. *Shubha* means "auspicious" and *iccha* means "wish." An auspicious wish is a good wish, a wish for good. That is why in India shubheccha is often used as a happy birthday greeting.

We have all been in situations when our life is in turmoil, we are anxious, things aren't going well. If we let that negativity linger and spiral out of control, it will destroy our innate peace of mind, and without that we won't have clarity and be able to find a solution. Being able to muster the strength to not allow those mental toxins to overwhelm us during difficult times indicates the presence of shubheccha. Goodwill arises when our love for life, love for others, love for God merges into a heart and mind that are serene and loving by nature. When we decide to focus our will on the good, goodwill becomes so strong that ill will won't have a chance.

All of us can easily succumb to confusion and negativity and feel like a victim of other people or situations. We can feel that we are powerless against the forces of evil, that there is just too much cruelty and injustice in the world and we can't do anything about it. We can feel that we don't have a right to be happy in the face of such suffering in the world. We can feel that to put the despair aside would be turning a blind eye, ignoring reality, and suppressing the horrors. Negative thoughts can consume us to the point where we identify with them to such an extent that we feel cut off from the goodness of our eternal soul.

There is an old Native American teaching from the Cherokee nation in which a grandfather is talking with his grandson and says: "There are two wolves fighting within me, it's a terrible fight, they are fighting for their lives. One wolf is evil—

he is anger, bitterness, blame, despair, fear, greed, guilt, inferiority, jealousy, pride, regret, self-loathing, selfishness, sorrow, and worry. The other is good—he is benevolence, compassion, courage, cheerfulness, faith, forgiveness, gratitude, happiness, hope, humility, joy, kindness, love, patience, and optimism. This is a fight that is going on inside each of us." The grandson reflects upon this for a moment and asks, "Which wolf will win?" The grandfather replies, "The one you feed."

The old adage "You are what you eat" covers everything you consume—not just food but subtle emotions too. We are expressions of our thoughts and attitudes. The choice is ours; still, bad habits are hard to break. It may take some willpower, the power of goodwill, to start "eating right." But once you start, you set goodness in motion, and it will take on momentum. Goodness will prevail and outshine evil because goodness is at the core of existence.

A desire for goodness is the first step and it is where the most struggle occurs. Shubheccha is the most important step, and it continues to inform all of the subsequent stages on the path. There are four means to cultivate shubheccha: *viveka*, *vairagya*, *shadsampat*, and *mumukshutva*.

Viveka

The first means to shubheccha is *viveka*, or discrimination. The word viveka is composed of *vi*, meaning "to separate or order," plus *eka*, meaning "one." Viveka allows you to discriminate between what is real and what is unreal—being able to see through the changeful and perceive the changeless. When one has developed viveka, they are able to separate or discriminate the one from the many, as well as to see the one in the many. To see the eternal, unchanging atman inside everyone, to see the essential nature within the core of every material temporary form, is to have viveka. What does viveka look like when it arises in a person? Have you had an experience of meeting someone for the first time and it doesn't seem like the first time? There is something about them that is familiar to you. They may remind you of someone else you know. You re-cognize them, and because of this familiarity, you feel at ease with them.

Here's an example. I was in India, staying in a rural ashram teaching for a couple of months. I was really missing my cat Miten. This ashram was a sanctuary that rescued cows and bulls. I would go every morning to visit them. There was one bull being kept isolated from the others. I was told that he was not friendly and was always in a bad mood and that I should not go too close. Well, I went to see him. As I approached his enclosure, he was lying down, but when he saw me coming, he stood up and walked over to the fence. We made eye contact and we both seemed to recognize a friend. I reached out my hand and he laid his cheek in my palm. There was a flash of recognition and I saw my little Siamese cat in this two-thousand-pound white Brahma bull! The outer form could not have been more different and yet he looked just like Miten to me.

You recognize one person, and then you go through life recognizing others, to the point where you start recognizing everyone, even those appearing in the form of another species. Then it dawns on you that you keep recognizing the same "one" appearing in multiple forms. You are beginning to glimpse the eternal soul in everybody. This discriminatory wisdom helps you to be unattached to temporary material forms. You are accepting as well as comfortable with things that come and go, because you hold to the eternal. It is the power of love that allows for this shift in perception.

To kindle this awareness, start by looking for similarities rather than differences. It may seem contradictory, because most of us think of discrimination in a negative way. That's because we are looking at the outer forms only—skin color, ethnicity, nationality, gender, religion, age, and species. But viveka is about looking through the changing appearances to recognize the unchanging reality within. Ultimately the full-blown manifestation of viveka allows for *sarvatmabhava*—seeing God everywhere and in everyone and everything.

Vairagya

The second means to shubheccha is *vairagya*, or loss of interest. The word *vairagya* is composed of *vai*, meaning "to dry up," plus *raga*, which means "passion." Vairagya is a drying up of passion. It happens not by force but when your passion for something becomes disinterest. Often vairagya is equated with abstinence and renunciation. Abstaining from something you really like to help you develop willpower or gain spiritual merit is not the same as vairagya. For example, during Lent a Catholic child might give up chocolate, vowing not to eat any for the forty days of the holiday. But for those forty days that child will be thinking of nothing but chocolate, and on Easter morning will jump out of bed and devour the chocolate rabbit waiting in the Easter basket.

There is a big difference between restraint and vairagya. Restraining yourself is when you tell yourself you are not going to indulge in something because you are trying to be good—maybe to lose weight or become healthier. But you can't really let go of whatever you want to indulge in, your mind keeps thinking about it, obsessing over what you gave up. A classic example is when a person stops smoking but replaces it with another oral habit—talking about it. Patanjali uses the word *nirodha*, which has a similar meaning to vairagya. His definition of Yoga, *yogash chitta-vritti-nirodhah* (PYS 1.2), is often translated as, "Yoga is the restriction of the fluctuations of the mind." This has caused people to equate self-imposed restriction with yoga as necessary to living a spiritual life. Thinking of nirodha, vairagya, or renunciation as overcoming natural tendencies through force of will is to misunderstand their true meaning.

Individuals who renounce the world and take religious vows, including celibacy, when they are not ready can cause themselves a lot of stress and anxiety. Or students who start taking yoga classes and become judgmental, criticizing others for doing things they themselves were doing last week and still want to do but have given up because now they think they are a "spiritual person." This is spiritual elitism, and it has nothing to do with true renunciation. As they say, a little bit of knowledge can be dangerous. I don't want to imply that self-control and restraint are not worthwhile. Refraining from indulging in things that are detrimental to your health and well-being can be an important step in freeing yourself from dangerous addictions and bad habits. Self-imposed abstinence could lead to vairagya but is not the same as vairagya.

True vairagya cannot be forced—it must evolve naturally. It is like letting the cucumber ripen until it gracefully falls off the vine. If you pick the cucumber too soon, it will retain a mark indicating where the stem was attached to the vine. But if you leave a cucumber alone, allowing it to soak up the sun and the nutrients from the soil, there will come a time in late summer when you go out into the garden and you see a fat, full cucumber lying all by itself, having rolled away from the vine. You pick it up and marvel that the smooth skin has no mark, no indication that it was ever attached to the vine. It appears to be self-originating, whole, and complete. The moksha mantra (*mahamrityunjaya*), found in the Taittiriya Upanishad, describes this process, using the metaphor of a cucumber (*urvarukam*) that has become *pushtivardhanam*, filled with ever increasing grace and thus liberated from death, from the attachment to perishable things for the sake of immortality: *Om tryambakam yajamahe / sugandhim pushtivardhanam / urvarukamiva bandhanan / mrityor mukshiya mamritat.*

Having vairagya doesn't mean you have a negative view of something. It means you have lost your interest in it; you simply don't want it anymore. You don't have to exert any willpower to stay away from it. Here's a mundane example that may provide a clue to what dispassion looks like: Did you have a favorite toy as a child, or a favorite game—something you cherished so dearly you could not bear to be parted from it? What was that toy? What was that game? Do you feel the same way about that toy or game now? As I have already mentioned in another essay, I was obsessed with the board game Clue—I could not wait to get up in the morning and play it and would beg people to play with me. The miniature figurines representing Colonel Mustard, Professor Plum, Miss Scarlett, and the others; the six tiny murder weapons: the candlestick, revolver, pipe, rope, wrench, and dagger, were all so precious to me. Then a time came, I don't remember when, when I just lost interest. I still have my Clue murder mystery game, it's in the closet, but I haven't played it in decades. I keep it around for when kids come to visit, and they seem to have a lot of fun playing it. Sometimes I join the game, but it isn't the same for me as when I was thirteen. It is not that I have a negative view about it and attempt to dissuade others if they show an interest in it, I just sincerely have lost my passion for it.

Vairagya can also be associated with subtle things, not just physical, material objects like toys and chocolate. Subtle things like impatience, greed, and unkindness—you come to a place where you just let them go, you're done with them, just like you are done playing with toys. You cease to identify with thoughts that pull you into samsara. You're drawn to the transcendental. True vairagya is dispassion for what is unreal. You are no longer moved by worldly pleasures; you know that they ultimately won't satisfy you. Temporary pleasures always lead to disappointment.

Is there a way to cultivate vairagya? Yes. You could look before you leap. Ask yourself if the activity you are about to engage in will increase your *bhava* or not. Shyamdas said that a yogi is "someone who has lost their taste for things that don't really taste good; they only want to eat in the best restaurants." It's not that you feel superior and in a place to judge others; on the contrary, you feel intensely humble. You become like a soul in wonder. Vairagya is an experience of relief that you are no longer attracted to things that won't boost your spiritual development.

Although it is not easy to be established in viveka and vairagya, when we sense their importance to our ultimate happiness, we find ways to increase their presence in our lives. Viveka and vairagya can be seen as wings of mercy enabling the soul to fly above confusion and delusion. When we want to feel the goodness of our eternal souls, we will seek out more means to cultivate goodness and then the six virtues will begin to manifest.

Shadsampat

The third means to shubheccha is *shadsampat*, or the six virtues. *Shad* means "six" and *sampat* means "virtues, qualities, or assets." The practices of these six disciplines are a form of yogic training for the mind. They bring the mind to a place of sattvic steadiness and balance. The six virtues are: *shama, dama, uparathi, titiksha, shraddha,* and *samadhana*.

a) Shama (the first virtue) is the ability to control the mind by controlling your thoughts. The word *shama* comes from the root *sham*, meaning "to be quiet, calm, tranquil, and resigned." Shama means equanimity of mind, neutral, devoid of agitation. When you possess this virtue, you can bring your mind back to equanimity when it gets distracted. Shama can be used as a synonym for *dhyana* (meditation). Meditation is the practice of focusing your mind, which entails being able to bring it back to your chosen object of attention when it wavers. You can heal a fragmented mind by fixing it into one-pointed focus. You can let go of distractions. When you have shama, you know how to protect your *chitta-prasadanam*—your innate serenity of mind. You know how to direct your attention back to the source; and with that ability you can reinstate peace and calmness.

b) Dama (the second virtue) is the ability to control the senses. Often it is translated as "punishment, taming, or subduing." The word *dama* actually means "to tune or train." The ability to fine-tune our senses so we can savor the highest enjoyment is what dama is about. To really be able to value what we smell, taste, see, touch, and hear is dama. If we did truly value our senses, we would live in a heightened, sensational, sensual state of gratefulness, appreciation, and delight. We would be what in Sanskrit is called a *rasika*—a connoisseur of taste (*rasa*). Instead, we often take the abundance that we have for granted and overstimulate our senses, then find ourselves bored and complaining that our lives are dull. When we expose ourselves to too many choices and overindulge, we dull our senses. With dulled senses we can't really enjoy, and we become out of tune. Hedonism, consuming too much, ironically, results in the dulling of the senses and does not lead to sensual enjoyment or delight, in this world or any other.

The antidote to gluttony is fasting. When you withhold or restrain yourself from overindulgence, it will reset your senses, increase your appetite, so that you can experience a heightened sensuality. For example, to truly enjoy eating dinner, it is best to come to the table with a good appetite. To have a good appetite it is best to be hungry; to be hungry you need to fast from food for a while. Temporary restriction can be applied to all the senses in order to heighten awareness. Fasting from food will increase your ability to smell and taste, as anyone who has gone on a seven-day, three-day, or even a one-day fast can attest to.

Fasting from sight can improve vision. Spending a few days in a completely dark room, removed from all visual stimulation, is a dramatic way to refine your sight. When you come into the light after such deprivation you see the objects of the world as the multidimensional, psychedelic miracles they are. To increase your sense of touch, try exposing yourself to extremes of heat or cold: hike into the forest on a snowy winter's day wearing a minimum of clothing and return after a few hours to a warm house, a blanket, and a wood stove blazing with fire. To deepen your listening abilities, reduce what you hear: stop talking and minimize your exposure to sound by going someplace quiet for a while, away from other people, television, radio, stereo, and phone, etc.

Most religious and spiritual traditions embrace these types of practices. But to appreciate them not as a sacrifice in the sense of punishment but as a way to increase enjoyment provides the key to go even beyond the normal level of sense perception and experience the transcendental. The physical senses are limited to physical existence. But like all things physical, they are but mere reflections of counterparts that exist in the celestial realms. The five material senses crave stimulation and expression. They use the tongue, eyes, nose, etc. to do their bidding. When the senses are given unbridled freedom to seek fulfillment in temporary material things the result is never fulfilling. Because the enjoyment is temporary, you can find yourself a slave to your senses, their unruly appetites never satisfied, always hankering for more.

But through the application of dama your senses become elevated, well-tuned instruments, able to extract and imbibe the highest transcendental bliss beyond this world. The yogic scriptures describe the transformation of an enlightened yogi as appearing as if they've been given a new glowing body and mind with heightened sensibilities able to receive, process, and transmit beyond the normal level of material sense awareness. Yoga philosophy speaks of the sense organs as the ten *indriyas*: five organs of sense, or the *jnana indriyas,* and five organs of function, the *karma indriyas.* The five organs of sense are smell, taste, sight, touch, and hearing. The five organs of function are the nose, tongue, eyes, skin, and ears. The yogi perceives the world through the jnana indriyas and responds by means of the karma indriyas.

c) **Uparathi** (the third virtue) is true mental poise or equanimity of mind. The word comes from *upa,* meaning "the way," and *rathi,* "a special form of affection." When we observe life, we see ups and downs continuously at play. Happiness and sadness are in constant flux. When life gets us down, we may feel a sense of disappointment. We are sitting in a chair in our room feeling down, and then by chance we look out the window and notice a bird singing on a branch. The sight and sound of the bird at that moment communicates something uplifting and we feel hopeful. We are having a great morning, our spirits are high, we are filled with optimism. Then we get a phone call from a friend with really bad news. We are driving down the highway with a friend, listening to music and talking happily, when a truck swerves and crashes into the passenger side of the car, instantly killing our friend. A woman is in the hospital giving birth to a baby while her mother is in the cancer ward of the same hospital dying.

Sukham aindriyakam daitya / deha-yogena dehinam/

sarvatra labhyate daivad / yatha duhkham ayatnatah (SB 7.6.3). In this verse from the Shrimad Bhagavatam, the child Prahlada is talking to his playmates and is telling them that both happiness and sadness are inevitable in life, they happen regardless of any effort on our part. They are both temporary conditions that arise because of our past karmas. We are all enmeshed in the net of samsara. It is best to accept it. It is futile to waste time and energy trying to fight distress or to work hard for happiness. The only thing we should focus our precious faculty of attention on in our short lifetime is discovering our eternal relationship with God—that is the only thing that will bring lasting happiness.

To have uparathi is to have mental poise, to be able to accept change. Even to gracefully embrace the flow of the pendulum. With uparathi you are able to witness the fluctuations of life with impartiality and draw opportunities for spiritual growth from them. You are not thrown off balance by *raga* and *dvesha*, by the things you like or dislike. You might have preferences, but you are not attached to your preferences. You are graceful with what comes. There is an elegance that arises from this benevolent attitude—you realize that to be complete, to be whole, to even be a holy being, you need both ups and downs. You begin to see your life, no matter what happens, as a great privilege. You feel grateful for every moment, you don't spend time wishing for things to be different. You don't see the calamities as mistakes. And you don't see the highpoints as what should always be. You accept what is. This acceptance is not the type of passivity in which you grit your teeth and grin and bear it. This acceptance of reality is wisdom that enables you to love what is; to have a special affection (rathi) for the way of life (upa).

The starting point is to be grateful for the changeful nature of reality. Gratefulness leads to mental poise. If we can be unafflicted by the highs and lows, the ups and downs, of life, we will glimpse what lies underneath the surface, beneath the flux, and discover the unchanging reality.

During a Jivamukti teacher training, I witnessed a student who exemplified uparathi in the following way: Each student had to get up in the front of the room and lead the group in a recitation of a Sanskrit chant. She chose a verse from the Brihadaranyaka Upanishad that translates as, "Lead me from the unreal to the real, from darkness to light, and from death to immortality": *asato ma sad-gamaya / tamaso ma jyotir gamaya / mrityor ma amritam gamaya.*

She was confident, her voice was loud, clear, and steady, but she left out the second line (*tamaso ma jyotir gamaya*). When she came to the end of the verse, she realized her mistake but instead of getting flustered, she remained calm and graceful. She did not fall apart, nor did she resort to defensiveness and apologize or try to explain to us that she was nervous, etc. Instead, in a serene manner she simply recited the chant again, this time inserting the second line, as if nothing unusual had happened, exemplifying great mental poise, or uparathi.

d) Titiksha (the fourth virtue) is to have forbearance, patience, and tolerance, the ability to endure external, physical conditions. The word comes from the root *tij*, meaning "to endure." When you are endowed with the virtue of titiksha, you are able to endure the physical changing conditions of life with an attitude of acceptance, without dejection or lamentation, devoid of any thought of retaliation. The weather is often used as an example to understand what titiksha looks like. You can't change the weather, and yet many people spend so much of their energy and time complaining about it and trying to push back against it. For example, living inside a house and wanting the temperature to always be at 72 degrees regardless of the season. When you have titiksha, you humble yourself to the weather, rather than try to conquer it. There are many old stories about yogis who go on retreat in desertlike places that get very hot in the daytime and cold at night. They subject themselves to these extremes in temperature to develop tolerance and forbearance in regard to external conditions they have no control over.

Titiksha is also the name of a goddess, the wife of the god Dharma. She is also known as "Diamond Heart," because she is the embodiment of patience, tolerance, and endurance and shines like a multifaceted diamond. The Hindi word *tike* (pronounced TEA-kay) translates into English as "okay." I think it must share the same root as the word *titiksha*, because when you say it you are saying that you are okay with what is.

e) Shraddha (the fifth virtue) means "faith, reverence, and trust." You need a certain amount of faith to get going on the spiritual path and to sustain you on your journey. With the virtue of shraddha, you have faith in things that can't necessarily be proven logically. For example, the existence of God, the goodness of the soul, the teachings found in scripture, and the words of the guru. *Shraddha* means "faith," but it doesn't mean blind faith. It is a faith that is cultivated and validated and arises over time with self-reflection and practice.

A lack of faith indicates a lack of practice. Faith increases with practice and experience. If you find yourself in a place of doubt about the worthwhileness of your spiritual practice, it is a sign that you haven't done it long enough. When you doubt the teachings of scripture or guru, it often indicates that you haven't put in enough hours of study. If you experience a lack of faith in your teacher, you probably haven't been with them long enough or haven't utilized the time you have had with them in the most productive or elevating way for your spiritual development. If you lack faith, don't worry about it too much. Instead, just go deeper into your practice and spend more quality time in study and with your teacher. Engage your teacher in *satsang* instead of focusing on your doubt and arguing with them. Something to remember about faith is that it can be illogical, nonsensical, and often goes beyond what can be proved empirically.

f) Samadhana (the sixth virtue) is remembering your connection to the eternal source. If you have samadhana, you are always thinking of God, your mind is God-centered. The word *samadhana* means "putting together, uniting, or remembering your true eternal connection with the divine nature of the soul." It can be thought of as contemplating your connection with God, keeping God as your priority—the foremost thought in your mind. When you engage in enough intentional spiritual practices and invest enough time in your day to focus on God, you start to remember God. This remembrance then spills over into everything you do in the day, even to what might appear like spiritually unrelated activities. When the virtue of samadhana arises, you see everything as helping you to remember and you find yourself looking for God in everything you do. You are practicing yoga all day long—it is not something that happens only on your yoga mat or meditation cushion. While sweeping the floor or washing dishes, you feel it as helping you. Work becomes prayer. The presence of God fills your day. Anxieties lift from your mind and heart, and you find yourself in a continuous state of gratitude. Samadhana even affects your sleep. As you drift off, you remember that you will be entering *sushupti* (the state of deep sleep), where you will experience oneness with God and be restored. This remembrance allows you to go to sleep with a peaceful heart and calm mind.

To cultivate samadhana, try to remember God in everything you do by inviting His presence. Make all of your activities offerings to God. Don't eat or drink anything without first offering it to God. Offer everything you do. Silently converse with God throughout your day. Let God be with you and with your spirit.

Mumukshutva

The fourth means to shubheccha is *mumukshutva*, an intense longing for the truth, a burning desire for liberation. A mind that is constantly preoccupied with lesser aspirations, with desires rooted in material goals, will be too busy to seek the truth, much less have a burning desire for it. At this stage the seeker understands with compassion the cycle of repeated births and deaths. The desire for liberation from samsara becomes their chief priority. If you are already well established in viveka, vairagya, and shadsampat, then mumukshutva will occur naturally.

The cultivation of the four means—viveka, vairagya, shadsampat, and mumukshutva—along with the six virtues entails a lot, and that's only the first bhumika, shubheccha. A person will persevere at this stage only if they really yearn to know God. They have had to have planted a lot of good karmic seeds in their past to be able to reap the fruit of those seeds in their present life and have a desire for enlightenment. But when those seeds do ripen into fruits, then the second stage, known as *vicharana*, appears.

2. VICHARANA

The second bhumika, *vicharana*, means "right inquiry"—from *vi*, "correct," and *charana* "seeking." Because of the effects of shubheccha, your mind and senses have become refined and are vibrating at a high level. You have pondered and gained some true spiritual knowledge; this enables you to discover teachings and teachers. You sense where and when to find what or who will help take you to the next step and you move accordingly. You don't hesitate; you go where you are supposed to go for your spiritual evolution. You trust your intuition and seem to find yourself in the right place at the right time. Here's an example: Some people may journey to India and encounter saints, yogis, and holy beings and witness miracles and have mystical experiences, while others may go but do not. Why this discrepancy? Because they don't have vicharana. They can't see the magic; the spiritual radiance of a person or situation eludes them. As Jesus says in the Gospels (Matthew 11.15), "Only those with ears to hear will hear," meaning that only those able to hear will.

3. TANUMANASI

The third bhumika, *tanumanasi* describes the thinning out of the mind—from *tanu*, "thinning or stretching," and *manas*, "mind." This stage indicates that a person, through concentrating the mind, by regular practice of meditation, has rendered it capable of grasping subtlety and can perceive the essence of a thing. At this stage the mind isn't cluttered with a lot of disconnected thoughts. The thoughts have thinned out. The person is not easily distracted; their focus on God is steadfast. This stage is the last point of separateness. There is still duality, but there is intense one-pointed focus toward the Supreme Self, which naturally results in progression to the fourth stage, *sattvapatti*, where *siddhis* (magical powers) appear.

But before we go into a description of the next stage, let's summarize the first three stages. Together, shubheccha, vicharana, and tanumanasi are known as the *sadhana bhumikas*. When a yogi has attained mastery of these three stages they are known as a *sadhaka*, one who is immersed in the process of purification. The qualification for knowledge has arisen, but knowledge itself has not yet been attained. That is yet to come.

4. SATTVAPATTI

The fourth bhumika, *sattvapatti*—from *sattva*, "light, purity, goodness," and *patti*, "lord or master of"—is the attainment of sattva, the attainment of knowledge, the realization of truth, the realization of the goodness of the eternal soul. At this stage there is true perception of reality. The perceiver becomes one with what is perceived. There is not the slightest shadow of a doubt about the existence of the atman, the aspirant has experienced Yoga—joining with the eternal soul. The purified chitta, or mind, is resting in the atman. The *jiva*, the individual self, has reunited with the atman, the eternal divine Self. The mind is merged with its source. This is *samadhi, samprajnata samadhi*, as the seed of dual consciousness is still operating, which means that the perceiver retains the awareness of their individual self (jiva) as well as the awareness of the absolute Self (Brahman). They are a knower of Brahman (a *Brahmavid*). The *mahavakya* (great saying) *aham brahmasmi* ("I am Brahman") applies to them because they have realized that they are part of the absolute divine reality. The atman (eternal soul) has become awakened. They no longer identify who they are with their body and mind but have expanded their consciousness to realize themselves as one with all that is. At this stage the yogi is no longer a sadhaka, no longer involved in practice, because through practice they have attained knowledge. They have reached the goal of practice.

It is at this stage that yogic siddhis, or magical powers, arise. The eight classical siddhis, or the eight great perfections, described in the Puranas are: 1) *anima*—the ability to become small, so you could go through a keyhole or pass through a solid object like a wall or even make yourself invisible; 2) *mahima*—the ability to become large; 3) *laghima*—the ability to become weightless or lighter than air and fly; 4) *garima*—the ability to become heavy or dense, which is helpful if you want to be immovable; 5) *prapti*—teleportation, the ability to travel instantaneously and go wherever you want; 6) *prakamya*—the ability to manifest what you want just by thinking of it; 7) *ishitva* —the ability to influence or even exert control over others, including human beings, animals, and even trees; 8) *vashitva*— the ability to control the natural forces, like earth, water, fire, and wind.

In the third chapter of the Yoga Sutra, Patanjali describes over twenty superpowers that result from the yogic practice of *samyama*, which combines concentration, meditation, and samadhi. The siddhis that arise include: knowledge of the past and future; the ability to understand the language of animals; knowledge of who you were in your past lives, as well as knowing when you will die in your present life; the ability to enter a person's mind and know what they are thinking, as well as to access their past memories; the ability to become invisible or make something disappear, to create darkness by stopping the flow of light, to see things that are remote, physically far away; knowledge about the movement of the sun, moon, stars, and planets; the ability to overcome hunger and live without food for long periods of time, to make your body stable and unshakable, to become as strong as an elephant, to be unsinkable in water, to fly through the air; the ability to hear others who are not nearby, even to hear the singing of celestial angelic beings and converse with them; control over the five elements—earth, water, fire, air, and ether—and to get nature to do your bidding, move mountains, redirect the course of rivers, etc.

In chapter 15 of the eleventh canto of the Shrimad Bhagavatam, Krishna also describes that the above-mentioned siddhis come to a yogi who realizes the atman: "When a yogi is connected to the absolute truth, has conquered his senses, and breathing, and has fixed his attention upon me alone and knows me to inhabit his soul, the mystical perfections of yoga, the siddhis, are at his disposal" (SB 11.15.1).

But all of the ancient texts warn against displaying siddhis, because to do so you risk identifying with their power. If you show your powers to others, your spiritual progress will be halted. Your ego could convince you that you are the doer manifesting these powers rather than God working through you. Because duality is still present at this stage of sattvapatti, the yogi still perceives themself as separate from others. If they were to display their powers to someone who didn't have those powers, they could easily create a separation between themself and others and feel superior. This separation, sense of duality, would incur karma, which would bind the yogi to future lives in which they would have to reincarnate to resolve those karmas. Karma and the sense of doership binds us to the world of phenomena. *Karma* means "action." *Karmashuklakrishnam yoginas trividham itaresham* (PYS 4.7): "The actions of ordinary people are good, bad, or mixed, while the actions of a realized yogi are neither good nor bad nor mixed, but clear, because the selfless yogi has ceased to identify with their actions and has realized God as the ultimate doer." Humility and loving devotion to God are the keys to true perfection. If the yogi can be unaffected by siddhis, they will evolve to the next stage, known as *asamshakti*.

5. ASAMSHAKTI

The fifth bhumika, *asamshakti*, means "leaning away from the world"—from *asam*, "not like," and *shakti*, "the power that manifests the world." At this stage the mind is silenced, the chitta-vrittis have been quelled. The yogi's consciousness is in *nirvikalpa samadhi*, which is likened to a dreamless deep sleep, but with conscious awareness. The yogi is absorbed in this samadhi for long periods of time. They have no more *sanchita karma* (the fruits of past actions) to burn. Others may prompt them to come out of their absorption to teach or give advice, but left on their own the yogi will not be much interested in anything but their mystical absorption. They still function and perform actions necessary to maintain their body, like eating, drinking, and walking. At this stage the yogi is known as a *Brahmavidvara* (a better knower of Brahman). The Indian saint Ramana Maharshi is often cited as an example of such a jivanmukta. He came out of samadhi only when someone asked him a question.

6. PADARTHA BHAVANA

The sixth bhumika, *padartha bhavana*, means "disappearance of visible forms"—from *pada*, "stepping" plus *artha*, "visible form" plus *a*, "not" plus *bhavana*, "appearance." The adept at this stage is known as a *Brahmavidvariya* (one who knows Brahman best). At this stage all individual mental activities dissolve. The yogi no longer wakes by themselves, nor do they perform actions to maintain their life. For example, when instigated by others, they may appear to eat, when food is placed in their mouth. The jivanmukta at this stage sees God everywhere in all things and beings, there is no duality. Sanchita and *agami karma* (the fruits of current actions) are gone. Only a small amount of *prarabdha karma* (the karmas that created the present body) keeps them in the body at all, and when that is exhausted, then turiya comes, the next stage, or final bhumika.

To explain the padartha bhavana stage, the metaphor of an electric fan can be helpful. The yogi is like a fan that is turned off but still rotates. The sanchita karma of the fan is electrical energy. The agami karma makes a nice breeze. At this stage, it is like the fan is unplugged but continues to revolve because of the momentum; eventually it will come to a stop and will not produce a breeze. The great saint Anandamayi Ma was thought to be at this stage—she would no longer eat or take care of her body. She spoke of the body as only appearing because of the actions and desires of her devotees, not because of her actions or desires. They would open her mouth and put food in, they moved her jaws to chew it, they dressed her, bathed her, combed her hair, etc.

7. TURIYA

The seventh bhumika, *turiya*, is perpetual samadhi. The Sanskrit word *turiya* means "the fourth." Turiya is the fourth dimension of being. It is what underlies, pervades, and transcends the three ordinary states of consciousness—waking (*jagrat*), dreaming (*swapna*), and deep sleep (*sushupti*). Turiya is the state of liberation, a total immersion in Brahman. It is pure nondual consciousness (Advaita Vedanta), measureless, blissful, changeless, self-luminous, imminent in all things, and transcendent. The yogi at this stage is called a *Brahmavidvarishtha* (the greatest knower of Brahman). They are said to be *gate gate, para gate, para samgate, bodhi swaha* —"gone, gone, real gone, gone beyond even the most gone." They have become one with Brahman. The body of such an enlightened being will usually drop approximately three days after entering this stage. Many times, if devotees are present, they will place the saint's body in *padmasana* and it will be entombed rather than cremated. Decay may not set in for many years.

Contemporary Sanskrit teacher Manorama d'Alvia, says: "*Turiya* means 'the fourth,' and what that implies is that you understand the three, you recognize that there is a beginning, a middle, and an end to manifestation. But the fourth is beyond that. Turiya signifies what is beyond the beyond, the incomprehensible, immeasurable, eternal soul."

Here's how the Mandukya Upanishad describes turiya: "What is known as the fourth is not inwardly cognitive, nor outwardly cognitive, not both-wise cognitive, neither knowing, nor unknowing; invisible, ineffable, intangible, devoid of characteristics, inconceivable, indefinable, ungraspable, nonthinkable, invisible, cannot be designated, having no distinctive mark, with which there can be no dealing, its sole essence being its own Self, without a second (*advaita*), the cessation of development, tranquil, benign, utterly quiet; peaceful. This is the Self, the atman—it cannot be found, only realized" (MU 7).

Liberation from samsara, moksha, turiya, merging with Brahman is considered the final stage, the ultimate attainment, by the *jnana* yogi, but the *bhakti* yogi does not perceive liberation as the final aim. The bhakta's supreme desire is to love Krishna, not to be Krishna. Liberation then is not the goal of spiritual life; it is only a by-product of loving devotional service. There is a teaching in some of the scriptures about liberation, or *mukti*, being just the beginning. Bhakti begins after liberation, after mukti comes *vimukti*. The Sanskrit prefix *vi* means "to separate," so the word *vimukti* means "to separate from mukti."

"The liberation of the bhakta is called not just mukti but vimukti, meaning a special mukti, and it surpasses the five kinds of liberation, *sayuja* (merging into Brahman), *salokya* (living on a heavenly planet), *sarupya* (getting a body that looks like Krishna's), *samipya* (close association with the Supreme Lord), and *sarshti* (having the same opulences that the Supreme Lord possesses)" (SB 10.1-13).

A bhakta rejects these five types of liberation and wants only to lovingly serve God. After becoming one with Brahman, the devotee steps through mukti and falls into vimukti, the transcendental arms of beloved Krishna, and will enjoy that ecstatic loving relationship beyond space and time forever more.

For easy reference, here's a summary of the Seven Bhumikas:
1. **SUBHECCHA** (good desire)
    Four means:
      I.Viveka (discrimination)
      II.Vairaga (dispassion)
      III. Shadsampat (six virtues):
            shama (mental control)
            dama (sense control)
            uparathi (poise)
            titiksha (forbearance)
            shraddha (faith)
            samadhana (God centered)
      IV. Mumukshutva (intense longing for liberation)
2. **VICHARANA** (right inquiry)
3. **TANUMANASI** (thinning out of the mind)
4. **SATTVAPATTI** (attainment of sattva—goodness)
5. **ASAMSHAKTI** (leaning away from the world)
6. **PADARTHA BHAVANA** (disappearance of visible forms)
7. **TURIYA** ("the fourth" —perpetual samadhi)

*From Vasishtha's Yoga, by Swami Venkatesananda.

V

CONTEMPORARY STORIES

*True life stories are historical
or in this case her-storical.
Be that as it may, these stories, rooted in
the past, have been pulled forward into the
present, where they are now finding a new
place for themselves in the future.*

Appreciation

At times our own light goes out
and is rekindled by a spark from another.
Each one of us has cause to think with deep gratitude
of those who have lighted the flame within us.
— Albert Schweitzer

When I'm in India I am always on the lookout for hungry dogs. There are many on the streets. I have gotten into the habit of never leaving my hotel room without being armed with provisions for any dog I might run into. Once, while David and I were in Mysore for a couple of months studying with our teacher Shri K. Pattabhi Jois, I came to know several street dogs as regulars, ready to accept my food offerings. There was one very sick and skinny female dog I had started to feed every afternoon. She was covered in mange—had oozing sores and most of her hair was gone; she was in very bad shape. A certain type of parasitic mite causes mange. Healthy dogs with strong immune systems can fight off this parasite, but starving and sick dogs are easy prey. If I had known that there was medicine I could have given her, I would have, but at the time I was ignorant of such things and focused only on providing nutritious food.

Before she would eat the food I brought her, she would always pause and look up into my eyes as if to say, "Thank you." She never grabbed the food and ran off with it, she never crowded out other dogs, and she never started to eat before showing thankfulness. I knew she appreciated my gifts, because she told me with her eyes. Making eye contact, she would hold my attention and convey her sincere gratitude. After a few days she began showing up to meet me around the same time, at the same spot on the street. David became very concerned. He was worried that I was making her dependent and that when it came time for us to leave India, she would be without any charitable human friend, which would be very disappointing to her. Wasn't I concerned about that? Of course I was, but I also knew, without a doubt, that what I was doing was good. I tried to explain it to David in the following way.

Remember, now we are in India, where the generally held belief is that wherever you find yourself in this life is a result of your past actions, your *karma*. If someone, anyone, human or animal, finds themself in an unfortunate situation, it is because they performed actions in a previous birth that planted the seeds to create the suffering they are experiencing now. Some people think that sick and starving dogs on the streets are receiving just punishment for their previous karmas and that we should not interfere. It is thought that if you were born a dog, then you must have done horrible things in your past life. In many cases, the attitude is to increase the pain and suffering by inflicting more pain and suffering. It is common practice in India to beat, kick, or throw stones at dogs simply because they are dogs.

I have come to reflect that if the law of karma is true, then how we treat others now will determine how others treat us in the future. So it seems to me that if we have the opportunity to show compassion to someone who is suffering, this will be beneficial for the one suffering, but also perhaps for ourselves at some point in our future. Maybe the people who kick the dogs will end up being a kicked dog in their future life. The point is, What is the harm in being kind? Kindness promotes humility and is a remedy for arrogance. I've come to see that if we hold on to negative emotions like pride, anger, and resentment, our hearts will have very little room for love, forgiveness, and compassion. If someone performed bad deeds in past lifetimes, which has resulted in their present birth, what will stop the cycle? If that dog's only experience of humans resulted in her feeling fear, anger, resentment, shame, and hate, what hope does she have of liberating herself from more and more miserable lifetimes? As long as she holds these negative emotions in her heart she is bound in misery.

If we can show that dog respect, unconditional love, a moment of kindness that can allow her heart to feel appreciation or forgiveness or gratitude instead of humiliation, pain, fear, and anger, she has a better chance of living out the rest of her life with a lighter heart, and perhaps when the time comes for her to die, she might die with the remembrance that someone cared for her. If a being can feel love in their heart, then their life is going to be better, and at the time of death their soul is going to be that much closer to rebirth in a better situation. Because of that, I am willing to do what I can to help that process along. Love and kindness are never wasted; they are valid, positive solutions and can enhance all situations.

Although, yes, she would most likely miss us when we left and we would also miss her, we had to remember that that should not stop us from reaching out with kindness during the time we were with her. Yes, it is true we had to leave her one day, everyone leaves everyone someday. Impermanence is the way of life. Nothing lasts forever. What seems to me to be important is the quality of time spent with another being, no matter how long that time may be. When kindness and respect are allowed to become the medium of exchange between two beings, then we are moving beyond impermanence into the eternal realm of the soul.

Daddy Dog

Clearly animals know more than we think
and think a great deal more than we know.
−Dr. Irene Pepperberg

David and I were visiting the holy city of Benares. On a street near our hotel, I would often see a very small, white, three-legged female dog. Most of her left back leg was missing. She always seemed to be in a hurry, constantly on the lookout for any bit of discarded food, and on the alert to dodge kicks. When she did find food, I noticed that she didn't eat it on the spot, but quickly ran away with her prize. One morning as I was walking down a busy, narrow street, so common in this city, I heard the whimper of a puppy. I looked under a rotting wooden board that was being used to cover an open sewer drain, and saw a tiny, white puppy crouching on the side of the gutter. I didn't have more than a two-second look when a white "blur" sped in front of me and to the side of the little waif-like puppy. It was the three-legged dog!

Now that I knew where they lived, I quickly went and purchased some food and brought it back for her and baby. I unwrapped a leaf containing a serving of rice and dal and placed it carefully next to her and she calmly accepted it. I decided to return later that day with more food, but when I did, she and baby had vanished. Every day I would look for them, but locating their living quarters proved to be a challenge. I realized she often had to change homes for security reasons. Sometimes I would be wandering around for hours with a bag of chapatis or a clay cup of yogurt or dal, but never see her. The food never went to waste, as there were always plenty of other hungry dogs.

One day while sitting on the banks of the River Ganga near the Benares Sanskrit College, with a full bag of chapatis, feeding a small troop of dogs, I became very intrigued with the behavior of one dog. He was quite polite and didn't push or shove his way to the front of the pack but waited patiently on the sidelines. I thought that maybe because of his humble demeanor the other dogs might be in the habit of bullying him, and that had made him shy. I asked David to distract the other dogs by feeding them while I walked closer to the shy one. Crouching down next to him I gave him a whole chapati. He took it in his mouth but then let it drop to the ground between his front paws and looked up at me imploringly. I was confused. I thought maybe he was too sick and couldn't eat, or maybe he didn't like chapatis. But the dog didn't walk away and leave the bread; instead, he remained stationed, looking up at me.

So I gave him another chapati, which he caught in his mouth, then dropped on top of the first one. I was surprised—he was building a stack! Then, with his mouth, he deftly scooped up both chapatis, quickly turned away, and began to run. I signaled to David that he should stay and keep the other dogs at bay while I took off, determined to follow him. I chased him through the narrow streets, dodging cows, people, and other dogs without losing him. Then he stopped abruptly, ducked his head beneath an old gutter board under a sari shop. I followed, and yes, there they were: three-legged mommy and little baby, his hungry family. Looking into their grateful eyes and seeing their wagging tails, I could tell they were all very happy. Dad was the breadwinner today, and what a haul—two big chapatis! I watched in awe, as valiant Little Daddy, as I called him, stoically stood guard in front of the gutter while his wife and child ate their dinner. When someone tells me that dogs are incapable of maintaining strong family ties, especially the males, I shake my head and say, "Hmm, perhaps you have underestimated the intelligence and emotional capacity of dogs?"

To see dogs as incapable of establishing strong, caring, and even selfless relationships with other dogs is all too common. We like to think that dogs belong to us alone and that their loyalty is reserved for their human owner. The custom of keeping pets has made most of us oblivious to the natural feelings that exist between friends and family members of other species. Dogs are more like people than we would like to admit. When we decide to adopt a puppy, for example, most of us never consider that we are breaking up a family. Whether we obtain our pet by buying them at a pet store or ordering directly from a breeder or rescuing from a shelter, the puppy we take home is an orphan. Some see buying a puppy as nothing more than acquiring a commodity, buying something cute that will provide them with companionship or a living toy for their kids to play with. Something warm, soft, and nice to touch—to pet. Perhaps that is how we came to call them pets. When you think of it that way, the term is a derogatory one as it diminishes the worth of a living being. Using the term *pet* is just one of the ways we relegate dogs and other animals to an inferior position.

We have become accustomed to seeing the adoption of a

pet as a noble gesture. But how many of us consider the feelings of the mother dog, whose baby she will never see again? How many of us even acknowledge that dogs have feelings? Taking a baby away from their mother is traumatic for mother and baby. Often, I have heard people justify themselves and say a puppy is old enough to be taken away from their mother when they're weaned. Would the same apply to a human baby who has stopped nursing? Just because a mother has ceased to breastfeed her child doesn't necessarily mean that she has stopped caring for her baby, or that her parental duties are over. In fact, for most mammals this stage signals that a new phase in the relationship between parent and child is just beginning. After protecting and nurturing, the job of a parent is to teach their child about life. Parents draw from their own experiences to impart their wisdom to their young. I don't think we consider that a dog might have anything to teach their children. Many humans like the idea of bringing a helpless puppy into their home. A vulnerable creature who is dependent upon us for everything gives us opportunities to train and shape them according to our desires. We like to maintain our sense of superiority when it comes to intelligence and emotional maturity.

Speciesism shares many similarities with misogyny. For one, they are both very old and ingrained prejudices. It takes a lot of deep reflection to recognize when our perception of others is colored by it. As civilized human beings, we seem to guard our ideas of culture and domestic lifestyle and feel entitled to protect it against anything and anyone who challenges it. Anyone who is wild and untamed is deemed a foreign invader to our world. If we care to think back, it wasn't that long ago that education was denied to most girls, because it was thought that it reduced their chances of finding a husband. Many men felt that an educated girl would be too wild and independent—to marry a girl like that would be a great risk to her husband, who would not be able to control her. We still feel this way about our pets. We like to own them and keep them under our control.

In most countries in the world today people keep dogs as pets. Because they are seen as owned by humans, they are afforded protection, to some extent, as property. Whereas the street dogs in India, or in other countries where they don't have a human home to go to, are seen as foreign invaders, pests, equal to rats or pigeons. Because they are not owned, they are given no protection or rights. They are untamed, uncivilized, and independent. Viewed as an eyesore for tourists and locals alike, these dogs are under constant threat of extermination. They are often poisoned or purposely hit by cars or beaten to death.

I hope the reader does not get the impression that I am against adopting a pet—I am not. But I would hope that if the reader is thinking about adoption that they would consider adopting from a shelter rather than buying a pet from a pet store or breeder and that they would adopt the mother dog along with her baby or babies, if possible. In an ideal world where dogs ran free and were healthy and happy and allowed to live within their own family groups and coinhabit this world along with human beings, the problem of stray dogs would not be a problem. But we live in an unnatural world, a world designed by and for human beings. We feel that we are the only species that deserves rights. We have taken over much of the wild forested land and have built our towns and cities, all according to our desires, excluding the needs of other creatures. This is not going to change anytime soon.

But we could start now to find ways to be more inclusive of the needs of other animals and to make life more comfortable for those who live in cities with us. It would behoove us to feel some responsibility toward those we have displaced. Everyone, including dogs, should have access to clean water, enough to eat, and a safe place to live. Every baby, regardless of what species they are, should be wanted and cared for. It would be a compassionate move on our part to provide medical assistance and birth control in the form of spaying and neutering for dogs who call the street their home. If we ourselves desire respect and to live a dignified life, we would do well to respect all others, including dogs. To see them as the people they are would expand our understanding of the interconnected web of life of which we are all a part.

Getting Across the River

I've got many rivers to cross / But I can't seem to find my way over
And this loneliness won't leave me alone
It's such a drag to be on your own.
—From the song "Many Rivers to Cross," by Jimmy Cliff

Shyamdas loved to go camping—to sleep under the stars, cook over an open fire, and offer food to Krishna. He loved to make *seva* out of doors, and he loved even more to make Krishna seva in the enchanted forests of Braj. Shyamdas loved good company. He would often say that to spend time with other *bhaktas* was what he lived for and that the *rasa* of good association only increased in Braj. I had the great privilege of going with him on several walking pilgrimages into the forests of Braj. The Braj *banyatra* is a special kind of pilgrimage unique to Braj and to the bhaktas who embark on such journeys. Most pilgrimages are taken with an aim or objective to get someplace or to get something and bring it back home. The banyatra, however, has no aim, as there is nothing to achieve. It is a pointless journey, which goes around in a circle. This externalized journey is synonymous with the internal *lila* of Shri Krishna's Path of Grace, where effort has no place.

We would leave Gokul, the small village where Shyamdas lived, set off on foot, and be gone for days or weeks at a time, far away from worldly pursuits and city life. This was the India that few Westerners got to experience—miles and miles of forests, fields, and jungles bereft of any normal, civilized human being. Sometimes we would encounter someone who even Shyamdas wasn't sure was of this mortal world. Shyamdas's trusted friend and devotee Mohan would always accompany us and help Shyamdas with the cooking and logistics of camping. Because Mohan was a native Brajbhashi, he was an essential traveling companion on these pilgrimages. Shyamdas relied on Mohan's sense of direction. Besides, Mohan was a great cook, and his prasad tasted even better when cooked over a cow-dung fire under a starry Braj night sky, serenaded by moon birds and the whispers of trees singing the praises of Hari.

One day it was decided that we were going to embark on a two-week journey that would take us to several *baithaks*, where we would camp and make seva. A baithak is a place where a saint was known to have sat and given teachings. There are eighty-four Vallabhacharya baithaks, sacred places where Shri

Vallabhacharya, the founder of the Pushtimarg, visited, throughout India, many in the Braj area. Mohan and Shyamdas had visited most of them already, but there were a few they hadn't seen in a long time and a couple they had never visited, because, as Shyamdas said, "they are quite off the map, hidden in remote, jungly places."

So off we went, David, Mohan, Shyamdas, Melu (Shyamdas's girlfriend), and me. All of us were wearing flip-flops except Shyamdas, who insisted on walking barefoot, because, as he explained: "I want to feel the ground directly. The land of Braj is the body of Krishna, and I don't want anything between me and the Beloved."

The first stop was Belvan, which wasn't that far away from Gokul. During the time Krishna lived in Braj, there was a large forest of bel trees across the Yamuna River from Vrindavan. Krishna and the gopis liked to go there to eat the ripe bel fruits. The bel forest is long gone, and most of the land is farmed now, but the sacred site remains. A boatman rowed us across the river. We stepped onto the bank. A falling-down stone temple was what remained of Vallabhacharya's baithak. An old man, Krishna Mukhiyaji, an exalted bhakta, lived there, worshiped, and cared for the place. Hundreds of elegant peacocks had also claimed this sacred site as their own and seemed to be continuously prancing and dancing their own *rasa lila*. As soon as we arrived, Mohan set up to prepare prasad. While he tended the breads roasting in the ash of the cow-dung coals, we walked around and came upon a three-foot-tall carved statue of a goddess. I asked Shyamdas, "Who's this?"

"This is the goddess Laxmi," he replied.

"Why is there a statue of her at this site?"

"Ah," Shyamdas sighed, and sadly shook his head back and forth. "Just look at her! There she stands, longingly looking across the river to Vrindavan. She wants so much to join in the rasa lila but lacks the eligibility."

"Why?"

"Because she's not a gopi. Only the gopis heard the call of Krishna's flute and were able to drop everything. Not everyone can do that. Everything they held dear, they just left it and rushed to the forest to meet their Beloved. On that full moon night, Krishna danced with each one of them and they each felt that he was dancing only with them."

"But why didn't Laxmi join the dance?"

"Laxmi didn't hear the flute, or if she did she was unable to drop everything and go. She is the great goddess, the consort of Narayan. She is beauty, wealth, and fame all rolled into one. But her many attributes mean nothing in Vrindavan, they can't get her through the door to the dance. So she stays here in exile, where it is said she is still performing austerities with the desire to hopefully someday get across the river and be invited to the dance."

This response plummeted me into deep despair. *Wow,* I thought, *if the goddess Laxmi lacks the eligibility to dance with Krishna, what chance is there for me?*

We spent the night under the stars camping with the peacocks, our sleeping bags rolled out on the ground a few yards away from the pining Laxmi. In the morning, we left Belvan and took a boat back across the river and set off walking along the banks, headed for a special, sacred pilgrimage site. Toward late afternoon, we arrived at the blessed kadamba tree where Krishna had acted out one of his holy pastimes thousands of years ago in another yuga. The story is a beloved one to Krishna devotees. While a group of young gopis were bathing naked in the river, Krishna mischievously stole their saris and climbed the tree with their clothes. When they realized He was in the tree with their clothes, they demanded that he give them back. He teased the girls, telling them that they had to come out of the water to retrieve their clothes. The message in the story is that we must go naked before God, devoid of all artifice, baring our souls. To surrender completely to the Lord demands that we give up everything, so there is nothing between us and Him.

The kadamba tree we saw before us had bits of colored cloth tied to its branches, as if the gopis had left their saris hanging on those branches for so long that they had been reduced to mere shreds of cloth. Although the tree did look like a very old tree, I asked Shyamdas if he thought it was the same tree Krishna had climbed thousands of years ago. He didn't give me a straight answer but responded by pressing his palms together, slowly moving his head back and forth, and said: "Jai Shri Krishna. What to say, Padma? There are many mysteries!"

The baithak near the tree was quite nicely kept up by a lovely, elderly woman who had been living there, alone, for some years. She was a very devoted bhakta, who besides caring for the temple, spent the rest of her time making seva to her Krishna deity. She invited us to stay the night, and we accepted her offer.

She insisted that we sleep on the stone floor of the temple, while she picked up her blanket and went to sleep outside. Before daybreak, we packed up and left so she could enter the temple and perform her deity worship before the sun rose.

It had been decided that Mohan would take a different route. Where we were headed was very remote and we would have to travel through uncharted rural areas. It would be better if we traveled light. So Mohan took our sleeping bags and all the cooking and seva utensils. He carried them to a place where he could find a car and driver for hire and then planned to meet up with us later.

Once again we had to find a boat and cross to the other side of the river. We then started walking toward a place Shyamdas said he had never been before, but he assured us that Mohan had provided a map before he left. We walked for hours and hours, never running into another human being, until we came upon some tribal-looking women wearing brightly colored yellow, pink, blue, and fluorescent-green saris and cholis. They were bent over, working in a rice field, their long, thin, dark arms completely covered by shiny bangles. As we approached, they stood up, and in unison each lifted one arm to shade their eyes from the sun, to get a better look at us. They all stared in disbelief, not having ever seen anyone with our color skin. Then Shyamdas, with what could only appear to be like magic to them, opened his mouth and spoke to them in Brajbhasha, the ancient language of the area, which predates Hindi. It was comparable to one of us walking through a jungle and coming across a monkey who talked to us in English with a Long Island accent. They were both delighted and baffled!

The women began to giggle uncontrollably, dropped what they were doing, and ran over to be near Shyamdas. With their strong, bangled arms, they grabbed hold of him and led him away to a cowshed as David, Melu, and I tagged along. We sat in that cool shed and watched while Shyamdas enraptured these women, engaging them in an animated conversation. When we asked him later what they were all talking about, he replied, "Krishna's lila, of course!" These women could have been gopis in a past life. It looked like the scene from the Shrimad Bhagavatam in which the gopis run into Krishna's cousin Uddhava and ply him with questions about their beloved Hari, whom they are missing terribly. After a few minutes, one of them gave us each a clay cup filled with buttermilk. This gesture moved Shyamdas to a spontaneous recitation of a poem by the sixteenth-century poet Rasakhan:

Narada, Shuka, and Vyasa are exhausted
from searching for Him.
They can never fathom His limits.
Yet, the dairymaids of Vrindavan
can make him dance—for a sip of buttermilk
from the palms of their hands!

Shyamdas asked me to take a photo of him as he was surrounded by the starstruck women feeding him buttermilk, and he said, "This is definitely something right out of *National Geographic*." After a while, Shyamdas felt it was time to move on and we set off down the road. We had walked only a little way when a couple of young kids came running after us, insisting that we come back and meet an important person. Shyamdas shrugged his shoulders, tilted his head, and with upturned palms said, "Radhe Radhe, okay, let's go meet the mayor," and our adventure continued.

We were led into a large hut with a thatched roof whose mud-plastered walls had been painted white. There were seven narrow wooden beds with rope woven across each to form a simple mattress of sorts. The beds lined the walls of this one room, with practically no space between them. Besides the beds, there was also a TV. The "mayor" gestured with his hand for each of us to take a bed, which we did. Immediately, Shyamdas laid down unselfconsciously on his and the mayor laid down on his, their heads next to each other. The rest of us sat on our beds and watched what was to unfold. Shyamdas spoke perfect Brajbhasha and communed with the mayor effortlessly. In a couple of minutes, they were laughing together as if they were old friends. Shyamdas introduced himself as coming from Connecticut, Melu from Malaysia, and David and I as being from New York. The mayor shook his head and said, "I don't know of these places—are they in India?"

"No, Connecticut and New York are in America! New York! New York! You know, New York City!" Shyamdas tried to explain.

"I don't know, where is New York?"

"It's in America."

"Oh, I never heard of it, but I have heard of Vietnam. Is New York near Vietnam?"

233

Shyamdas translated and we all laughed. The mayor asked his wife to make us some chai and to turn on the TV. He was very proud of the TV, although all the channels played the same show: static. It couldn't pick up any stations. After chai and some more chitchat we left, back on the road toward our destination, the remote jungle baithak that Shyamdas had allegedly never visited before.

We again walked and walked through fields and forests so remote that we didn't run into another human being, although we did get the rare darshan of a family of blue deer grazing. That was a sight! Shyamdas spotted them first and told us to approach very, very slowly so as not to frighten them. We were excited, but Shyamdas made us control ourselves. We crouched low to the ground, covered by tall grasses, and were able to get closer. When he felt we were close enough, he motioned for us to sit down and be quiet. There we sat, observing in wonder these exceptional beings. I took out my camera, but Shyamdas's eyes told me to put it away and be present in the moment. It was like seeing mythical creatures from another realm.

There were seven of them. They were tall and had very long legs. Their bodies were not as slender as white-tailed deer, being filled out, more like elk. Their faces resembled horses'. The two males had silvery white antlers. But it was the heavenly, misty blue hue of their fur that was the most enchanting. They were also very shy. When it was time for us to move on, Shyamdas made us walk slowly and softly in silence until we were out of their range of sight so as not to frighten them. Once on the road, Shyamdas spoke about the deer: "These deer are so rare that no one from *National Geographic* has ever been able to photograph them. Not many people in the world have ever even seen them. They are considered creatures from another time or planet, like unicorns." He kept reminding us that we had been blessed by Hari's grace to have their darshan.

It was dark by the time we finally arrived at our destination. How Shyamdas was able to navigate through the dark I can't even imagine. He only said, "With Hari's grace, all is possible." As we approached the baithak we saw a fire burning. Mohan had arrived before us and was already preparing kitchari. When we walked into the camp, we were greeted not only by Mohan, but by an old sadhu and his family of dogs. Dogs of all ages, including many puppies, energetically and affectionately welcomed us. Dogs love strong smells, and no doubt we weary travelers, all exuding pungent odors, were hard to resist. Mohan was concerned and did not like that all these dogs were about, jumping all over us and begging for attention. I pressed him to tell me why he had such an aversion to dogs, and he replied: "It's their tongues, Padma, they might defile Thakurji's seva by licking something with their tongues. They are dogs and touch unclean things with their tongues. I don't like them here."

The old sadhu who lived and traveled with these dogs was very easygoing and patient. We learned that he and the dogs had been traveling together for some years. They had been living at this baithak for several months. The sadhu wore the *Vaishnav tilak* on his forehead and was a Krishna bhakta.

We ate the prasad and then prepared a place to sleep. The baithak was quite dilapidated but still contained a small structure with stone walls and a wooden door, although the wood at the bottom of the door had rotted out, allowing for the puppies to crawl into the house. The sadhu had been accustomed to sleeping together with all the dogs inside this little house, but of course graciously offered it to us. It was decided that the dogs, the sadhu, and Mohan would sleep outside. The room was roughly eight by eight square feet, just big enough for us to sleep compactly side by side. When Mohan saw the puppies crawling into the house under the door to sleep with us, he became upset and put stuff in front of the door to block them from coming in.

Shyamdas knew the words and tunes to many Broadway musicals, and often when we were in situations like this, he would break into song. I would try to follow him, but his memory for lyrics far surpassed mine. So we were all lying down in this small room, and he propped himself up on an elbow and started singing, "When I joined this firm / as a brash young man. / Well I said to myself now brash young man. / Don't get any ideas. / Well, I stuck to that / And haven't had one in years," from *How to Succeed in Business Without Really Trying*.

To which I belted out in response, "OOOOklahoma, where the wind comes sweepin' down the plain," from *Oklahoma*.

David and Melu got a bit annoyed and got up and went outside, as they couldn't sleep amid our raucous belting out of show tunes. When they pushed open the door, some of the dogs rushed in, wagging their tails and wanting to play. David and Melu sat by the campfire with Mohan and the sadhu while Shyamdas and I went through our repertoire accompanied now by howling dogs. After a while it got late, and I was getting tired.

Shyamdas, who never seemed to sleep, went outside to join the others. I'm not sure how long they stayed up, but the next thing I knew it was morning and Mohan had prepared some chai.

The sadhu was so devoted to his dogs. We gave him some money, and he left with it, returning in the late afternoon with some food, which he prepared and offered to all of the dogs. We could see how grateful they were to him for that. I remember that when he placed their food lovingly on leaves on the ground and then said prayers, each one of those dogs waited patiently until he had blessed and offered the food before they ate. He told us that the dogs were not ordinary dogs, they were bhaktas, elevated souls who longed for God. He loved those dogs so much.

Mohan was still bothered by the dogs, so later that evening, after dinner, Shyamdas told us all a "dog story" that comes at the end of the Mahabharata:

After the Pandavas won the battle of Kurukshetra, Yudhishthira, Arjuna's older brother, became the king and reigned for some time. He was a righteous ruler. But when King Yudhishthira became elderly, he put his nephew Parikshit on the throne and became a renunciate. With his four brothers and their wife, Draupadi, he traveled to the Himalayas. Their intention was to live out the rest of their lives as yogis. On the way, Draupadi and his brothers all died.

Yudhishthira is left to carry on. He continues to travel, accompanied by his little brown dog, who had been a faithful companion to all of them during the journey. As Yudhishthira and the dog are making camp one night in the snowy mountains, they watch as a bright star seems to fall from the sky and land in front of them. It is a vimana, a celestial spacecraft. The radiant god Indra, the king of heaven, disembarks from the luminous ship and tells Yudhishthira he has come to take him to heaven. Yudhishthira bows to him with deep respect and walks toward the ship, his little dog trotting after him.

Indra stops them and says sternly, "The invitation is for you only, Yudhishthira, there is no room in heaven for a dog." Yudhishthira stops and reflects on how much love and devotion this dog had shown him, much more than most human beings he had known, so he thanks Indra but declines the invitation.

At this point, with tears in our eyes, having listened with rapt attention, Shyamdas says, "But that's not the end of the story —should I continue?" And of course, we say yes, and he resumes:

Yudhishthira turns to walk away, with his little dog following behind. There is a flash of light, and Yudhishthira turns to see the dog transforming into a celestial being who introduces himself as none other than the god Dharma, Yudhishthira's true father (!), who says, "Come my son, it is time." They both enter the ship and speed away to Svarga Loka, Indra's heavenly abode.

With that, we all sigh with relief. Shyamdas says, "Okay, boys and girls, the bedtime story is over, time for us to take a trip to *swapna loka*" (dreamland).

We stayed two nights with that sadhu and the dogs. On the morning of the third day, we packed up our stuff and prepared to start walking again. After reviewing the map and asking a few directions from the sadhu, we bid farewell to Mohan, who gave *pranams* to our sadhu friend, and surprisingly to his dogs as well, and then left in the car. Four of the dogs insisted on following us, even though we tried to shoo them away.

The first leg of our journey took us to a desert, and after walking for about two hours through nothing but parched ground and dried shrubs, two of the dogs started to whimper and restlessly turned back, yelping to try to convince us all to do the same. We told them to go and tried to get the other two to leave with them, but they wouldn't go. So, we continued with those two dogs, a black male and a female with a golden-colored coat who had the most yearning and determined look in her large brown eyes. We started calling her Goldie Girl and her dark boyfriend Shyam. Goldie Girl had decided that whatever it took, she was going with us. We walked all day. There were no paths. The land was dry and desertlike. It was hot, the terrain challenging, not easygoing for any of us.

By late afternoon we came to a high cliff next to the river. Shyamdas said we had to cross the river. We looked in the direction we were going and saw that the steep cliff continued for a long way, perhaps some miles. We walked along the cliff for some time, hoping it would get less steep, and it did somewhat, so at that point we decided to descend to the river. The dogs were worried and paced back and forth barking. As we started to climb down, Goldie Girl showed us her resolution by going before us. The ground was so dry it started to crumble, and she helplessly began to slide several feet. But she deftly managed to turn around and pull herself back up the slope with her front paws. She looked up at us and barked, as if to say, "Too dangerous guys, best to go back."

We ignored her and started down the slope. She tried to push us back up the incline, even though she herself was slipping. At this point, her dark Shyam became very worried and started down the embankment. He slipped, then fell on his side, and dangerously started to slide. He managed to right himself and succeeded in climbing back up to the top of the cliff. We tried to encourage Goldie Girl to go back up too, but she wouldn't go. She wouldn't leave us. So, we slowly made our descent, with her next to us, all the way down to the river. Shyam was on the top of the cliff frantically barking, trying to get his Goldie Girl and us to forgo the river crossing. He was warning us. The current was swift, and we had no idea how deep the river was. Shyamdas told us we had to cross and to wrap our clothes tightly around us, as we might have to swim. Melu and I were wearing saris, David and Shyamdas *dhotis*.

"What about our dog?" I asked.

"Don't worry, Padma, she's smart, she won't go in this river," Shyamdas assured me.

Shyamdas went first and we followed. The current was strong, but it seemed like we were going to be able to manage it. We were able to walk in, as it wasn't too deep at first. Goldie Girl stayed on the bank. We were up to our necks near the middle of the river when Goldie Girl jumped in. "No, go back!" we shouted. She was swimming desperately toward us, but the current began to take her. We panicked and shouted louder, "Go back." She seemed to hear us and was able to resist the current, turn around, and pull herself out of the water and onto the embankment. What relief we felt—now she will go back home, surely. The current was pulling us quickly downstream, and the water got deeper, so we had to swim. We made it to the other side.

The two dogs were beside themselves—black Shyam on top of the cliff running in worried circles, and Goldie Girl at the river's edge, strategically trying to determine when to make her jump. And then she did. She jumped in and started to swim with all her strength and courage toward us on the other side. She was fighting against the current, which was winning, carrying her tiny, lithe body downstream. We started running along the river's edge. Then she went under. We all jumped in, swimming toward her. We saw her head as she surfaced. The force of the river had carried her far downstream, but she was still trying to swim in our direction. Shyam was now making his way down from the cliff, sliding down toward the river and her.

The current switched direction and succeeded in taking Goldie Girl away from us and toward the embankment. There she was able to pull herself out of the water. We made our way out of the river onto the embankment opposite her. She stood there so still, so filled with sorrow and longing, that I could feel her heart breaking. She wanted so much to go with us, but it was obvious that her past karmas did not match her present intention.

We stood watching as black Shyam, having quickly slid all the way down to the river and run along the rocky shoreline, finally made his way to her. He was licking and nuzzling her and letting out some loud yelps of relief. After a few minutes, he seemed to have convinced her to abandon the idea of following us. We watched them, transfixed, as they painfully climbed back up the steep incline, using their front paws to pull their bodies onward. When they finally made it to the top, they stood at the edge of the cliff watching us as we stood on our side of the river watching them. We saw Shyam nudging Goldie Girl, trying to get her to turn and travel back. He even walked away from her, but she remained motionless, watching us. The sun was setting, and its light was focused on her, illuminating her goldenness. She looked like a radiant celestial being. I could not help seeing her as Laxmi, so resolute, so sure of what she wanted, and so filled with longing, but lacking the necessary eligibility at that time.

We watched until our wet clothes were dry. Then Shyamdas said we had to resume our journey. As I looked back, I could still see Goldie Girl, although her body was getting smaller with the distance. At one point I stopped and let the others go on ahead. Although she was tiny in my view, I could make out Shyam joining her. Then they both seemed to disappear. I moved on to catch up with my companions, but I could not stop thinking about her. I identified with her, sure that I also lacked the necessary eligibility to reach my heart's desire—no matter how hard I tried, it still continued to elude me.

The great saint Shri Anandamayi Ma said, "The sheer desire for God is itself the way to God." But even with the consolation of these wise words, it seems that desire alone only reveals the path and that it takes more than just one's own effort to reach the goal. It takes relinquishing the goal all together. But how many of us can do that? To live without an aim or objective, to let go of all ambitions, and leave your destiny totally in the hands of God takes a lot of courage. One's sense of adventure must be fueled by fearlessness, and only unconditional love can make one *that* fearless.

The profound teaching embedded in the story of Laxmi at Belvan, unable to gain access to the rasa lila, reveals something of this deep mystery of how love works. The name *Laxmi* comes from the Sanskrit root *lakshya*, which means "to aim, point, or indicate." So of course, since there is no point to the rasa lila, it can contain no Laxmi. Those of us who embark upon a pilgrimage to go somewhere or to achieve something will, like the goddess Laxmi, not be able to penetrate the forests of Braj, where the exalted delights of the lila are accessible only to those grace-filled souls who have surrendered all objectives.

Yes, we must have the intense desire for God—that will put us on the path. But we would do well to remember that God is not a goal we can achieve. What can we really do, but make ourselves available? The practice of letting go of all aims may provide space in our hearts, enabling us to surrender to His grace. Grace is the only eligibility that matters in Shri Krishna's lila. Still, the cultivation of intense longing will contribute to our eligibility. It must! Either way, as Shyamdas would say: "What to do? Radhe Radhe!" Meaning, remember God. What better way to spend your day, but in such delightful, pointless revelry?

Tea Miracle

Miracles occur naturally as expressions of love.
The real miracle is the love that inspires them.
In this sense everything that comes from love is a miracle.
—Marianne Williamson

The laws of faith govern the laws of nature.
—Franz Liszt

Shyamdas was visiting me one evening in August at my home in Woodstock. It was the day before I was scheduled to give a talk at the Omega Institute, in Rhinebeck, New York, just across the river from where I live. The talk was to be part of the opening evening event for their annual Being Yoga Conference. I had been asked, along with a few other yoga teachers, to share a "yoga story." I had decided to tell a story describing a time I was in India and had witnessed a miracle. The story featured a saint who lived in Vrindavan and was known simply as Little Maharajji. He was given that name by Westerners who had come in the 1960s with Ram Dass to the Neem Karoli Baba Ashram, also in Vrindavan, just down the road from Little Maharajji's place. Whenever I was in Vrindavan with Shyamdas, we would visit Little Maharajji, or Choti Maharaj, as Shyamdas called him. *Choti* is a Hindi word meaning "short, small, or little."

Although his body appeared little—he was only four feet tall—his spirit was large. He also had very long hair, which over the years of his asceticism, had turned to *jetta*, dreadlocks. His hair was so long, it dragged on the ground, several feet behind him. Most of the time he coiled it all on top of his head, extending his height by at least a foot. All the Westerners were enthralled with the saint Neem Karoli Baba, who was called Maharajji. But as many of us would come to understand, India is full of saints and they often live near one another. That was the case with Little Maharajji, who lived down the road from Neem Karoli Baba. The story I planned to tell at Omega was about a time Little Maharajji manifested a miracle for me, or at least I thought he was responsible for the miracle.

Since I had met Little Maharajji through Shyamdas and he knew Little Maharajji much better than I did, and most importantly, he was there with me when the miracle occurred, I asked Shyamdas if I could tell him the story. I knew it would help me to practice before I had to get up on stage the next day, at the conference, and tell it to a roomful of people. I hoped that

241

Shyamdas would correct me if I left anything out or got any information wrong. Shyamdas, who called me Padma, heartily agreed, but before I began, he said: "You know, Padma, Little Maharajji is still alive. I saw him a few months back, and you know how old he is, right?"

"Well, you always told me he was ancient."

"Yeah, but how old do you think?"

"I don't know, a hundred?"

"Nooooo—more!"

"What? No way!"

"Yeah. This past year I was visiting the Neem Karoli Baba Ashram on my way to see Little Maharajji. After I left the ashram, I was on the road walking to Choti's and I met a policeman. He stopped me to ask where I was going. I told him and then we got to talking about Little Maharajji.

"He's older than you think," the policeman said.

"How old?"

"Ask him," the policeman said. "Ask Little Maharajji how old he was during the Battle of Jhansi."

"*Hmm*, I think, *the Battle of Jhansi?* Well I never heard of it, but I thought, *Okay.* So when I get to Little Maharajji's place I asked, 'Choti Maharajji, how old were you during the battle of Jhansi?' "

He didn't hesitate and replied, "Oh, I was twelve."

"Then, later on, I Googled it: 'The Battle of Jhansi 1858—an important battle fought for Indian independence between the British and the beautiful Queen of Jhansi, Lakshmi Bai, who, riding on her horse, led her army.' *Oh*, I thought, *this is veeery interesting! The battle happened in 1858.* Okay, so I do the math. If he was twelve when the battle happened, he must have been born in 1846. So if it's now 2012, that would make him 166 years old! Wow! I knew he was old, but not *that* old. Okay, Padma, tell your story, let me listen."

Miracles do happen, but they don't always have to be big, spectacular, fireworks-going-off types of things; they can be as subtle as the miracle of a cup of tea. This miracle story takes place in Vrindavan, the sacred city in North India where Krishna spent a lot of his teenage years. Vrindavan is filled with holy sites and holy saints. I used to travel to India to visit Shyamdas when he lived in Gokul, a small medieval town on the banks of the Yamuna River about ten miles or so from Vrindavan. Gokul was where Krishna lived, five thousand years ago, as a small child with his adoptive parents, Yashodha and Nanda, and where he played and enchanted all of the residents, including the gopis, cows, deer, birds, trees, and even the clouds. Often, Shyamdas and I would take day trips to Vrindavan to visit temples, pilgrimage sites, shop in the bazaar, eat at the famous ISKCON restaurant, and hang out with old friends and holy people.

We planned to take such a trip, and Shyamdas made the arrangements—getting a car and driver, planning who we would see and where we would go. Creating an amazing magical day for his friends was one of his specialties. He decided that we should get an early start so we could make the most of our day and not get home too late. It was dangerous to drive from Vrindavan to Gokul at night because of bandits, who would ambush the car. At that time, during the 1990s, the roads were just dirt and very bumpy, so you couldn't drive very fast if you wanted to get away from a bandit. And at night it was very dark—the rural country roads were not lighted.

"Okay, Padma, 5 a.m., be ready to go."

"Can we have tea first?"

"Oh, sure, chai and then we go."

Shyamdas knew how much I liked tea. The fact is, I like tea very much. Once, when Shyamdas and I were contemplating joining the Hare Krishnas, Shyamdas said to me, "I found out what we have to do to join up."

"Okay, great—what?"

"Well, we have to give up a few things: no meat-eating, no intoxicants—alcohol, drugs, even chocolate—no sex, and no coffee or tea."

"What, no tea? I gotta think about that one."

He laughed and said, "Well maybe they would make an exception for you, Padma."

So, back to Gokul. The next morning comes, and I'm in the big room that served as Shyamdas's kitchen, bedroom, living room, book-translation department, and kirtan hall. I'm trying to get a fire going to boil water to make tea when Shyamdas runs up the stone stairs of the dharmshala and says: "Padma, come on, the car is downstairs. We gotta go now, we don't want to miss *darshan*."

"Wait, can't I have tea first?"

"No. We can stop on the way. Hey, we're going to Vrindavan, where there are a million places to get tea. It's the chai capital of the world—*chalo*, let's go!"

243

Well, we don't stop on the way, as all the usual chai stalls are closed. Maybe it was too early, I don't know. We arrive in Vrindavan and go straight to the Jai Singh Ghera ashram to meet our friend Asim Krishnadas, who is waiting for us, standing at the ashram gate.

"Hurry—if we run, we can arrive in time for Banke Bihari darshan," Asim says, as he is waving at us from down the road.

"But wait," I say to Shyamdas, "the temple priests never wake up the deity before 9 a.m. It's still too early, isn't it? Why don't we go and have tea someplace and wait till the temple opens?"

"Don't question the *bhav* of a God-intoxicated Asim Krishnadas. *Chalo*, Padma, let's go!"

We run down the road trying to catch up with Asim. We get to the temple, and it's closed. Asim switches gears and directs us: "Quick! We can still make the Radha Ramana darshan, *chalo!*"

Although I know both Asim and Shyamdas have visited these temples and had these darshans hundreds of times, they act with such an urgency, as if it is their last chance. We actually do arrive at Radha Ramana in time to see the miraculous *shaligram murti* of Madan Mohanji, the flute-playing Krishna. But we don't stay for long, as it is nearing 9 a.m. Asim signals us, and we rush out of the mandir and back to Banke Bihari in time for the Shringar darshan.

The Banke Bihari mandir is perhaps the most popular temple in Vrindavan. The deity, Banke Bihari, is a form of Krishna—a composite of Krishna and Radha entwined, merged as one entity. *Banke* means "bent," and *bihari* means "enjoyer." Banke Bihari is bent in three places and knows how to enjoy themself. The first darshan at most Vrindavan temples is at 4 a.m., but the *pujaris* who serve Banke Bihari don't like to wake the deity up early, because, they say, Banke Bihari's been out late the night before playing love games in the forest and needs to rest in the morning.

The scene in the Banke Bihari temple is hard to describe adequately. To use the word *ecstatic* falls short—it is just not juicy enough. The atmosphere in the temple before the curtain is raised to reveal the *svarupa* (form) of the deity is heavy, weighted with intense longing. Devotees swoon and fall to the floor, writhing in convulsions, crying and moaning, unable to bear even the slightest glance toward the deity, who cannot even be seen yet. The deity resides behind many curtains and doors. The pujaris

244

take their time revealing the murti. First the outer doors have to be opened, then curtains and more curtains, and another set of doors, and more curtains—this foreplay goes on for a long time. Even before the last curtains are parted, finally revealing the svarupa, devotees are dropping to the ground, grabbing at their clothes, singing, and crying out in agonized rapture.

It is quite a sight, and an even more extraordinary bhav permeates the room. Asim is thoroughly turned on; his body is trembling with *prema*, he's barely able to stand, and tears are jumping out from his eyes, which are fixated on the deity. All of this lasts only about three or four minutes, after which the pujari comes and closes the innermost curtains. Devotees scream and tear at their hair. Then, after a few minutes, the pujari comes back and closes another layer of curtains. The devotees start to moan. It goes on like this with layer after layer until the outer heavy wooden doors are at last closed, completing the physical barrier between the deity and the devotees until the next darshan scheduled for later that day.

The three of us stumble out of the temple, as if intoxicated. Asim invites us back to his place for chai. We are on the way, when we run into a friend of Asim's who convinces us to come with him to Raman Reti to roll in the sands. He says a saint who just arrived yesterday is staying in the temple there. So off we go —and then on to the next event, and so on. Throughout the day as we go from one place to another, I ask if we can stop for tea, but we are always rushing to the next holy place or to visit a saint. This is how it goes until we end up at the ISKCON restaurant. There is no chance of getting a cup of tea there, as no caffeine is allowed at the ashram. But by this time, I have resigned myself and let go of that morning cup of tea. The fact is, it is late afternoon.

Shyamdas reminds me that we should be heading home soon, but we can't leave Vrindavan without visiting the Neem Karoli Baba Ashram. I agree, and when we arrive we are fortunate to find Siddhi Ma there. Shyamdas knows her well. She is a great saint and was an intimate friend of Neem Karoli Baba's while he was alive. She greets Shyamdas, and they speak in Brajbhasha, the ancient language, predating Hindi, which is still spoken by the locals in the area. Shyamdas asks her, "Mataji, how was it when you played Holi with Maharajji?" She looks right at Shyamdas, her eyes get big, she opens her mouth to speak, and just then her eyes roll back in her head and she goes into *samadhi*! Yeah, just like that!

One of her close devotees annoyingly says to Shyamdas, "Look what you've done!"

I ask innocently: "What? What did he do?"

"Because he mentioned her being with Maharajji, it pulled up more than a memory, it was enough to transport her into the lila. Who knows how long she will be gone from us now? It is best you leave right away."

Shyamdas looks at me, lifts up his hands, and says: "So what to do? *Chalo*—let's go. Let's visit Little Maharajji. Padma, you'll finally get your cup of chai."

Little Maharajji's ashram is about a quarter of a mile down the road from the Neem Karoli Baba Ashram on the Parikrama path that encircles the holy city of Vrindavan. As we walk on the timeworn sacred path toward Little Maharajji, Shyamdas, being the gentleman he is, apologizes for letting the whole day go by without serving me tea. He assures me that Little Maharajji will make me tea, saying, "Tea is what Little Maharajji always gives to visitors as *prasad*!" I feel embarrassed by his concern, as the incredible spiritual adventures he took me on all day far surpassed what a cup of tea could deliver. As we walk together in the dusk, on the dusty road, about to visit yet another living saint, not only am I over tea, but I am filled with intense gratitude, realizing that I am only hanging onto the coattails of Shyamdas's good karma (or should I say *dhoti* instead of coattails?). I am filled with wonder that all of this is happening. What did I do to deserve Shyamdas's presence in my life?

We arrive at Little Maharajji's. He is sitting in front of his place, which is covered with larger-than-life paintings that he himself painted. They are all paintings of God. We sit on the ground at his feet, along with a few devotees, his long jetta cascading over his small body and trailing in the dust around him. He gracefully gathers them up and lifts them into the crook of his right arm, rearranging them to make more room for us to sit. His beloved cows are nearby, having come home from a day of grazing to gather together near their beloved Govinda in the form of Choti Maharaj. Little Maharajji does cow seva. He rescues many sick and abandoned cows from the street and cares for them. He is now gazing lovingly at them and asks us to look at them too.

"Take their darshan!" he says. "Look at them, have you ever seen cows more beautiful? This is my most favorite time of day, when my cows come back to me as the sun is setting." He goes on with a bit of mischief in his voice, "Their eyes are filled with light, with rapture, because they have been in the forest all day with their beloved." Shyamdas translates it all for me.

We sit with this gentle saint for some time, when Shyamdas says, "Maharajji, chai?" Little Maharajji, seemingly obedient to Shyamdas's request, calls one of his devotees and instructs them to prepare the chai. The devotee bows as if to say "of course," and leaves, only to come back a minute later holding an empty 3 Roses tea tin in front of Little Maharajji. Shyamdas lifts up his hands and exclaims, "*Kyaa baat hai!* Unbelievable! Never, in the thirty years that I have known Little Maharajji, have I ever witnessed a time when he was out of chai! Unbelievable! Padma, *chalo*, let's go." With folded hands and waving head, Shyamdas bids farewell to Little Maharajji.

With folded hands and our heads bowed, we walk backward, as it is disrespectful to turn your back to a saint, until we are out of sight. Then we turn to walk up the dirt road. We take just a few steps, when one of Little Maharajji's devotees calls us back for prasad. In India, you never leave the presence of a saint without receiving prasad. So we return and prostrate at his feet.

He puts his hands on our heads as a blessing and says, "Take prasad, take prasad." We sit up and hold out our hands, and he puts sweet balls in our palms.

"Thank you, Maharajji."

"Now you go," he says, laughing, and waves us on.

We back away and then turn to go. Shyamdas quickly pops the sweet ball into his mouth and is walking quickly up the road ahead of me. By this time, it is dark, and we need to get back to Gokul soon. I know this, but I am walking slowly in a sort of a reverie, holding the sweet ball in my palm. Because I am not fond of sweet things, I usually pass them on to Shyamdas when I am given them. This time, however, for some reason I chip off a small piece and place it in my mouth. I receive a shock and say quietly, "Oh, my!" Then I call out, "Shyamdas, what did Little Maharajji give us?"

Shyamdas, without turning around, says impatiently: "Prasad! Look if you don't want it, just give it to a dog or someone. Padma, come on, we gotta go." And he hurries up the road faster.

I take another bite of the sweet ball and have to stop in the middle of the road. "Shyamdas, what did he give us?" I persist.

"A ladoo."

I run toward Shyamdas and say, "You have to taste this." I put a big piece of the ladoo in Shyamdas's mouth.

He looks at me and closes his eyes, then exclaims: "*Kyaa baat hai!* Amazing! Wow, Hari bol, Radhe Shyam! He gave you your tea, Padma! This is definitely extraordinary! Unbelievable! This is a miracle, you know! But *chalo*, we gotta go, let's go."

Shyamdas hurries onward, with me next to him. We find our car and driver, and with a bit of urgency Shyamdas shoves me in and we drive back to Gokul. We sit in silence, both of us reflecting on the events of the day, as the driver takes us home. You see, it is hard to explain what it was like to eat that ladoo. It was not like eating something that tasted *like* tea, that had the flavor of tea, but it was exactly the experience, the experience of drinking a cup of tea. Yes, Shyamdas recognized that it was magical and unexplainable, but I got the feeling that to him it was just another blessed day in Braj.

Now fast forward to us sitting at the dining room table in my house in Woodstock and I have just finished recounting the Little Maharajji tea story. Shyamdas says: "Yeah, Padma, I remember that day—it happened all as you say. Amazing! You tell the story well. It will be good for people to hear it at Omega tomorrow. But Padma, as you were telling it, I was reminded of another story, a story about the Pushtimargi Vaishnav Padmanabh. Can I tell you that story?"

"Yeah, of course," I say, and he continues:

Padmanabh was so poor that he could offer only chickpeas in his seva, and his chickpeas weren't even cooked, they were just sprouted—he was too poor to buy fuel to cook with. Yet because his devotion was so pure, when he prepared the chickpeas to be offered, each chickpea became a particular dish while still retaining its chickpea form. Padmanabh would place little bowls of chickpeas in front of his Krishna deity, then after he performed aarti (the ritual waving of light), he would invite other bhaktas for lunch and share the prasad. He would say to them, "Please, take prasad, have some dal, some rice, subji, take rotis, here, have some delicious mango chutney."

The guests would become confused and say, "But there are only chickpeas here."

To which Padmanabh would insist, "Please taste the

prasad."

When the guests finally gave in and tasted the chickpeas from each of the different bowls, they would be amazed, because one tasted like dal, another like rice, while another just like a roti.

Shyamdas then explained:

Because everything is Bhagavan, and Bhagavan lives in everything, everything contains everything else. Nothing but Bhagavan exists in this world, although he may be concealed. So even though something might appear as a chickpea, Bhagavan is concealed inside that chickpea, so that chickpea holds inside its form the potential for anything and everything to be revealed. So a chickpea could manifest itself as a roti or rice or whatever, it all depends on what Bhagavan wants to reveal. And in the case of a pure devotee, who has managed to get Bhagavan under his or her control, that devotee can pull out from a chickpea its concealed potential. Wow! The truth is truly unfathomable by the thinking mind!

Being with Shyamdas was a cascade of millions of magical moments, and many miracles, some major, some minor. He seemed to be able to orchestrate subtle and acute shifts in perception for his friends. He always seemed to be in a state of wonder. He was also so incredibly humble and would never accept praise or credit for anything. I still ponder my experience of that ladoo—who turned it into chai? Was it Little Maharajji? Or was it Shyamdas? It will remain a mystery. Shyamdas was extremely generous, and his *bhakti*, his loving devotion to God, manifested as spiritual accomplishments. These exalted faculties instigated great mercy to flow into the lives of his friends, the people fortunate to have his association and to receive his love. He wanted so much to share with all of us the bliss of devotion that he experienced. He was always there waiting to open the door for anyone who wanted to enter into the lila that he knew so well. Shyamdas was a blessed vessel for grace. How can his story ever be fully told?

Attachment to Preferences

The Great Way is not difficult for those who have no preferences.
—From "Hsin Hsin Ming," by the Third Chinese Patriarch

On April 30, 1975, the last few Americans still in South Vietnam were airlifted out of the country as Saigon fell to communist forces, marking the official end of the Vietnam War. But for many, the ghosts of war never ended and they lived with the horror for the rest of their lives. I met Jake Mannerly in 1974. That's not his real name—but I'll use it to respect his privacy. Jake had been honorably discharged from the army after serving his term as a soldier in Vietnam. He ranked as a sergeant and came home with a few medals. He was a painter and suffering from PTSD. Back then, post-traumatic stress disorder was not recognized as a serious condition and soldiers were pretty much on their own to find ways to deal with it. Jake, like many Vietnam vets, took drugs to ease his pain.

One rainy Seattle night, he dropped several hits of acid, smoked some hash, took the bottle of vodka he had been drinking, and sped off in his car, the radio blaring, onto the freeway. The car spun out of control and crashed into a railing. He was flung through the windshield. Whether or not Jake was intending to kill himself, I don't know, he doesn't even remember if he was or not. Regardless, he ended up in a hospital and spent months recovering from his injuries. The smashup left his face scarred—wide, deep red lines crisscrossing his face. Jake was very forthcoming about his past. His experiences in Vietnam had left deep wounds in his soul, which had surfaced in his face.

He painted in the cubist style; his paintings presaged the scars on his face. To me, they resembled his face—a map of intersecting lines and planes. His use of color and nuanced shading was effective in portraying the promise of light coming up through the cracks made by the lines dissecting the planes of color. To me, his paintings were optimistic, like a sunrise. Painting was therapeutic for him, as was storytelling. It didn't take much to prompt him to tell a story. His stories were all from his time in Vietnam. This is one of them:

Before the war I had a strong sense of right and wrong. I believed that America was the greatest nation in the world, and so I enlisted voluntarily and wanted to be sent to Vietnam to fight the enemy. My wish was granted, but once there, my idealism was challenged and with it my naïve concepts. The army teaches you to adhere to a rigid belief system that divides the world into black and white, into good guys and bad guys, friends and foes. A trained soldier must make split-second decisions and doesn't have the leisure to contemplate gray areas. It sounds simple and direct, but when you are on the front lines in the stench of battle, it becomes confusing, because it isn't black and white—it's all gray, very dark gray. You start out thinking you are one of the good guys, but very soon you aren't so sure. It was like that for all of us.

We were in the jungle somewhere; it was dinnertime. I lined my men up to get served. During wartime preferences become extremely important to men who are living on army rations. We all dream of the food we are missing, as well as everything else we left behind. It is a dangerous thing for a person to be caught in a place they don't want to be, as it takes you out of the present. Your mind, body, and heart become disconnected, fragmented. You yearn for the past or for an imagined future. To try to hold on to a sense of identity, you adhere strongly to your preferences, as it gives you a reason for living. To a soldier on the front lines of battle, under intense pressure, attachments to likes and dislikes can become perversely exaggerated.

I remember this one soldier standing in line for food. He looked ahead and saw that there was a pan of red Jell-O for dessert. "I love red Jell-O—my favorite!" he exclaimed with a hoot and yowl and started to sing an impromptu crazy song in praise of red Jell-O:

Red, red, slimy, slippery, red
goes to my head
gonna slurp you up good cause like I said,
J-E-L-L-O, Oh, Oh, Oh,
I love you Jell-O!

But by the time he made it to the front of the line, the guy in front of him had taken the last of the red Jell-O and a pan of green Jell-O had been brought out, which the server was about to put on the soldier's plate.

"Hey man, I ain't takin that sh!t," he said. "Give me the red Jell-O!"

"Sorry, the guy ahead of you got the last of it," the server apologized.

The soldier threw his empty plate at the server, took out his machine gun, and fired a round of bullets at him, then aimed at the guy who had taken the last of the red Jell-O and started firing. Both men lay dead. Jake lurched for the shooter, pulled him to the ground, and disarmed him. Lying on his back, with Jake's knee pressed against his chest, he laughed maniacally and spittingly said, "Yeah, so whatcha goin' do now, Sarge, send me to Nam?"

This story might sound extreme, but it provides a lesson in how detrimental attachment to preferences can be. Having real needs is not wrong, but wants, on the other hand, can become problematic, for ourselves and others. Each of us must figure out the difference between a real need and a want. The problem with desires—wants or preferences—arises when we become so attached to them that we allow them to cause us and others distress. For example, when we demand that others provide us with what we want and blame them for our unhappiness when they don't deliver, or when we allow ourselves to become so rigid and fanatical about getting what we want that we lose the innate serenity of our minds.

Without serenity of mind, true happiness is beyond reach. Patanjali cites *raga* (what we like) and *dvesha* (what we dislike) as two of the five obstacles to Yoga. The other three are *avidya* (ignorance of who we really are; forgetting our eternal Self and thinking we are our body and mind), *asmita* (attachment to the ego and with it the sense of I, me, and mine), and *abhinivesha* (fear of death).

In a 1979 lecture, Ram Dass told a great story about not getting caught up in preferences based on a teaching found in the "Hsin Hsin Ming," by the Third Chinese Patriarch of Zen. He called it the "Ah, So" story:

The Great Way is not difficult for those who have no preferences. Just look at your life and think how many preferences you have. Do you prefer pleasure over pain? Life over death? Friends over aloneness? Freedom over imprisonment? Praise over blame? Love over hate? Where are your attachments? Where are your clingings? Are you stuck in polarities? That is what the Third Chinese Patriarch is asking.

"Make the slightest distinction, and heaven and earth are set infinitely apart," he says. Make the slightest distinction, and you've already created hell. "If you wish to see the truth, then hold no opinions for or against anything. To set up what you like against what you dislike is the disease of the mind." Are you ready to live like that? Do you realize how spacious you have to be, to live by that kind of philosophy?

That's the fiercest kind of philosophy I know. But I like to have that kind of fierce friend to hang out with me, to keep reminding me how much I "hold opinions": this should be like this, that should be like that, and I want everybody to be thus and so, and wouldn't it be better if ... ? Instead of just being spacious with it, we're full of opinions. Not to "hold opinions" doesn't mean we don't have them—it means we are not attached to them. It doesn't mean we don't have preferences; it means we're not attached to our preferences. I can prefer red over green, but if I end up with green, ah, so.

"Ah, so"—remember the "Ah, So" story? There was a monk who lived in the monastery up on the hill. The local girl down in the village got pregnant by the fisherman. She didn't want to cause problems for him in the village, so she said that the father "was the monk up in the monastery." When the baby was born, the townspeople carried it up the hill to the monastery. They knocked on the gate, and the monk opened the door; they said to the monk, "This is your baby—you raise it." And the monk said, "Ah, so." And he took the baby and closed the gate. I mean, the guy's whole life changed just like that, in that moment, and his only reaction is, "Ah, so."

Nine years later the girl was dying. She didn't want to die without admitting what had really happened, so she said to the people: "Look, I lied. It really wasn't the monk; it was the fisherman." The villagers were horrified! They went up to the monastery and they knocked on the door. The monk opened the gate, and there standing next to him was this nine-year-old child. The villagers said: "We've made a terrible mistake. This isn't your child after all. We'll take him back down to the village to raise him, and you are free to go back to your monastic life." And the monk said, "Ah, so." He was so much right here that whatever new change arose, "Ah, so."

Contemporary teacher Byron Katie teaches Loving What Is as the key to discovering serenity of mind amid upheaval. We are very attached to our preferences regarding how we think other people should act, and when they don't behave the way we want them to, we become disappointed. Disappointment often leads to serious disturbances like anger, blame, depression, and even overt violence. Loving what is goes far beyond mere passive acceptance. It doesn't mean you grin and bear it, pretend you are happy but inside are seething with anger and plotting revenge from your position as a victim. It doesn't mean you turn a blind eye or stay in an abusive relationship or that you condone the atrocities happening in the world.

We may have preferences regarding how we would like things to be, but if we are blinded by our preferences and can't see what is actually happening, then problems arise. Too often when reality doesn't match how we think it should be, we fight it. Katie says, "When we fight with reality we will lose." To be able to accept a situation and honestly see it as it is, not as we wish it to be, is the first step to serenity of mind. Getting involved in other people's business is a sure way to unhappiness. We all know how this sounds: "I want him to do this, I would like him to pay more attention to me, I would like it if he was vegan, or if only she wouldn't do that, I don't like that she nags me all the time about watching TV," and on and on it goes. When we try to mind other people's business, we neglect our own. Katie says: "If I had a prayer, it would be this: God spare me from the desire for love, approval, or appreciation. Amen." If we could ease up on our desires and wants, we could give ourselves a chance to be happy.

My teacher Shri Brahmananda Sarasvati was very keen on this practice of letting go of preferences. He defined Yoga as, "Mind, your own business!" Stop judging and making tyrannical demands upon others; instead, purify your own mind. Krishna gives this fundamental wisdom teaching in the Bhagavad Gita when he suggests renouncing the fruits of your actions. Do your best to act with perfection and let God take care of the rest. Let go of obsessing over the way you think God should act or how other people should act. You can't control God or other people. Can you control yourself? The investigation into how to control your own mind is called yoga practice. It is a practice of exercising choice rather than reacting to impulses. If you don't like the world you are living in, getting angry about it will not change it and ultimately won't make you any happier. Krishna explains it like this:

Endowed with a pure mind, controlling yourself with firmness, purifying your speech, turning away from the noise of distractions, letting go of likes and dislikes, you take refuge in the peace of your own eternal soul, the divine atman.
—Bhagavad Gita 18.51-53

The important choices are not about getting what you want, but rather refraining from getting upset if you don't get what you thought you wanted. To paraphrase Mick Jagger's encouraging advice, if we try sometimes, we just might find we'll get what we need.

To gracefully embrace each moment, no matter what life provides us with, is to discover the path, the Great Way.

An Ice Cream Sandwich
for Mother Superior

patram pushpam phalam toyam / yo me bhaktya prayacchati
tad aham bhakty-upahritam / ashnami prayatatmanah
*Whatever is offered to me with a pure and loving heart,
no matter if it is as small as a leaf, a flower, or a piece of fruit,
or a sip of water, I will accept it.*
—Bhagavad Gita 9.26

This is a story about my first experience of *prasad*. When I was in grade school, Richard Bowers was my best friend. We both were students at Saint Louis Catholic School in Alexandria, Virginia. The school was run by Franciscan nuns. Richard's mother always packed a lunch for him. My mother was not so conscientious and never packed a lunch for me—I guess she expected me to figure out my own lunch. My grandmother would usually make sure I had a nickel to buy a carton of milk. But the fact is, I usually came to school without lunch. Richard would often share his lunch with me, including his iced tea. His mother made iced tea for him in a thermos. This tea was the most delicious drink I had ever tasted. Still, to this day, when I think of Richard, I can taste that tea. Often, I try to duplicate it. Over the years, I have had a fair amount of good luck in this endeavor, especially while traveling on airplanes.

Here's a few things to consider: The tea should not be ice-cold and there should be no ice cubes in it. It shouldn't be warm either, or even lukewarm, but close to room temperature. It should be made with black tea but very diluted, not strong, and with sugar, but not too sweet. There should also be a hint of lemon. When I'm on a plane and the flight attendant asks me if I want tea, I say yes. She brings it and I start my own alterations, attempting to recreate the perfect "Richard Bowers cup of tea." I get quite excited when I feel I have it just right. If someone I know is traveling with me, I ask them if they would like to taste the amazing concoction. Unfortunately, no one has ever responded with the same delight as I experience while drinking the perfect Richard Bowers' cup, but most likely that is because they don't have the same memories I do of Richard Bowers.

How can I describe him? To speak of his physical appearance hardly portrays his inner soul, but allow this brief visual to at least serve as a window into the personality of my friend. Not very tall, he was a little, skinny boy with straight blond hair. He wore a uniform, like all the other boys in school, navy-blue trousers, a white shirt, and navy-blue tie, but he had a way of making his uniform appear natural and elegant. He managed to be always very well-put-together. His clothes were always clean and pressed, his clip-on tie never crooked. Besides that, he seemed comfortable in his clothes, they never hindered his gracefulness.

Unlike him, I felt awkward in my dark-blue jumper and felt it never fit me well. And since I tried to save time in the morning by sleeping in my school clothes, they were always wrinkled and stained with coffee and bits of food. Besides his clothes, the most impressive thing to me was that Richard Bowers liked me and was very nice to me. He always seemed to be able to cheer me up and say something supportive and positive. He tended to look on the sunny side of situations. School was difficult enough, most of us kids were so scared, and afraid of doing something wrong, and being punished in this world, or in hell, so it was great to have a friend.

The mother superior at our school at that time was Mother Mary Margaret. She seemed quite young and very beautiful. I remember my parents making comments about her like: "What a shame that she's a nun. It's a crime to lock someone so beautiful up in a convent." Mother Mary Margaret was not only beautiful, but also angelic as well as very kind. Whenever any of us kids would have the rare opportunity of seeing her, she seemed to be floating a few inches off the floor, drifting along the school corridors. Sometimes she would stop to speak to us, and when she did, she would look directly into our eyes, one by one, with hands folded in prayer, and say with the sweetest voice: "God be with you, children. God be with you, children. God be with you, children. ..."

We all loved her, and some of us, like Richard and myself, dreamed of someday being invited to move into the convent to live with her. One day Richard and I were sitting together in the school cafeteria, drinking some delicious iced tea, and we saw Mother Mary Margaret enter the lunchroom. She looked like a black-and-white angel gliding on an invisible magic carpet. Richard's mom had put extra Oreo cookies in his lunch to share with me. As he gave me one, I had an idea. I said: "Richard, don't eat the cookies yet. I have a nickel, I'm going to buy an ice cream. Wait here."

I bought one Dixie cup of vanilla ice cream, returned to my

seat, opened one of the cookies, and using the little wooden ice cream spoon, scraped the cream filling off the Oreo, replaced it with ice cream, and put the other cookie on top. I mused over my creation.

"Look, Richard, it's black and white, like her!"

"Wow, that looks yummy—can I have a bite?" he asked politely.

"No, I'm making this one for Mother Mary Margaret. You can make another one for yourself."

"You made that for Mother Mary Margaret? Are you really going to give it to her?"

"Yes," I said with resolve.

"Should I go with you?"

"No, better stay here."

"Okay, but be careful—we aren't supposed to leave our seats until the bell rings."

I put the custom-made ice cream sandwich in my hand and got up to go across the room to the mother superior. I wanted to surprise her, so I crouched low and zigzagged my way between the lunch tables. Some kids started to laugh at me, but I kept going. When I made my way to the other side of the room she was gone. "Oh, no!" I panicked.

Then she miraculously emerged from the kitchen, and when she did, I quite boldly ran up to her.

"Excuse me, Mother Mary Margaret."

She turned slowly and gracefully. "Yes?"

"I made something for you."

"Who are you, what is your name, little one?"

"Sharon Gannon."

"What have you made Sharon Gannon?"

I extended my hand, palm up and opened my fingers.

"Oh my, what is this?"

"It's an ice cream sandwich. I made it especially for you 'cause it looks like you."

She bent down close to my hand, then lifted her eyes and looked right into my face.

"Oh, I see."

"Will you take it?" I said fearfully, seeing that what was in my sweaty hand was now melted mush dripping through my fingers.

"Of course," she assured me, as she picked up the goop from my palm, stood up straight and held it in a loose fist close to her heart.

"Arrre you reeeally gggoing to eat it?" I stammered shyly, as I was so embarrassed that it didn't look like the original.

"Something as good as this?" She lifted her eyes upward, toward heaven, and said, "I'm going to take it to my Lord." Then she looked down into my eyes, nodded, and smiled so sweetly and kindly I couldn't stand it, so I quickly ran back to Richard.

"I saw you talking to her! Did she take it? What did she say?"

"She said she was going to give it to her Lord."

Richard smiled at me and held my messy hand. "Oh. Sharon, wow, I didn't know Jesus ate Oreo ice cream sandwiches! Do you think he lives in the convent house with her?"

"I guess so," I said, worried, trying to process this possibility.

Richard matter-of–factly stated: "My mom said that the nuns are brides of Christ. Mother Mary Margaret is way too busy with *nuns' stuff* and can't be cooking for him like a normal wife; she probably must bring him all of his food from the school cafeteria. And because of you he will have something very special to eat today."

Air Ventures

vastu-samye chitta-bhedat tayor vibhaktah panthah
Each individual person perceives the same object in a different way,
according to their own state of mind and projections.
Everything is empty from its own side
and appears according to how you see it.
—Patanjali's Yoga Sutra 4.15

It was August in Tucson, Arizona, 1967. I had turned
sixteen a month before. My stepfather had been working on a
plan for a new business scheme named Air Ventures—a vacation
club. He would talk people into buying a membership to the club,
which would entitle them to be flown, by him, in a small plane, to
a different exotic location to be determined every month. To this
day, I am not sure if he intended to actually carry this out or
whether he planned to collect the money for memberships and
then skip town. He was a seasoned con man—very skilled in
persuasion. He had swindled a woman who ran the local dog
grooming business into lending him the startup capital. He rented
a hangar at the airport and enlisted my mom, my brother, and me
as decorators. Unbelievably, he somehow procured three Cessna
172 four-seater planes.

The opening party was a full house, the wealthy of Tucson
sitting at rented tables being served tropical drinks by my sister
and me in demeaning hula skirts and coconut-shell bras, my
brother in a gorilla costume, which must have been stifling. We
gave the drink orders to my sarong-clad mother, who was behind
the bar mixing the drinks. My stepfather showed 8 mm "travel
films" of faraway places like Tahiti and Bora Bora, accompanied
by a glib sales pitch that no one seemed to be able to resist. At the
end of the night, every guest offered up their support in the form
of a personal check, making Air Ventures an overnight success
with a hundred-plus members. My stepfather, who had imbibed
many mai tais, as well as other brightly colored drinks along with
his standard vodka, throughout the evening, was noticeably
intoxicated. So, when the last of the happy new Air Venturers
departed, and he announced to us, "C'mon, let's celebrate—get in
the plane, we're going for a joy ride!" I defiantly said, "No way,
you're drunk."

Nonetheless, he coerced my mom and brother to get in the
plane as he readied it for takeoff. My younger sister, Ivy, who had
been overwhelmed, by the whole evening, was scared and

confused, looking for a place to hide. Realizing that my stepfather intended to fly, I became very worried and ran after him, yelling and threatening: "I'm going to call the tower and tell them you're drunk. They won't give you clearance." He responded by cursing me with ugly words. I ran to the passenger side and hopped up on the metal support piece that attaches the wing to the body of the plane.

"Mom, this is crazy," I yelled. "Get out now while you can."

Mom tried to reason with me, and in her sweet way said: "Honey, he just wants to celebrate. Let's have some fun—you're always so serious."

"Yeah, I'm serious—and so is he," I said. "He's serious about killing you and Marty and himself! Get out now!"

"Lighten up, this is his big night, please don't argue now," my mom insisted. "C'mon, get in, he wants all of us to get in." Meanwhile, my brother Marty was cowered beside her with a look of terror and helplessness on his face.

"You're so pessimistic! Sherry, just get in!" She laughed and said gleefully, "Look at it this way—if we die, we will all die together!"

"No."

I became more desperate and reached through the window to try to pull my brother toward me. My stepfather abruptly turned and slapped him back and told me to go to hell. As the plane started to roll down the runway I had to jump off.

I ran back into the hangar to call the airport tower. Ivy was standing in the doorway crying. She followed me into the office. I was shaking but able to dial the number for the tower, and luckily someone answered right away. I told them what was up, then Ivy and I ran back to the plane, which was already taxiing down the runway. It was very windy, because of the propeller and because a summer storm was coming on fast, contributing to the drama of the situation. "Please stop!" I cried anxiously. "Mom, Marty—jump out!"

It took a few minutes for the airport cops to arrive. They circled the plane, causing it to come to a halt. Using megaphones, they commanded my stepfather to deplane. He did and ran immediately to me, grabbing me by the neck and really laying into me with his fists, calling me quite demeaning names. The police intervened and pulled him away from me. He reacted by turning and attacking them, which caused my mom to jump on the police officers, hitting and biting whomever she could. Soon more police arrived and broke up the fight. My parents were forced into a police car. My brother, sister, and I were put in the back seat of another police car. We were scared and silent. My stepfather managed to break free of the car he was in and ran over to the car we were sitting in. He poked his head through the open window, spat on me, and cursed me more, but as he was about to hit me, he was restrained and handcuffed and led back to the other police car, where my mother was.

A policeman who was sitting in the front seat of our squad car turned around and said to me, "Don't worry, kid, when he sobers up in the morning, he will be thankful that you saved his life as well as your family's." I just hung my head and turned to look at Marty and Ivy. Marty said sarcastically, "Yeah, sure." We were taken to the Youth Center, my parents to jail.

The next morning there was a picture on the front page of *The Tucson Daily Star* of the Cessna with my stepfather in the pilot's seat. The story, a sensationalized version of what had actually happened, went something like, "Frantic daughter hangs on tail of plane trying to save her family." Of course, all the people who had just become members of the new Air Ventures Club canceled their checks after seeing the paper. Our kind next-door neighbor was able to get us out of the detention center and bring us to his house. He also put up the bail to release my parents from jail. When we saw the police car bring them home, our neighbor said, "You better get over there, quick."

"Do we have to go?" I pleaded. "Can't we stay here?"

"No," he said sadly.

And so, with hearts heavy with fear and trepidation, we went home.

As soon as my stepfather saw me, he said sardonically: "So, are you happy now that you succeeded in ruining your family's life? We could have been rich. You stupid, stupid, self-righteous little girl, how could you have called the cops on your own family? What kind of a monster are you? Do me and everyone else a favor, shut up. Don't open your ugly, f*ckin' mouth again. You are worse than sh!t. Get out of my sight."

I was mortified and went to my room without protest and cried myself to sleep. The next day, I asked my mother if she hated me. She replied: "No, I don't hate you, but I am mad at you. You know that you shouldn't have done that. We are really in trouble now, we've lost everything."

At home the curtains were all drawn and the shades pulled

down. Only our stepfather was allowed to leave the house, and he did that only after the sun went down. For several days we had to pretend no one was home, while the bill collectors and curiosity seekers rang the doorbell and phone nonstop.

One night my stepfather came home and placed a map of the United States on the floor and asked my mother, "So Evlyn, where do you want to go now?" She closed her eyes, pointed her finger on the map and giddily said, "How about here?" As she opened her eyes, we all saw that her finger had landed about halfway between Tacoma and Seattle, Washington.

"Okay," he said, "we'll go to Seattle, no one knows me there. We will drive out of here tomorrow morning. Each one of you kids can take one shoebox filled with your stuff, that's all. We're leaving everything else here."

My cat, Taffy, who had traveled with me from West Virginia, fit perfectly into the box. We took off, my mom driving, but about thirty minutes into the exodus Taffy started howling. It was really hot in the car, since the air conditioning wasn't working. The windows had to be open, and he was desperate to get out no matter how much I tried to console and calm him down. As we reached the outskirts of town, my stepfather told my mom to pull off the highway.

"Where are we going?" I asked from the back seat.

"You shut up," he said angrily, as he gestured to slap me with the back of his hand. When we arrived at the animal shelter, he forcibly took Taffy out of my arms and in his intimidating voice said, "Don't open your mouth—remember you have no rights." Inclining his head toward his left, where I knew he wore a shoulder holster with a loaded gun under his shirt, he said, threateningly, "Shut up or I'll kill you and this ugly rodent."

I watched him go through the door holding Taffy with his right hand. I started to cry. My mom turned to me and said, "We're just going to leave him here, honey, until we find a new home—then we'll send for him, don't worry." I was so desperate that I actually believed her at that moment. I looked at my brother and sister, who tried to comfort me by saying, "It's going to be all right." But they were scared and crying too and we all knew it wasn't going to be all right.

After a brief stop in Los Angeles, where my stepfather borrowed money from his cousin, we were on the road again, heading north. We stopped to spend the night in a low-end roadside motel somewhere in Oregon. My stepfather had gone

263

out, saying he was going to bring back some food. It had been hours and he hadn't returned. My mom decided that we should get into bed and try to sleep. She turned out the lights, but none of us could sleep. I was feeling scared, lonely, and very worried about Taffy. I had worked myself into a dark place full of regret and grief. I asked my mom when we were going to get Taffy back. She told me the truth, that he wasn't coming back. I was delirious with grief. She tried to console me by saying, "But, hey, he's a good-looking cat, I am sure someone has adopted him by now." Ivy and Marty, to help me feel better, agreed.

Their comforting words didn't help me, though, and the truth hit me hard. I knew that Taffy had received a death sentence. I realized that no amount of pretending and lying to myself could change that. I was the one person in the world he trusted, and I had betrayed him. I fell into deep despair, knowing that there was nothing I could do to change the situation, and I blamed myself. I totally believed that my stepfather was right—I had destroyed my family. Because of what I had done, Taffy was most likely dead and we were homeless.

The finality and irreversibility of all that had occurred flooded my mind along with the realization that I had instigated the course of events by what I had done at the airport: Taffy was gone. Our family's future looked bleak. My stepfather hated me. My mother, although she was being kind to me, agreed with him about me being a terrible person who called the cops on our own family and plunged us all back into poverty. I kept hearing my stepfather's words of condemnation in my head and started to spiral downward, reviewing in my mind other times I had instigated a catastrophe that affected the lives of others.

My mother heard me sobbing in the dark and said, "C'mon, kids, let's get up and watch some TV." She switched on a light. The motel room had two large beds. The one that we kids slept in was pushed up against a wall. As my mom and brother and sister sat around the TV, I stayed in the kids' bed as close to the wall as possible. I tried to stifle my sobs and settle into what I knew was coming.

In a short while, my hand began to involuntarily twitch, and I recognized the pattern that was beginning to unfold, because it had happened to me at other stressful times in my life when I felt hopeless. I knew that I would become very still soon. My mom, brother, and sister, engaged in what they were watching, were unaware of what was happening to me. This was

264

not the first time I had experienced a catatonic seizure. It had happened before when I realized that I had been the cause of a traumatic experience that had affected others, even though my initial intention had not been to cause them harm. I had come to recognize and welcome the symptoms, which would lead to complete rigidity of my body in a few minutes.

First, I would feel very sad, hopeless, and overwhelmed with self-loathing. I would try to find a place to be alone. I would try not to cry or make any noise. A part of my body, usually a hand or a foot, would begin to twitch, then some involuntary repetitive movement would set in—like two fingers touching together, over and over again, while the rest of my body was completely still. Eventually, in a few minutes, the rubbing of the fingers would trigger something, and a sort of paralysis would set in. My breath would slow down, and my body would become rigid. I would be motionless for minutes or hours. Usually no one noticed.

In that motel room, on a bed by myself, I felt like I had years before, when my grandmother would remind me that I had destroyed my mother's life. My mother had trained to become a professional musician but had become pregnant with me at seventeen. My grandmother had arranged for an abortion, but my mother was afraid and refused to go through with it. She married a boy she had gone to high school with, and everyone assumed he was my father. My brother was born two years later and my sister a year after that. My mom had to let go of her aspirations for a musical career in order to raise a family. As she was a high school dropout and unskilled in any vocation besides music, she had to accept minimum-wage jobs to help make ends meet.

When I was around eight, our dad started to drop in and out of the picture. (My parents would officially divorce when I was twelve.) My grandmother (actually my great-grandmother, my mother's grandmother) moved in with us to help. Being a single mom was hard. Whenever we would fall into some difficulty—financial usually—Grandma was quick to remind me that I was the cause of our family's predicament: "You destroyed your mother's life. She had been destined to be a concert pianist, not living like this!" Around this time the catatonic seizures began.

Now, in this motel room, en route to Seattle, I was overcome with guilt, believing that I had destroyed not only my mother's chance for a music career, but now my family's chance of success as well. I had also destroyed the life of my cat, my only real friend, and now there was no one I could talk anything over with, there was nowhere to go, all options were closed. I saw myself as a person to be despised. I prayed to God that I might be able to find a way to disappear myself so as to not cause any more trouble in other people's lives. I was a very troubled young girl.

We did settle in Seattle, and my stepfather tried a few more get-rich-quick schemes, though nothing as grand as the Air Ventures venture.

Through the exercise of writing this story, I was provided with the opportunity to see the emptiness in the experience. At the time, I felt extreme self-loathing and saw my stepfather as an adversary, whom I feared and hated, coming at me. When writing this story, I faced the karmic truth that I *had* been the cause of the demise of the Air Ventures scheme, as my stepfather had said— but not exactly as I had understood his accusatory words then. Now, through distance and time, as well as yogic *sadhana*, my perception is colored by compassion for everyone involved, including myself.

As a yoga practitioner, I have continued to work on letting go of blaming my stepfather and the perception of myself as a victim of his unfairness, my own self-loathing, and the anger and confusion I directed toward my stepfather. I try to see it all as a karmic play, the program for which I must have set in motion a long time before the events of the story—most likely in past lives. It is said that we choose our parents, or rather that our past actions do the choosing for us. The yogic teachings tell us that we cannot escape the karmic results of our actions. We write the script for our future with each action we take now. We are bound to others; how we see ourselves is in relation to the others in our life.

To understand *shunyata,* or "emptiness," is to understand how each person and situation we encounter arises from our own karmas. The people in our lives are phantoms arising from our own past karmas. From our past actions, we project onto the world and others. The reality we experience is in accordance with those projections. We can't change what we did in the past (past lives included). The past creates the present. The only semblance of control we have is to act in the present moment in a way that will create the kind of future we want to see. As Gandhi suggested, "Be the change you want to see in the world." Ram Dass advised, "Treat everyone you meet as if they were God in Drag." In other words, God in disguise presenting to you an opportunity for spiritual growth—to choose love over hate, forgiveness over anger.

When you understand shunyata, you understand that there is no reality out there coming at you—it is all coming from you. Grasping that, you will obviously be careful never to blame others or to play the victim when you engage in self-reflection. If you were to ask yourself what percentage of your reality is coming from other people and what is coming from you, what would you say—50-50? Or 100 percent is coming from other people? Or could you take responsibility and see that 100 percent is coming from you—from your past karmas?

Certainly, in our culture, children are dependent upon adults, and it is often very difficult for a child not to see themself as being controlled 100 percent by parents or others in authority positions and to resent it. This can plant the seeds in a child to grow up into an adult who easily sees themself as a victim. We have only to read or hear the stories in the news to know that we live in a victim-orientated culture. We are quick to blame and find fault with others. We even blame the weather and God and seem to equate freedom of speech to mean the freedom to say mean and unkind things to others or to curse the weather or God.

Yes—but what if other people *are* really doing horrible things? I remember one of my teachers answered a question like this by saying: If you are in a situation where someone seems to be acting in an angry or unfair way toward you, the yogic reaction would be to immediately say to yourself, "I have to stop treating other people like this." With such an uncommon response, you are not condoning the other person's bad behavior or setting yourself up to be the recipient of their abuse. On the contrary, you are freeing yourself from the victim trap.

Yes, it can be risky business to take on 100 percent of the responsibility for the situations in your life you find yourself in. The risk is that you could easily disconnect from your innate serenity (*chitta-prasadanam*) and fall into the dire straits of disappointment, sadness, guilt, anger, and blame. Those negative emotions can feel justified and provide a false feeling of being in control. But such negative, dark emotions never lead to the light. When overwhelmed by such dark emotions, most people feel that the only way to deal with them is by expressing them outwardly or absorbing them inwardly, as I did as a young girl. Those emotions then imploded inside me, resulting in a debilitating psychological and physical condition. At the time, I accepted and felt deserving of the darkness and didn't realize there was an option other than expressing or suppressing. I didn't know that the light was available to me or that I was deserving of it. I had yet to experience the miracle of forgiveness.

"Blame," as the poet Hafiz said, "keeps the sad game going." Forgiveness releases us from the chains of blame. Forgiveness allows us to tap into the power that can truly change our perception of ourselves and others and free us from the most abject conditions of despair, distress, and misfortune. Forgiveness awakens compassion within us together with inner serenity of mind and ease of heart. Compassion provides us with a broader vision—enabling us to see ourselves and others as players, all acting out our entangled karmic destinies on the stage of life.

Compassion allows us to see so deeply into another that otherness disappears and only love remains. Compassion enables us to pierce through the veil of illusion (*maya*) and see the emptiness in a situation and in another. This shift will lead to the direct perception of reality, the realization of the *atman*—the joyful eternal soul that resides inside us as well as inside everyone.

To transcend the gap between self and other, to let go of blame, whether directed at another or at yourself, and awaken compassion, is no easy task. Forgiveness takes tremendous courage. It takes great spiritual maturity to come to a place where you can let go of justifying negative reactions, and renounce anger and blame toward yourself and others. That road is certainly the road less traveled and not for everyone. But when you come to a point in your present life where you no longer find yourself attracted to suffering, seeing yourself as a victim, identifying with your unhappiness, you will reach for that key to your freedom and use it to unlock the door to your heart, and to your soul.

It took me many years and many trials to find that key and many more attempts to muster the courage to use it to forgive myself. But eventually I did allow my soul to take flight from Air Ventures and embark on an adventure into the blue sky of infinite possibilities.

Mom and Joe

Optimism is a strategy for making a better future.
Because unless you believe that the future can be better,
you are unlikely to step up and take responsibility for making it so.
—Noam Chomsky

The outrageous story that you are about to read is all true. It's a story about my mother, Evlyn, whose sense of adventure and optimism were beyond what anyone would call normal.

It must have been around 1978, in Seattle, Washington. As I remember, it was a couple of years after my stepfather Paul Evans died, after Mom had taken a job as a waitress at Russ's Coffee shop in the U District, and after she left that job to fly to Washington, DC, to get back together with her ex-husband, Don Gannon, which ended in a major disaster.

Mom had a high-strung, elderly chihuahua named Prudence Penny, who was put in the cargo section of the plane when Mom checked in at the airport. When the plane landed, Mom went to the baggage claim to find poor Prudence in the carrier dead of what she presumed was a heart attack. She should have seen this as a bad omen of things to come, but she never was quite able to recognize a bad storm brewing on the horizon.

Don had sweet-talked her over the phone. He told her he had separated from his wife and wanted to try making another go of their relationship and had sent her a plane ticket. They had been divorced since 1963 and hadn't had much contact during all that time, until recently. She was a forgiving person and didn't think she had anything to lose at that point, so she took him up on the offer. He met her at the airport and drove her to a small, run-down apartment outside DC. They spent the night together, and then he left, telling her he would return in a couple of hours. He didn't. She was stranded. She didn't really know where she was, had no food, no phone, no car, and no keys to the apartment. She left the apartment anyway to look for a pay phone. She called his number and he answered.

"Hey, babe, I told you I'd be back soon, just gotta take care of some business."

"Yeah, but where are you? You left me stranded," she cried.

"Hey, things are getting tight here, can't talk now, the ol' lady's here." He hung up.

It turned out that while Don had told Mom that he had

separated from his wife, it wasn't true. She called Ivy, my younger sister, who lived in DC. Ivy drove to get her. In about a week Mom was on a plane back to Seattle. She got a job as a barmaid at the Yesler Tavern downtown, and in a few weeks she met Billy George there.

It was summer break, and I was working at Jimmy Woo's Jade Pagoda, a Chinese restaurant-bar in the Capitol Hill District of Seattle. I worked in the dining room, while Jimmy and his wife, Pearl, ran the bar, which was famous for its exotic parasol drinks. All of us waitresses wore uniforms that were long kimono-like dresses made of light polyester fabric. Each of us had a different color and print. The uniforms were quite elegant, although the long Japanese-style sleeves were not so practical for bussing tables. Mine was permanently stained with soy sauce and mustard, and no matter how many times I washed it, my kimono always smelled like sweet-and-sour chicken.

One night, Pearl pulls me out of the dining room to tell me that my mother is in the bar and needs to see me immediately.

"Sherreeee, I've been sitting here for hour-ers and you haven't come in to say so much as a hello to your mother."

"Mom, I'm working."

"Yeah, but Jimmy knows I'm a regular—you can make an exception at least for me and stop for a minute to take a break, especially because I want to introduce you to Billy George," she says a bit tipsy-ish.

She puts her arms around a guy wearing a dirty, beat-up cowboy hat sitting in the booth close to her. "Isn't he handsome? Doesn't he look just like a cross between Kris Kristofferson and Paul Newman? I met him downtown at the place where I've been working. He's a transient—doesn't have a permanent address anywhere."

"Uh-huh," I say, unimpressed.

"Yeah, and I'm leaving with him tomorrow. We're headed for Oregon. Just wanted to come in and say goodbye—to my daughter. Give your mom a hug and say hello to Billy George," she says pleadingly.

"So how long have you been a transient, and what is that anyway?" I ask.

"I'm a bum, I'm a hobo, I'm freewheelin'—go where the action is. Been livin' like this for a few years, no one to answer to but me."

"Yeah, okay, but now you'll have my mom too."

"Ah, she's a winner, she's my lucky charm, her and me we be up to no good! We're gonna raise some hell!" He picks up his bottle of beer and guzzles the whole thing down in one swallow, then belches as my mom giggles, swirling her melting margarita. She picks up the parasol, holding it high with one hand, and takes a dainty sip, her green eyes flashing dangerously.

The next day, Mom and Billy George hopped a freight train going south. They traveled the country pretty much like that for over two years. They drove a broken-down car at one point, but they reverted to the easy travel afforded by open boxcars so they didn't have the expense of gas. I would receive periodic letters and postcards from her. During the winter months they would usually camp in The Dalles, Oregon, by the Columbia River. She let me know that she could receive mail addressed to her in care of a local church there. I wrote to her and told her she was a renunciate, like an Indian wandering ascetic who gives up everything in search of the truth. I called her my sannyasi.

She and Billy George made their way back to Seattle and decided to camp for a couple of weeks under the freeway next to the house I was living in with my boyfriend, Bill. I invited them to stay with us, but Billy George rejected that idea and said: "Unless you want to host us and our friends, thanks but no thanks. Besides, hey, we like to cook our meat over an open fire, and I don't think you'll be letting us light fires on the floor in your living room—ha-ha!"

Since they were camping with a couple of traveling buddies and a dog, it made sense for them to stay under the freeway. So I didn't try to convince them otherwise. Even so, I tried to get Mom to come and stay inside with us. "No, honey, it is best I stay with him—I can keep him out of trouble, you know," she said, laughing.

She did come in and take advantage of our bathtub, which she greatly appreciated. I had some sandalwood-scented soap from India that she loved. At the time, I was reading *Autobiography of a Yogi*, by Paramahansa Yogananda, and would read passages out loud to her while she was relaxing in the tub. On the day they packed up and were getting ready to hitchhike to catch a train out of the railway freight yard at Interbay, I gave her the book. I thought if she read it, she would identify with the lifestyle of a wandering yogi and see its spiritual possibilities for herself. Mostly, I wanted her to know that I supported her decision and was proud of her. I realized that her transient life was by no means easy and could only hope that Billy George was a good traveling companion.

Although I didn't have a phone, she would call my next-door neighbors when she wanted to talk to me, and they would come and get me so I could talk with her. She only called when there was an emergency, when things were getting bad between her and Billy George. She would always call collect, usually from some bar when he was drunk and causing a ruckus or from a police station when he was in jail or from a church when she was hiding from him because he had beat her up. I would always say: "Mom, leave him! I'll send you money for a bus ticket. You can come and live with us."

"Thanks, honey, but I don't want to leave him," she would always say. "He's a good man most of the time. He just has a bit of a drinking problem—what guy doesn't? I'm just calling to let you know I'm okay."

I remember one letter postmarked from The Dalles that I received toward the end of her second year on the road with him. She had written proudly to tell me that she had been crowned the "Queen of the Hobos!" She explained that the old-timer hobos, who all came together every year at The Dalles, held an award ceremony, and she was declared the winner that year. She went on to clarify that she was the only contestant in the beauty pageant. She described how she and Billy George had built themselves a little shack in the hobo settlement near the Columbia River. She insisted that she was very happy with her life and that she had even been able to amass a small library of books. She said that of all the places she had traveled to, The Dalles was the best place for transients. The weather was temperate, and the local churches were very helpful—provided clothes, shoes, books, and regular meals. "They even give vouchers to us to eat in restaurants!" she wrote. "The Olive Tree is my favorite—it's Italian, you know!"

My mom was in her mid-forties. Billy George, she had told me, was in his early thirties when they met. My mother was still a very attractive woman, with porcelain-like skin, auburn hair, and green eyes. Having been trained as a classical singer in her youth, she had a very musical and soothing voice, almost hypnotic. She was easygoing, trusting, kind, and generous. She saw the good in others and rarely got angry with anyone or anything. When she was with you, she made you feel special and focused all her attention on you. She was a great listener. With an outgoing nature, incredible optimism, and a spontaneous sense of adventure, she was compelling to be with.

One day our next-door neighbor comes over to the house to let me know my mom is on the phone, calling from a hospital, and that she sounds desperate. I drop what I'm doing and run over. When I pick up the phone, my mom says, quite calmly: "I need you to come to see me. I'm in a hospital in The Dalles. Please borrow a car or something and get here as fast as you can. Bring your brother too, if you know where he is."

"Mom, what are you talking about, what's going on? Why are you in a hospital? Are you hurt?"

"I'm okay, I just have some very bad burns, actually third-degree burns, but mostly on my legs—my face is fine."

"Wha-at? Mom, what happened? Tell me!"

"I'm fine, really, but I need to see you."

"You better tell me what happened, and tell me now."

"Oh, Sherry, well, it was Billy George, I'm sure you guessed that. You see, Joe and I were sleeping in the shack and Billy George came around drunk and set the place on fire."

"Mom, wait, who's Joe?" I ask confusedly.

"Oh, Joe? Joe is the man that I am in love with," she says matter-of-factly. "We've been going together now for a few weeks. Things really weren't working out with Billy George and me. He can get so violent, and he really has a drinking problem, you know. Joe is really this great guy. I think we're soul mates."

"So, Billy George was jealous and tried to kill you by setting your house on fire?" I ask desperately.

"Well, he did more than that—he tried to kill Joe too. He shot Joe in the head."

"Mom! What are you saying? Did he kill Joe?"

"No, thank God! When he set the shack on fire, we were asleep, but woke up amid the blaze and ran out. Billy George was waiting for us with a gun. That's when he shot Joe, and then pointed the gun at me, but you know me, I talked him out of it and then he ran off. There was poor Joe, still alive, but bleeding terribly. I only had a small piece of burned blanket to cover me and ran up the embankment to the road. No one would stop for me! I don't blame 'em, a half-naked woman at three o'clock in the morning. So what could I do? I walked to the police station, which is more than a mile, and I walked with my feet and legs burned! The cops went and got Joe—luckily he was still alive. They brought us both to the hospital last night. Please, come soon, 'cause Joe may not make it."

I find my brother, Bill borrows his mother's car, and the three of us drive to The Dalles. It's about a four-hour drive from Seattle. We find the hospital and when we walk in, the nurses in the reception area are waiting to welcome us: "Oh, you must be Evlyn's kids, come on, we'll take you up to her. We've all been dyin' to meet y'all. Your mom is pretty special."

When we walk into her room, she is sitting up in her hospital bed smiling, with all her makeup on, and the first thing she says, as chipper as a robin, is: "Look at my hair. Isn't it amazing? A perfect shag—the fire burnt it off in just the right places!"

And you know, she did look pretty good, and, wow, what about a positive attitude! She then goes on to theatrically retell the story about the fire, the shooting, and her walk to get help. Then she says: "I'm so glad you came. I really want you to meet Joe—he is the love of my life and he's in critical condition. They don't know if he's going to pull through, the bullet is still lodged in his head. The doctors are debating about the operation, he only has a 50-50 chance to come through, so that is why you have to meet him now, because he may not be alive tomorrow!"

"Okay, let's go!" we all agree enthusiastically. "But will they let us into the intensive care? Is he conscious?"

"Oh, yes, I told him you were coming. He's been waiting all day to meet you." She gets out of bed and starts to walk with her bandaged feet. Bill says, "Oh, no, you don't—you gotta ride in a wheelchair, lady." He asks the nurse to bring a wheelchair and we all go to the ICU.

Before we enter the swinging doors to the unit, she tells us to stop and says: "Oh, wait, there is one more thing I need to tell you about Joe. He's twenty-four years old! Yeah, you know he's the same age as your little sister, Ivy, but it doesn't matter to us, so don't worry 'cause we really love each other."

We then wheel her through the ICU doors and are greeted by a nurse, who takes us right in to see Joe. Joe is lying on a bed with his head all wrapped up in bandages, only his eyes are visible, and he's hooked up to all kinds of IVs and electronic devices. Mom wheels over to him and kisses him. "This is my Joseph," she says proudly, and introduces us: "This is my daughter Sherry, this is my son, Marty, and this is Bill, Sherry's boyfriend—he's an artist."

Joe tries to talk, but the bandages are too tight around his mouth; he motions with his hands to the nurses that he wants to write something. They give him a pen and a small piece of paper on a clipboard, which they hold for him. On the piece of paper, he writes slowly and painfully, "I love your mom I would do it all over again to be with her." All of us are amazed beyond words. Then Mom says, "You see, that's why I wanted you to meet him—isn't he amazing!"

The nurses tell us that we need to leave because he needs to rest. We take Mom back to her room. We've brought her a few little presents: a carton of her favorite cigarettes, some chocolate, and a bit of cash. Marty asks her if she wants to smoke a joint. She says, "Yeah, I'd love to, but we have to go outside for that, and they won't let me off the floor, so thanks, but no."

We visit with her for about another hour and then it is time for us to go, as we have to get the car back. I ask her if there is anything more I can do for her. She says: "Yes, there is one more thing. You know they caught Billy George, and he's in jail, and because I'm here in the hospital, he has no one to visit him. Could you go and visit him?"

"No, Mom, I can't do that," I say.

"Oh, okay, I understand, but still I had to ask. Honey, it's so wonderful that you all drove down here and that you got to meet Joe. Thank you, I love you."

We drove back to Seattle. Two days later, Mom called from the hospital to tell us that Joe had his operation, and they removed the bullet, and that he was okay. They both stayed in the hospital for several weeks to recover. In the Spring an envelope arrived in the mail addressed to me from Mom. I opened it to find the front page of *The Dalles Chronicle* with a picture of Mom and Joe arm in arm at the top of the stairs in front of the entrance to the hospital. The headline read, "Newlyweds Survive Fire and Bullets." On April 30th, 1980, the day after they were released from the hospital, they were married in a small old-fashioned church in nearby Goldendale, Washington, with their favorite nurse from the ICU as the maid of honor.

Wow—what a story. They became the sweethearts of the town. All doors opened to them. They got on welfare, and disability assistance provided them with an apartment and food stamps. She wrote me several letters during this time, describing her life as a continuous fairytale honeymoon. Then one day, the tide turned, and I received this letter:

Dear Sherry,

How are you, Honey? Me and Joe were doing well living a dream life—until today. FBI agents knocked on our door, this morning! They've arrested Joe, it's so sad. They are transporting him to Michigan in a few days. I just got back from the jail, where I got to talk with him, thank God!

I guess all this time he forgot to tell me that he was an escaped convict. When we met at The Dalles, he had been on the run for some months. He broke out of a prison in Michigan. That's pretty cool, eh? It was a robbery charge. But he didn't do it. He's <u>innocent</u>. He was framed. The FBI tracked him down because of the publicity we attracted with our wedding picture in the paper! Now he must serve out his time in prison in Michigan. But that's okay, 'cause I'm going to Michigan as soon as I can save up enough money.

I love you, please say a prayer for Joe.

Your Mom

She called me a week later to say she had gotten a waitress job at a local club, was making a lot in tips, and would have enough money to leave for Michigan soon. "And you will never guess who's playing this weekend at the club! Steppenwolf! Wow, can you believe it, Sherry? *Born to Be Wild*! You know they were always one of my favorite bands!"

That's how she was, always finding something positive in every situation, no matter how challenging. She worked at that club for two months, saving everything until she felt she had enough to go to Michigan. Although I offered to send her money, she wouldn't take it. She insisted that she had to do this on her own. She took a Greyhound bus to Michigan and found an apartment close to the prison. She got a job answering phones for a battered-women's hotline. She visited Joe every visiting day and after he served his seventeen months they were reunited again.

They stayed in Michigan, where he was from originally, working together at various seasonal jobs, which Joe had done a lot of when he was on the run. In the summer they worked as farm laborers in fields, harvesting vegetables, and in the autumn, picking fruit for a large fruit orchard corporation. Then Joe hurt his back, falling from an apple-picking ladder. Winters in Michigan are harsh, and they decided to move back to Oregon. They worked odd jobs for a few years and managed to save enough to put a down payment on a small lot in the woods, then with a bit more bought a modest two-bedroom prefabricated house that they put together on the land. They lived in that house together in Astoria, Oregon, until 2000, when my mom died at the age of sixty-seven.

Mom was very specific about what she wanted to have happen after she died. While on her deathbed she told me and Joe, "I want to be cremated. Afterwards, promise me you will go to the Blue Ridge Mountains, with my ashes, hire a pilot to take you up in a small plane and pour the ashes out the window so they are scattered over those mountains and the Shenandoah River Valley. Then when that is done, I want you to go to a nice Chinese Restaurant for dinner and tell each other stories about me. A few months later, we met at an airport in Front Royal, Virginia and fulfilled her wishes.

Glossary

Aarti—a ritual consisting of waving a light in front of a deity or honored person. The ritual reminds us that the real form of the Divine is light and that that light is within each of us.

Abhinivesha—fear of death. One of the five *kleshas,* or obstacles to the attainment of Yoga, that Patanjali describes in his Yoga Sutra.

Abhyasa—practice; to sit with something.

Acharya—a teacher, preceptor, expert instructor, vehicle.

Adipurusha—supreme person, the first person, Lord Vishnu.

Adishesha—a thousand-headed snake upon whom Lord Vishnu reclines. Also known as Ananta, which means "endless." Adishesha as an avatar appeared with Vishnu in the Treta Yuga as Lakshman, brother to Lord Rama, and at the end of the Dvapara Yuga as Balarama, Lord Krishna's brother. Shesha is the *nagaraja,* the king (*raja*) of the *nagas,* one of the primal beings of creation.

Advaita—the term used in Vedanta philosophy to express nondualism, or the belief that there is only one reality (*Brahman*); from *a* = not + *dvaita* = two.

Agami karma—future karma; from *agam* = to return + *karma* = action. The effects, or fruits, of our current actions that we will have to deal with in the future. One of the three types of karma, including past (*sanchita*) and present (*prarabdha*).

Ahamkara—the ego, the sense of I-ness.

Ahimsa—nonharming; from *a* = not + *himsa* = to harm. One of the five *yamas,* or behavior restrictions, that Patanjali describes in his Yoga Sutra.

Ajna chakra—the eye of intuition, commonly referred to as the "third eye." It is located between the eyebrows and is one of the seven major *chakras* (levels of perception). *Ajna* = command.

Alice Coltrane (1937-2007)—Swami Turiyasangitananda. A Self-realized saint, born in Detroit, Michigan, she was a musician and composer and married to jazz musician John Coltrane from 1965 until his death, in 1967.

Anahata chakra—the lotus of the heart. One of the seven major *chakras* (levels of perception). *Anahata* = unstruck sound.

Ananda—bliss.

Anandamayi Ma (1896-1982)—an Indian saint, considered to be a *jivanmukta*. Her name means "bliss-permeated mother."

Ananta—endless, infinite. The name of Shesa, the serpent god whose body is Vishnu's couch. Ananta supports Vishnu and accompanies the avatar when He incarnates. For example, when Vishnu appeared as Lord Krishna in the Dvapara Yuga, Ananta appeared as his brother, Balarama.

Anjali mudra—placing the hands together in front of the chest in a prayer position, representing, composure; returning to one's heart.

Antar-kumbhaka—inner savoring; the inhale retention.

Apana—one of the five *prana vayus*, or vital airs. Apana flows downward from the navel to the feet and is necessary for defecation, urination, ejaculation, and childbirth.

Aparigraha—not being greedy, taking more than we need. One of the five *yamas*, or behavior restrictions, that Patanjali describes in his Yoga Sutra.

Apsara—a celestial nymph, heavenly fairy. As ethereal, angel-like beings, apsaras can fly through time and space and visit other worlds and realms. They are magical beings who can change their shape at will. They excel in the arts, especially music and dance, as well as the art of seduction, and are forever youthful, elegant, and beautiful. They enjoy assuming the role of a muse to inspire mortal beings.

Arjuna—One of the major characters in the Indian epic Mahabharata, in which he is depicted as the third of the five Pandava brothers, a *devaputra* (half-god, half-human). He was the son of the god Indra and the princess Kunti, who was married to Pandu at the time of his conception. He was the best archer in the world and the cousin and friend of Krishna.

Artha—object, thing, wealth. According to Vedic tradition, artha is one of the four pursuits of life: *artha* (material wealth), *kama* (sensual desire), *dharma* (profession), and *moksha* (liberation from the *samsaric* material world).

Asamprajnata samadhi—*samadhi* without seed. Also called *nirvikalpa* or *nirbija samadhi*. The individual self is completely merged with the absolute Self. Duality disappears. It is considered by some to be the highest stage of samadhi, in which all sense of an individual separate self disappears. Unlike *samprajnata samadhi*, in which the yogi's sense of ego still operates.

Asamshakti—leaning away from the world; from *asam* = not like + *shakti* = the world. The fifth *bhumika*.

Asana—seat, connection, relationship to the Earth and all earthly manifestations.

Ashaya—resting place, where the reservoir of karmic impressions, or *samskaras*, are deposited and reside in the subconscious.

Ashraya—assistance, shelter, protection, refuge. In terms of Vaishnavism, the living entity, the *jiva*, is dependent upon Bhagavan (God) and to find His shelter, His refuge, is the goal of life.

Ashtakshara—the eight-syllable initiation mantra of refuge, *Shri Krishna sharanam mama,* given as the first level of initiation in the Pushtimarg, Vallabhacharya's Path of Grace.

Ashtanga Yoga—the eight-limbed path described by Patanjali in his Yoga Sutra, consisting of *yama* (behavior restrictions), *niyama* (personal observances), *asana* (seat), *pranayama* (breath control), *pratyahara* (sense withdrawal), *dharana* (concentration), *dhyana* (meditation), and *samadhi* (ecstasy). Ashtanga Yoga is also known as Raja (royal) Yoga and is considered one of the four classical spiritual paths in Hinduism, the others being Bhakti, Karma, and Jnana Yoga; from *ashta* = eight + *anga* = limb. Ashtanga Yoga is also the name of the style of yoga popularized by Shri K. Pattabhi Jois.

Asmita—ego identification. One of the five *kleshas*, or obstacles to the attainment of Yoga, that Patanjali describes in his Yoga Sutra.

Asteya—not stealing. One of the five *yamas*, or behavior restrictions, that Patanjali describes in his Yoga Sutra.

Asura—demon. A race of powerful celestial beings mentioned in the ancient Indian scriptures along with *devas* (benevolent demigods), *yakshas* (nature spirits), *rakshasas* (vampires), *bhutas* (ghosts), *gandharvas* (elves), and more.

Atha—now.

Atma-jnana—knowledge of the Divine Self.

Atman—the Divine Self; the indwelling eternal soul.

Avatar—to descend; referring to an incarnation of God in the appearance of a physical body.

Avidya—ignorance; pertaining to being ignorant of your true identity as transcendental, as *satchidananda*: eternal truth, consciousness, and bliss. One of the five *kleshas*, or obstacles to the attainment of Yoga, described by Patanjali in the Yoga Sutra.

Ayodhya—an ancient city in the North Indian state of Uttar Pradesh. It used to be the capital of the ancient Kosala Kingdom. It is the birthplace of Shri Rama, an avatar of Lord Vishnu.

Ayurveda—the science of life, an ancient Indian system of medicine and healing; from *ayur* = life + *veda* = knowledge, science.

Bahya-kumbhaka—outer savoring, the exhale retention.

Baithak (also bethak)—a seat or place to sit; also a shrine built over a place where a holy teacher once sat and gave teachings.

Ban (also van)—forest.

Bandha—lock, bind, knot; a psychokinetic energy lock used to direct the flow of *prana*; from *bandh* = to bind.

Banyatra (also vanyatra)—journey through the forest.

Bardo—Tibetan term for the intermediate, transitional state we experience between death and our next rebirth.

Belvan—one of the twelve main forests in the Vrindavan area in the state of Uttar Pradesh, in North India. Located on the other side of the Yamuna River from Vrindavan, it is named Belvan because when Krishna lived in Vrindavan there were lots of bel trees growing in that area, which yielded tasty bel fruits. It is the place where Laxmi performed austerities in the hope of being invited across the river to dance with Krishna in the *rasa lila*.

Bhagavad Gita—the Song of God. The most widely read of all the yogic scriptures. Written by Vyasa as a dialogue between the Pandava Arjuna and his friend and adviser, Krishna, while on the battlefield on the verge of war. It is an important philosophical text that presents a synthesis of Hindu ideas about *dharma*, death, and God, as well as *Bhakti, Jnana, Karma,* and *Raja Yoga.* It is part of a larger work, the Mahabharata.

Bhagavan—a name indicating *Brahman*, the Divine, the Absolute in personal form as Krishna.

Bhakta—one who is passionately devoted to God.

Bhakti—devotion to God.

Bhakti Yoga—the Yoga that is attained through loving devotion to God. The Bhakti Yoga practices purify one's emotions and awaken within the practitioner the remembrance of God. They include chanting and singing the names of God, listening to and reciting stories about God, deity worship and prayer. Bhakti Yoga, or the "Yoga of Love," is one of the four classical spiritual paths in Hinduism, the others being Jnana, Karma, and Raja Yoga.

Bhav(a)—the ultimate good mood, transcendental mood, atmosphere of heightened devotional intoxication for God, or enlightened emotional perception akin to the feeling of being in love with God. Feeling God's blissful presence.

Bhumi—earth. Bhumi can refer to the planet Earth, the element of earth, and the ground, as well as a particular stage or level of practice. Also the name of the Earth goddess.

Bhumika—stage, state, degree; step toward enlightenment, according to the Yoga Vasishtha.

Bija mantra—seed syllable. Bija mantras are akin to "shorthand," in that they are monosyllabic sounds that represent the quintessence of more complex sounds. Bija mantras are the building blocks for words and eventually things.

Brahma—the name of the creator in the Hindu trinity of Brahma, Vishnu, and Shiva.

Brahmacharya—God's path, the way to God. One of five *yamas*, or behavior restrictions, that Patanjali describes in his Yoga Sutra. Meaning "to refrain from abusing others sexually"; from *Brahma* = creator + *charya* = vehicle.

Brahman—God, absolute reality, vast expanse; from *bri* = to expand.

Brahmarandhra—passage (*randhra*) to and from God (*Brahma*). The opening at the top of the skull corresponding to the anterior, or bregma, fontanelle, or the *sahasrara chakra*.

Brahma Sambandha—the mantra initiation that reestablishes the soul's connection to God. The term means "to be bound to God." The initiation is like a marriage, in which you tie the knot. This initiation was first given to Shri Vallabhacharya by Shri Krishna Himself and now is given to followers of the Path of Grace (Pushtimarg) by Shri Vallabha's descendants, who perform *seva* (devotional service to a Krishna deity).

Braj (also Vraj)—an area in the state of Uttar Pradesh, North India, associated with Krishna. The region comprises places on both sides of the Yamuna River where Krishna lived as a cowherd boy. Today it is known as Mathura District.

Brajbhasha (also Vrajbhasha)—the language spoken in Braj, an area in the state of Uttar Pradesh, North India, associated with Krishna. It predates Hindi and is the language that Krishna spoke.

Brajbhashi (also Vrajbhashi)—a person who lives in Braj and speaks Brajbhasha.

Buddhi—the wisdom faculty of the higher mind/intellect.

Chai—Hindi word for tea, a beverage prepared by pouring boiling water over the leaves of *Camellia sinensis*, a shrub grown in China as well as in India and other Asian countries.

Chaitanya (1486-1534)—an Indian Vaishnava saint from Bengal whose mode of worshiping Krishna with ecstatic dancing and singing spearheaded a revolution in *Bhakti Yoga*, popularizing *kirtan*, and especially the chanting of the sixteen-syllable Hare Krishna mantra. He is the founder of Gaudiya Vaishnavism, which follows the teaching of the Vedantic *acharya* Madhava.

Chakra—wheel, circle, turning, energy point; from *char* = vehicle, to move. *Chakras* are doorways of perception, entryways into different realms or dimensions.

Chalo—how to say "let's go" in Brajbhasha.

Chela—a disciple or student.

Chitta—mind; from *chit* = consciousness.

Chitta-vritti—the whirling fluctuations of the mind; from *chitta* = mind + *vritti* = fluctuations or whirlings.

Choli—a woman's blouse, usually worn with a sari.

Choti—Hindi word meaning "short, little, or small."

Daksha—a son of the creator god, Brahma. He is known as Prajapati, because he was given the role of progenitor of many living beings. He had many daughters, including Sati, the wife of Lord Shiva. *Daksha* = able and dexterous.

Dama—to tune, to train, to control the senses. Dama is one of the six virtues (*shadsampat*) that must be cultivated for *shubheccha,* the first *bhumika,* to arise.

Darshan—to see, usually associated with seeing something divine—the vision of God, a saint, a holy place, or a deity.

Das—follower, servant.

Deity—a form or image that is worshiped as God. Sometimes discovered as a self-originating stone (see *shaligrama*), but often a man-made statue made of stone, metal, or other material.

Dharamshala—a guesthouse reserved for spiritual pilgrims.

Dharma—to maintain or hold in place, the law or order that upholds, usually used to mean righteous or correct way for one to behave according to established social or religious rules.

Dhoti—traditional way men dress in India, consisting of a simple cloth wrapped around the lower part of the body, folded and tucked in at the waist, sometimes also drawn between the legs to create a sort of trousers-like effect.

Dhyana—meditation.

Divine—that which is beyond the mundane material world, transcendental, celestial, heavenly, Godly.

Dosha—a fault or defect. According to the Ayurvedic system, *dosha* refers to a bodily humour, and health is achieved by balancing the three doshas: *vata*, *pitta*, and *kapha*.

Duhkha—suffering, sorrow, grief, stress, dissatisfaction; from *duh* = bad + *kha* = state.

Dvesha—aversion, dislike, repulsion, hatred. One of the five *kleshas*, or obstacles to the attainment of Yoga, that Patanjali describes in the Yoga Sutra.

Ego—the sense of "I," or the individual self of any person, distinguished from the self of others or the Divine Self.

Four Kumaras—the oldest beings in the universe, the first mind-born children created by Brahma. They eternally appear as naked five-year-old little boys. *Kumara* = prince.

Gandharva—elf. In Hinduism, Buddhism, and Jainism *gandharva* is a race of celestial beings who especially excel in the arts of music and dance.

Ghritachi—an *apsara*, a beautiful celestial nymph, a dancer in Indra's heaven. She is the wife of Vyasa and the mother of their son, Shukadeva Goswami, who recites the Shrimad Bhagavatam to King Parikshit during the final week of his life. She is also the mother of Drona, who was the teacher of the Kuru and Pandava princes.

Gokul—a small village in the Braj (also Vraj) region of North India; where Krishna spent his childhood.

Gopala—a name for Krishna, usually used to denote Him when he was a young child; from *go* = cow or senses + *pala* = protector and friend or pal (a friend is someone you can rely on, someone who will protect and defend you). Gopal is the friend and protector of the cows as well as the senses. *Gopal*, with the final "a" dropped, is the Hindi version of the name.

Gopis—dairy maids. The gopis of Braj were the intimate beloveds of Krishna and are considered the gurus of the path of devotion. Because they were born enlightened sages from a past *yuga*, their minds and senses were exalted, not worldly.

Goswami—a yogi who has mastered their senses; from *go* = senses + *swami* = master. A renunciate who is at home with their eternal Self and needs nothing more.

Govinda—a name for Krishna that means "cowherd" or "the one who can find the cows and bring them home"; from *go* = cow (also senses) + *vinda* = finder. *Govind*, with the final "a" dropped, is the Hindi version of the name.

Guna—quality, the constituents of nature: *sattva* (brightness, goodness), *rajas* (activity, passion), and *tamas* (inertia, darkness).

Guru—the remover of darkness or ignorance, the enlightenment principle, a teacher; from *gu* = darkness + *ru* = remover.

Hanuman—the Hindu monkey god and son of the wind god, Vayu. The companion, friend, protector, and devotee of Lord Rama.

Hari—a name for Krishna that means "the one who takes away all material pain and afflictions."

Haribol—an exclamation meaning "speak/say/sing the name of Hari" and invoke Him; from *bol* = to say. In contemporary times, Haribol is often used in parts of India as a greeting much like hello, goodnight, or have a nice day.

Harirayaji (1591-1711)—a prolific writer, poet, scholar, philosopher, and major contributor to the literature of the Pushtimarg (Path of Grace) who is believed to have lived an exceptionally long life. *Shiksha Patra: 41 Letters of Spiritual Counsel* is his most widely read work and is held in high esteem by Pushtimargis. He was the *bhakti* master Shrimad Vallabhacharya's great-grandson.

Hatha yoga—the joining of the sun (*ha*) and the moon (*tha*); the Yoga that is attained through forceful means.

Hatha Yoga Pradipika—fourteenth-century scripture written by yogi Swatmarama outlining the methods of hatha yoga, including *asanas*, *pranayamas*, and *kriyas*.

Hazrat Inayat Khan (1882-1927)—*nada yoga* master, professor of musicology, singer, exponent of the vina, poet, and philosopher. He was instrumental in bringing the teachings of Sufism to the West.

Hiranyakashipu—an ancient *asura*, the demonic son of Kashyapa and Diti. *Hiranyakashipu* = clothed in gold and describes a person who is very materialistic, fond of wealth and sensual comforts, and has no interest in worshiping God. In his early life, Hiranyakashipu underwent intense yogic austerities and earned a boon from Lord Brahma that made him almost indestructible. He became a cruel, demonic king bent on destroying anyone who didn't worship him. He tried to kill his son Prahlada, because of the boy's pious devotion to Vishnu. Vishnu appeared in the form of Narasimha (half-man, half-lion) and saved the boy by killing the demon king. Hiranyakashipu was not always a demon. He was once known as Jaya, one of the gatekeepers of Vaikuntha, Vishnu's heavenly realm, but was cursed by the Kumaras, along with his brother, Vijaya, to take birth three times in the earthly realm as a demon.

Holi—an Indian spring festival in which devotees spray each other with colored powders and water, emulating a time when Krishna did the same with his beloved *gopis*.

Ida—the moon stream, left *nadi*, feminine, or receptive channel.

Indra—an ancient Hindu deity, the king of heaven (Svarga Loka) and the demigods. He controls rain, storms, thunder, lightning, the flow of rivers, and war.

Ishta Devata—one's own chosen favorite form of God; from *ishta* = cherished, preferred, personal, choicest, favorite + *devata* = deity.

Ishvara—Lord, God, the special Supreme Self who lives in the hearts of all beings. A person's own personal choice of whom to worship; from *ish* = owner, ruler, chief + *vara* = best, excellent, choice.

Ishvara-pranidhana—surrender to God, commitment to God, devoting your life, offering your life force (*prana*), and all your actions to your personal form of God. One of the five *niyamas*, or personal observances, described by Patanjali in his Yoga Sutra.

ISKCON—the International Society for Krishna Consciousness, also known as the Hari Krishnas, a Gaudiya organization founded in the twentieth century by Shri A. C. Bhaktivedanta Swami Prabhupada.

Jagrat—waking state of consciousness.

Jai—victory, an exclamation akin to the word *hurrah* in English.

Jai Shringera—A Gaudiya ashram in Vrindavan, India, presided over (at the time the "Tea Miracle" story took place) by Purushottam Goswami, a follower of Shri Chaitanya.

Jala neti—one of the *shatkarma kriyas*. It is performed by pouring salt water in the nose, to cleanse the nostrils; from *jala* = water + *neti* = not this.

Janmashtami—the festival celebrating Krishna's birthday; from *janma* = birth + *ashtami* = eighth. He was born as the eighth *avatar* of Lord Vishnu, the eighth child of Vasudeva and Devaki, on the eighth day of the eighth month.

Japa—the repetition of a *mantra*, usually done with prayer beads (a *japa mala*).

Jaya—one of the gatekeepers, along with his brother, Vijaya, of Vaikuntha, the heavenly abode of Lord Vishnu. Because of a curse by the Four Kumaras, Jaya and his brother had to take birth three times as demons who are killed by different *avatars* of Vishnu. In the Satya Yuga, Jaya is Hiranyakashipu, who is killed by Narasimha; in the Treta Yuga, he is Ravana and is killed by Rama; and in the Dvapara Yuga, he is Shishupala and is killed by Krishna.

Jetta—dreadlocked, matted hair. Many *sadhus* (ascetics) in India have *jetta*. It is considered a sign of renunciation to stop combing your hair; it is also considered a yogic *tapasya* (austerity) to have to carry around the weight of all that matted hair.

Jiva—individual soul.

Jivanmukta—a liberated soul, one who is living liberated; from *jiva* = individual soul + *mukta* = liberation. *Jivanmuktas* are classified into four categories: 1) *Brahmavit* (knower of Brahman); 2) *Brahmavidvara* (better knower of Brahman); 3) *Brahmavidvariya* (one who knows Brahman best); and 4) *Brahmavidvarishtha* (the greatest knower of Brahman).

Jivanmukti—the state of liberation.

Jnana—knowledge.

Jnana-vritti—knowledge of the *vrittis*; worldly knowledge, as opposed to *atma-jnana*, which is knowledge of the *atman*, or the eternal soul, the Divine Self.

Jnana Yoga—the Yoga that is attained through purifying the intellect. The Jnana Yoga practices include the study of scripture and self-inquiry, asking the question, "Who am I?" in order to pierce through the layers of ignorance and illusion. Jnana Yoga, or the "Yoga of Wisdom," is one of the four classical spiritual paths in Hinduism, the others being Bhakti, Karma, and Raja Yoga.

Kali Yuga—the dark age, the present eon, typified by moral and spiritual decline; from *kal* = to incite, to count + *yuj* = join. According to Hinduism there are four yugas: Satya, Treta, Dvapara, and Kali.

Kama—desire, passion. Usually refers to sexual desire or sensual pleasure. According to Vedic tradition, *kama* is one of the four aims, or pursuits, of life, the others being *dharma* (career), *artha* (wealth), and *moksha* (liberation).

Kapalabhati—skull-shining; a *kriya,* or purifying technique.

Karma—action; from *kr* = to do. It includes all actions, whether considered good, bad, mixed, or neutral. *Karma* is classified into three types: past (*sanchita*), present (*prarabdha*), and future (*agami*).

Karma Yoga—the Yoga that is attained through selfless service. The karma yogi engages in work to benefit others with no aim for personal reward or acknowledgment. By renouncing the fruits of their actions, the practitioner hopes to purify themself from selfishness and the sense of doership in order to become an instrument for God's work. Karma Yoga, or the "Yoga of Action," is one of the four classical spiritual paths in Hinduism, the others being Bhakti, Jnana, and Raja Yoga.

Karuna—compassion; to feel together. *Karuna*, or compassion, is the desire to relieve the suffering of another, understanding that when you relieve the suffering of another, your own suffering will be relieved too.

Katha—storytelling.

Kevala kumbhaka—the spontaneous, effortless retention of the breath that occurs in *samadhi.*

Kirtan—to cut through, to recite, to sing the names of God; also call-and-response group singing of the names of the Divine.

Kitchari—a simple thick porridge-like dish made of lentils and rice cooked together in one pot.

Klesha—obstacle or hindrance; from *klish* = to suffer or be in distress. In his Yoga Sutra, Patanjali lists five *kleshas*, or obstacles to Yoga: *avidya* (ignorance), *asmita* (ego), *raga* (attachment to likes), *dvesha* (aversion to dislikes), and *abhinivesha* (fear of death).

Kosha—sheath, layer envelope; from *kush* = to enfold. Yoga philosophy says that the individual is not just their physical body but is composed of five bodies, or sheaths (*koshas*), that envelope the soul, the transcendental Self. From gross to subtle, those sheaths are known as: *annamaya* (physical) kosha, *pranamaya* (energetic) kosha, *manomaya* (emotional) kosha, *vijnanamaya* (intellectual) kosha, and *anandamaya* (blissful) kosha.

Krishna—the all-attractive one, your deepest heart's desire. Krishna is the supreme, absolute God who incarnated as an *avatar* of Lord Vishnu during the Dvapara Yuga to his royal parents, Devaki and the Yadava prince Vasudeva, around five thousand years ago in a jail in Mathura, North India, and was raised by His foster parents, Yashoda and Nanda, in the small village of Gokul, where he enchanted Radha and the other *gopis*, as well everyone and everything, before traveling to the city of Dwarka to assume his position as a king and adviser to Arjuna and the Pandavas during the great battle of Kurukshetra.

Kriyas—purification actions, rituals, or exercises done to awaken *kundalini*.

Kshatriyas—warriors, rulers, administrators. One of the four castes recognized in India.

Kumbhaka—to hold, savor, or cherish.

Kundalini—coiled snake, consciousness.

Kunti—the mother of the five Pandavas, as well as her firstborn child, Karna. Kunti was Krishna's aunt, being the sister of Krishna's father, the Yadava prince Vasudeva. Her story is told in the Mahabharata and the Shrimad Bhagavatam.

Kurukshetra—the battlefield in North India where the great, terrible war at the end of the Dvapara Yuga was fought between the Kurus and the Pandavas, described in the epic scripture the Mahabharata. Kuru is the name of the dynasty that reigned from the capital city Hastinapura (modern-day Delhi); *kshetra* = a field.

Kusha—a type of tall grass with sturdy canes. Used for centuries in India to make woven mats. In the Bhagavad Gita, Krishna recommends it as the ideal seat for meditation.

Kyaa baat hai—a phrase meaning "amazing, wonderful, or wow" in the Brajbhasha language spoken in northern India.

Ladoo—Indian sweet ball usually made of chickpea and wheat flour, sugar, and ghee.

Lakshman—Lord Rama's half-brother and close friend.

Laxmi (also Lakshmi)—the consort of Lord Vishnu, the goddess of beauty, wealth, and prosperity; from *lakshya* = aim, point or objective. The granter of prosperity. She is also known as *Shri* (beauty) and is closely associated with *padma*, the lotus flower.

Lila—the eternal loving plays or pastimes of Shri Krishna with his *bhaktas* and associates that exist sort of like a parallel universe to the finite world that most of us mistakenly assume is reality.

Lokah—location, place, world, realm.

Mahabharata—an ancient Hindu epic, the longest poem ever written, consisting of one hundred thousand verses, divided into eighteen chapters, written by Vyasa. The epic focuses on the story of the five Pandava brothers. Within Book 6: The Bhishma Parva of the Mahabharata, the Bhagavad Gita is found.

Maharaj—great king; from *maha* = great + *raj* = king. Often used as a respectful, affectionate title for a saint. The expression of affection is increased when you add *ji*, to make *maharajji*.

Mahavakyas—great sayings; from *maha* = great + *vakya* = speech, utterance. The *mahavakyas* are found in the Upanishads and declare the relationship between the individual soul and God. There are four mahavakyas:
1. *Aham Bramasmi*, meaning "I am Brahman" or "I know myself as part of Brahman" or "I know myself as one with the Self"; from the Brihadaranyaka Upanishad.
2. *Tat tvam asi*, meaning "That you are"; from the Chandogya Upanishad.
3. *Prajnanam Brahma*, meaning "Knowledge is Brahman"; from the

Aitareya Upanishad.

4. *Ayam Atma Brahma*, meaning "This Self is Brahman"; from the Mandukya Upanishad.

Maitri—friendliness.

Mala—garland, necklace, rosary, prayer beads. Malas can be strung on a string or chain and made of flowers, leaves, wood, stone, gems, etc.

Mama—my, mine.

Manas—mind, or heart and mind combined.

Mandir—temple.

Manipura chakra—the jewel in the city, the navel center, the third *chakra*, located in the region of the solar plexus; from *mani* = jewel + *pura* = city.

Mantra—protection for the mind; from *man* = mind/heart + *tra* = to cross over. A magical spell.

Marg(a)—path.

Mataji—an affectionate title given to a respected female saint.

Matsya—fish.

Matsyendranath—the founder of hatha yoga. One of the eighty-four *mahasiddhas* (ancient yogis who had attained magical superpowers).

Maya—the manifesting power or agent of *Brahman*.

Moksha—liberation; from *muk* = to free. Freedom from *samsara*, the wheel of time, the cycle of birth, death, and rebirth. See also *mukti*.

Mudra—seal, stamp, or gesture; from *mud* = joy + *ra* = to give. Some mudras involve the entire body, but most are performed with only the fingers and hands.

Mukti—liberation, freedom, enlightenment, *moksha*. Liberation from *samsara* (the cycle of birth and death). When the word *moksha* is used it implies *sayuja mukti* (becoming one with God). There are said to be five types of mukti: *sayuja*, in which the soul merges with God; *salokya*, in which the soul goes to heaven; *sarupya*, in which the soul gets a body similar to God's form; *samipya*, in which the soul gets to be near God; and *sarshti*, in which the soul obtains the six opulences God has (knowledge, wealth, fame, strength, beauty, and renunciation).

Muladhara chakra—the first *chakra* (energy center, level of perception); from *mula* = root + *dhara* = place.

Mumukshutva—intense longing for the truth, a burning desire to know God, a desire for liberation, being in hot pursuit of emancipation. The fourth means to cultivate *shubheccha*, the first *bhumika*.

Murti—embodiment; a representation of a divinity, usually a statue made of stone, wood, or metal that serves as a means to worship a deity.

Nada(m)—sound, divine music, primal vibration.

Nada Brahma—sound is God.

Nadi—channel, river, current, stream, sounding, conduit for *prana*. There are seventy-two thousand *nadis* in the subtle body, but three main ones: *ida* (left), *pingala* (right), and *sushumna* (center) nadi.

Nadi shodhana—channel-cleansing, a *pranayama* technique that purifies the *nadis* through alternate-nostril breathing.

Naimisha Forest—an ancient sacred forest mentioned in both the Ramayana and the Mahabharata; from *nimisha* = in the twinkling of the eye. Known as the abode of many *rishis*, sages, and yogis. It was a place where the *puranas* (ancient stories of God) were first narrated. Located in what is now the Sitapur District of Uttar Pradesh, in North India.

Namaste—a traditional greeting in India, often accompanied by *anjali mudra* (prayer hands); from *na* = not + *ma* = mine + *te* = to you. Literally meaning "not mine, but Thine," *Thine* referring to the Divine. By saying namaste to someone you acknowledge the divine within you who is bowing to the divine within them.

Narada—a god-sage famous in the Hindu tradition as a traveling musician, storyteller, and *guru* who bestows enlightening wisdom on those in a crisis who are ready to hear. Also known as the celestial spaceman, because he can travel throughout the universe as well as through time. Narada is the mind-born son of the creator god, Brahma.

Narasimha—the man-lion, the fourth *avatar* of Lord Vishnu, who incarnates on Earth to kill the demon Hiranyakashipu and rescue the demon's son Prahlada, a saintly devotee of Lord Vishnu.

Neem Karoli Baba (1900-1973)—Indian saint, devotee of the Hindu deity Hanuman. Known as Maharajji to his followers, he was the *guru* to many well-known Western spiritual practitioners, such as Ram Dass, Shyamdas, Bhagavan Das, Krishna Das, and Jai Uttal.

Neem Karoli Baba Ashram—the place in Vrindavan, North India, where the saint Neem Karoli Baba lived with his devotees. His other ashrams are in Kainchi and Rishikesh.

Nidra—sleep.

Nirodha—ceasing, stopping; the state of absorption of one's consciousness into Shri Krishna, the Supreme Lord, Bhagavan.

Niyamas—observances. Patanjali, in the Yoga Sutra, describes five *niyamas*, or personal observances, suggested guidelines for a yogi to follow: *shaucha* (cleanliness), *santosha* (contentment), *tapas* (self-discipline), *svadhyaya* (study of the Self), and *Ishvara-pranidhana* (surrender to God).

Om—the *pranava*, the eternal sound from which all sounds arise.

Padartha bhavana—disappearance of visible forms; from *pada* = stepping + *artha* = visible forms + *a* = dis + *bhavana* = appearance. The sixth *bhumika*.

Padma—lotus, a name for the goddess Laxmi.

Pandavas—five brothers (Yudhishthira, Bhima, Arjuna, Nakula, and Sahadeva) who are the main characters in the epic scripture the Mahabharata. Kunti was their mother. They were regarded as the sons of the Kuru king, Pandu, but were, in fact, *devaputras* (half-god, half-human): fathered by divine beings—Dharma, Vayu, Indra, and the Ashwini Twins. They shared a wife, Draupadi. The Pandavas waged war against their cousins the Kauravas, known as the battle of Kurukshetra in the Bhagavad Gita. The Pandavas won.

Paramatman—the Supersoul, the Divine Self; the aspiring yogi wants to unite their *jivatman* (or individual soul) with the *paramatman* (the absolute or super soul).

Parampara—an uninterrupted series or succession. The word is traditionally used to describe the succession of teachers and students who keep a lineage alive by passing the teachings down through the generations.

Parikrama—to travel in a circle; the road or path that encircles the town of Vrindavan is known as the Parikrama.

Parikshit—the great Kuru king of Hastinapura who lived at the very end of the Dvapara Yuga. He succeeded his great uncle, Yudhishthira. *Parikshit* = belonging to the people. He was seen as a righteous ruler much beloved by the people. At the age of sixty he was cursed by Shringin (the grandson of the yogi Shamika), to die of a snakebite in seven days. On hearing this, he renounced his kingdom, put his second son, Janamejaya on the throne, and sought enlightenment on the banks of the Ganga. It is there that the king encountered the boy-sage Shukadev Goswami, who enlightened him by reciting to him the Shrimad Bhagavatam.

Pashupati—protector of the animals; a name for Lord Shiva; from *pashu* = animal + *pati* = lord or protector.

Patanjali—complier of the Yoga Sutra, thought to be an incarnation of Shesha, the divine serpent. *Patanjali* = fell into her hands; from *patta* = fell + *anjali* = joining of the hands in reverence. Anjali is the name of Patanjali's mother.

Pingala—the sun stream, the right *nadi*, the masculine channel.

Prahlada—a saintly boy who, although he was a demon, was devoted to Lord Vishnu. His father, the demon King Hiranyakashipu, tried to kill him because of his devotion, but Vishnu appeared as Narasimha (his half-lion, half-man *avatar* form) and saved the boy by killing his father. Prahlada lived during the Treta Yuga (the second age). His story is told in the tenth canto of the Shrimad Bhagavatam.

Prakriti—nature, the primal material energy of which all matter is composed. *Prakriti* is personified in Hinduism as female, in contrast with her male counterpart, *purusha*, pure consciousness. *Prakriti* = matter; *purusha* = spirit.

Pramana—means of proving or gaining knowledge about something.

Prana—life force, vitality, one of the five *vayus*, or winds; *prana vayu* is the upward-moving wind.

Pranam(a)—to respectfully bow, to show obeisance.

Pranava—ever-renewing, the sound of *Om*.

Pranayama—the yogic practice of breath control; from *prana* = life force + *yama* = to restrain, regulate, or control. The fourth limb of Patanjali's Ashtanga Yoga.

Prarabdha karma—present *karma*. *Prarabdha karmas* are part of the *sanchita karmas*, a collection of past karmas that are ready to be experienced in an individual's present incarnation. Prarabdha is that portion of one's past karma that is responsible for their present body.

Prasad(a)—food (or anything) that has been first offered to God and then given to the *bhakta* filled with God's grace and eaten by the bhakta so they can become filled with God's merciful, consecrated gift.

Pratyahara—sense withdrawal from external reality; from *prati* = to withdraw + *ahara* = food. In this case, food refers to any external stimuli one might consume. The fifth limb of Patanjali's Ashtanga Yoga.

Prem(a)—divine love.

Pujari—a temple priest, one entrusted with performing *puja* (ritual worship), making offerings and caring for the deity who resides in a temple.

Puraka—inhalation.

Purana—ancient; the sacred literature of Hinduism written in a narrative style.

Purusha—person, self. When spelled with an upper case "P," the word refers to God, the eternal, authentic divine spirit.

Pushti—well-nourished, fat, grace-filled.

Pushtimarg(a)—the Path of Grace; from *pushti* = grace + *marg* = path. A *bhakti* devotional movement founded by Vallabhacharya (1479-1531) focused on the worship of Krishna. The philosophy is aligned with the *shuddhadvaita* (pure nondual) Vedantic teachings of Vallabhacharya, in which everything is dependent on Krishna's grace and the world is not seen as something to renounce but to cherish as the creation and abode of Krishna. The main practice among Pushtimargis is taking refuge by chanting the mantra *Shri Krishna sharanam mama* and performing Krishna *seva* daily.

Radha—the beloved of Krishna, his favorite *gopi*. *Radha* = the one who praises, or the one who excels in love for, Krishna. She is considered a form of Laxmi.

Radha Ramana Temple—famous temple where the *shaligram* form of Krishna playing the flute resides. Notable for the fact that for five hundred years the deity has not left the temple. Even during the seventeenth-century Mogul invasions, when many deities were removed from temples for safekeeping, this deity remained in the temple unharmed.

Raga—passion, attachment. One of the five *kleshas*, or obstacles to the attainment of Yoga, described by Patanjali in the Yoga Sutra.

Rajas—passion, dynamic, active; one of the three *gunas*.

Raja Yoga—the Royal Yoga. *Raja* = royal, kingly or chief, as in "best of," so Raja Yoga means "the best yoga." The term Raja Yoga is usually used in reference to the eight-limbed (*ashtanga*) system found in Patanjali's Yoga Sutra. Raja Yoga, or the "Yoga of Meditation," is one of the four classical spiritual paths in Hinduism, the others being Bhakti, Karma, and Jnana Yoga.

Ram(a)—the seventh *avatar* of the Hindu god Vishnu. He is also known as *Ramachandra* (Rama of the moon). The hero of the Sanskrit epic poem the Ramayana.

Ramana—merriment, amour, enjoyment, delighting in playing with the Lord, sporting with the Lord, to engage in love plays with God; from *ram* = to be delighted.

Ramana Maharshi (1879-1950)—an Indian saint, a great jnana yogi, considered to be a *jivanmukta*.

Raman-Reti—playing in the sand; from *raman* = play + *reti* = sand. A place in the Vrindavan forest of North India where Krishna and Radha, as well as Balarama and the other *gopis* and *gopas,* used to go to play—to frolic together, delightfully rolling in the sands by the banks of the Yamuna River.

Ramayana—an ancient Indian scripture that tells the epic life story of Lord Rama. Written by Valmiki, in poetic form, consisting of twenty-four thousand verses.

Ram Dass (1931-2019)—born Richard Alpert; an American spiritual teacher, psychologist, and author who in 1971 wrote *Be Here Now,* the best-selling book that helped to popularize yoga in the West. He was a devotee of Neem Karoli Baba.

Ras(a)—juice, essence, nectar; referring to the loving sweetness of the Divine.

Rasakhan (1534-1619)—a Pushtimarga *bhakti* poet, devoted to Shri Krishna; one of the 252 main disciples of Shri Gusainji.

Ras(a) lila—a circle dance performed under the autumn full moon in the forest of Vrindavan, where Krishna multiplied himself to be able to dance with each *gopi.*

Ravana—the demon king who steals Rama's wife, Sita, and imprisons her in his palace in Lanka. Rama, with help from his friends, rescues Sita and kills Ravana. This epic story is told in the Ramayana. In a previous incarnation, Ravana was the demon Hiranyakashipu, but before that he was Jaya, and along with his brother, Vijaya, was a gatekeeper of Vaikuntha, the heavenly abode of Vishnu.

Rechaka—exhalation.

Rishi—an accomplished, enlightened, wise person; a sage, a great yogi.

Roti—a simple unleavened, flat, round bread made of whole-wheat flour, water, and salt; also called chapati.

Sadhaka—one who is engaged in conscious spiritual practice (*sadhana*).

Sadhana—conscious spiritual practice.

Sahasrara—thousand-petalled. The crown *chakra,* the seventh primary chakra, thought to be located hovering an inch or so above the top of the head.

Sama—calm, tranquil, balanced, same. *Sama* is one of the six virtues (*shadsampat*) that must be cultivated for *shubheccha,* the first *bhumika,* to arise.

Samadhana—to set your sights on the highest, to restore your whole being into a single one-pointed focus on what is true and eternal. *Samadhana* is one of the six virtues (*shadsampat*) that must be cultivated for *shubheccha*, the first *bhumika*, to arise.

Samadhi—enlightenment, *Yoga*, ecstasy, cosmic consciousness; from *sam* = same + *adhi* = highest, supreme.

Samavritti—same fluctuation; from *sam* = same + *vritti* = fluctuation. A *pranayama* practice in which the parts of the breath—the inhalation, exhalation, and retentions—are given the same duration. For example: Inhale for a count of four, retain the breath in for a count of four, exhale for a count of four, retain the breath out for a count of four.

Samprajnata samadhi—*samadhi* with seed. A level of samadhi, or ecstatic spiritual realization, that arises through deep reflection, where the individual becomes aware of *Brahman*, the Self as the ultimate reality. Unlike *asamprajnata samadhi*, in *samprajnata samadhi* the yogi is aware of their own individuality as well as of the presence of other objects around them. Duality is still operating, but they know themself as one with all that is.

Samsara—same agitation; from *sam* = same + *sara* = agitation. The wheel of birth, life, death, and rebirth; the cycle of repeated births: the world of suffering, the wheel of time.

Samskara—activator, indelible psychological imprints in the subconscious, vestiges left behind by our daily experiences (*karmas*), whether conscious or unconscious, internal, or external, desirable, or undesirable. *Samskaras* propel a person's consciousness into action.

Samyama—the simultaneous practice of concentration (*dharana*), meditation (*dhyana*), and ecstasy (*samadhi*).

Sanchita karma—past *karma*, one of the three types of karmas. *Sanchita* = heaped together and refers to the sum of all karmas—all actions, good and bad, that a person has performed throughout many lifetimes. Often referred to as the storehouse of past karmas waiting to be dealt with and resolved.

Sannyasi—an ascetic, one who has entered into the renounced order of life, is detached from material concerns and focused on spiritual pursuits. The ancient Indian Vedic system speaks of the stages of human life as the four *ashramas*: *brahmacharya* (student), *grihastha* (householder, marriage, and career), *vanaprastha* (forest-dweller, retired from work and family responsibilities), and *sannyasa* (asceticism).

Santosha—contentment. One of the five *niyamas*, or personal observances, that Patanjali describes in the Yoga Sutra.

Sarvatmabhav(a)—seeing and feeling God's presence everywhere; from *sarva* = all + *atma* = the eternal, divine soul + *bhav* = blissful, divine mood of being loved and in love with God. The mood of being loved and in love with God in which a person sees God in everyone and everything.

Satchidananda—truth, consciousness, and bliss; the attributes of the eternal, Divine Self.

Sati—Lord Shiva's first wife, who was the daughter of Daksha. *Sati* = truthful. After her death by self-immolation, she was reborn as the goddess Parvati to become Shiva's second wife.

Satsang—attachment to the truth, keeping the company of others who are interested in remembering God.

Sattva—light, pure, balanced, one of the three *gunas*.

Sattvapatti—the attainment of *sattva*; from *sattva* = light, purity + *pati* = lord or master.
The fourth *bhumika*.

Satya—truth. One of the five *yamas*, or behavior restrictions, described by Patanjali in the Yoga Sutras.

Seva—service; loving, caring service performed by a *bhakta* toward a personal deity or respected person.

Shabda—word, speech, sound, an utterance.

Shabda Brahman—word is God. *Shabda* = sound or word + *Brahman* = God. The universe is a creation of *Shabda Brahman*.

Shadsampat—the six virtues that are a means to *shubheccha*, the first *bhumika*: *sama, dama, uparathi, titiksha, shraddha*, and *samadhana*.

Shakti—cosmic power, the animating force, female power.

Shaligram(a)—a fossilized stone having the shape or form of a god. A *shaligrama* is not carved by human hands. The shaligrama in the Radha Ramana Temple, mentioned in the "Tea Miracle" story, is in the form of Krishna playing the flute.

Shamika—ancient Brahmana sage whose grandson, Shringin, would curse King Parikshit.

Shanmukhi mudra—A hand gesture performed with the fingers to close the gates of perception: the two eyes, ears, nostrils, and mouth. Covering the ears with the thumbs, the eyes with the index fingers, the nostrils with the middle fingers, and the mouth with the ring and little fingers. Its practice induces *pratyahara* (sense withdrawal) and is used by yogis to be able to hear the inner sound, the *nadam*

Shanti—peace, a state free of conflict.

Sharanam—refuge, shelter, protection.

Shastra—scripture, instructional text, particularly on religion or science.

Shatkarma—six actions; from *shat* = six + *karma* = action.

Shaucha—cleanliness. One of the five *niyamas*, or personal observances, described by Patanjali in the Yoga Sutra.

Shavasana—the seat or position of the corpse; the practice of dying.

Shiva—the destroyer in the Hindu trinity of Brahma, Vishnu, and Shiva.

Shraddha—faith, having faith in *guru*, scriptures, or God; reverence, trust. One of the six virtues (*shadsampat*) that must be cultivated for *shubheccha*, the first *bhumika*, to arise.

Shravana—hearing, to know or acquire knowledge through hearing.

Shri—divinely, eternally, beautiful; also another name for the goddess Laxmi.

Shri Brahmananda Sarasvati (?-1993)—Self-realized saint from Uttar Pradesh, North India. A yogi, medical doctor, Sanskrit scholar, and teacher. Founder of Ananda Ashram in Monroe, New York, and the Yoga Society of San Francisco, California. Author of *The Textbook of Yoga Psychology*, the definitive text on the Yoga Sutra of Patanjali. Also known as Ramamurti S. Mishra, MD.

Shri K. Pattabhi Jois (1915-2009)—yoga *guru* and Sanskrit scholar from South India who popularized the *vinyasa* style of yoga known as

Ashtanga Yoga. Author of *Yoga Mala*. His guru was Krishnamacharya.

Shrimad Bhagavatam—also known as the Bhagavata Purana, one of the great Hindu scriptures; authored by Vyasa. It primarily focuses on *bhakti*, or devotion to the Supreme God as Krishna, and includes a complete telling, in eighteen thousand verses, of all His incarnations in twelve cantos, or volumes. Scholars date it between 500 BC and CE 100.

Shringar darshan—to see the deity bathed, dressed, and adorned with jewelry.

Shruti—that which is heard; refers to the ancient Hindu scriptures that are believed to have been revealed to the ancient *rishis* (sages) by God.

Shrutidhara—someone who can memorize anything immediately; from *shruti* = hearing + *dhara* = one who can capture.

Shubheccha—good desire, good will, good wanting, the first *bhumika*, or step on the path toward enlightenment; from *shubha* = good, auspicious + *iccha* = wish. There are four means to cultivate *shubheccha*: *viveka, vairagya, shadsampat*, and *mumukshutva*.

Shuddha—pure, good, clear.

Shuddhadvaita—pure nondualism. The philosophy propounded by Vallabhacharya, the founder of the Path of Grace (Pushtimarg).

Shukadev(a)—a *jivanmukta* (liberated soul). He was born enlightened because he heard the Shrimad Bhagavatam recited by his father, the sage Vyasa, while in the womb of his mother, the *apsara* Ghritachi. In his previous birth he was Shuka, the pet parrot beloved of Radha of Vrindavan, and recites the Shrimad Bhagavatam to King Parikshit on the banks of the Ganga in Hastinapura during the final week of the king's life. He was also known as Shukadeva Goswami, because he was a master of his senses.

Shunyata—Sanskrit term, often translated as emptiness, referring to reality being subject to the interpretation of the perceiver.

Shyamdas (1953-2013)—born in Connecticut as Stephen Ted Schaffer, Shyamdas traveled to India in the early 1970s and met Neem Karoli Baba. He then took initiation into the *Pushtimarg sampradaya* (spiritual lineage) of Vallabhacharya and studied under the tutelage of Shri Prathameshji, a direct descendent of Vallabhacharya. Shyamdas was a Sanskrit scholar who spoke many Indian languages. He was an accomplished classical Indian musician and *bhajan* (devotional) singer. He was a wisdom teacher who wrote and translated many books pertaining to the Vaishnava Pushtimarg sampradaya. Most importantly, Shyamdas was a saintly *bhakta* devoted to Shri Krishna. He tragically died in a motorcycle accident in Kerala, South India.

Siddhi—supernatural, paranormal, magical powers that arise from the practice of yoga. *Siddhi* = perfection or accomplishment. The eight classical *siddhis*, or great perfections, are: *anima* (to become small), *mahima* (to become large), *laghima* (to become very light and to fly), *garima* (to become very heavy), *prapti* (to materialize objects out of thin air), *prakamya* (to enter into the body of another, also to live underwater without breathing), *ishitva* (to bend others to your will), and *vashitva* (to control the five elements and override the laws of nature).

Siddhi Ma (?-2017)—an Indian female saint who was the most intimate devotee of Neem Karoli Baba.

Sita—a Hindu goddess, the daughter of the earth, the wife of Lord Rama, and heroine of the epic story the Ramayana. As an infant, she was found in a field by King Janaka, who called her Sita, which means "furrow."

Spanda—movement, motion, or vibration; from *spand* = to move, quiver. The subtle, pulsing, radiating energy that emanates from *Brahman*, the Supreme Consciousness.

Speciesism—a human-supremacist world view. A prejudice held by humans against all nonhuman animals that allows humans to exploit them. Not respecting other animal species for having their own desires and ambitions.

Subji—Hindi word for vegetable.

Sushumna—sweet shrine, ray of light, gracious channel, the central channel. The *nadi* that moves from the base of the spine to the top of the head.

Sushupti—deep sleep where there is no dreaming, no REM (rapid eye movement). One of the three states of ordinary consciousness, including *jagrat* (waking) and *swapna* (dreaming).

Suta Goswami—a great sage, a disciple of Vyasa, endowed with powerful hearing abilities, a *shrutidhara*. He narrated several *puranas*, including the Shrimad Bhagavatam, Mahabharata, Padma Purana, and Shiva Purana. He lived during the Dvapara Yuga.

Sutra—thread; teachings given in concise, terse statements.

Svadhishthana chakra—her favorite standing place, the second *chakra*, or level of perception. The creative or sexual center.

Svadhyaya—study of the Self. One of the five *niyamas*, or personal observances, described by Patanjali in the Yoga Sutra.

Svarga Loka—one of the seven heavenly realms.

Svarupa—the divine form of a deity.

Swami Nirmalananda (1925-1997)—Self-realized saint from Kerala, South India. Known as "the anarchist swami." He lived for the last thirty years of his life secluded in the forest of B. R. Hills, Karnataka, South India. A vegan, social activist, and prolific writer. Author of *A Garland of Forest Flowers* and *Flowers from the Forest*. He took *prayopavesha* (self-willed death) on January 10, 1997.

Swami Satchidananda (1914-2002)—born C. K. Ramaswamy, he was an enlightened saint and spiritual teacher from Tamil Nadu, South India, who came to America in the 1960s and influenced the popularization of yoga in the West. He translated the Yoga Sutra and the Bhagavad Gita in a way that was easily understood by modern readers. He is also known as the "Woodstock guru," because he gave a riveting talk from the stage at the 1969 festival.

Swapna—dream state.

Takshaka—The ancient king of the *nagas* (serpents). His kingdom was known as Takshasila. Takshaka, at the request of Shringin (the grandson of the yogi Shamika), killed King Parikshit. After Parikshit's death, his second son, Janamejaya, took revenge by attempting to massacre all the snakes in the world and almost succeeded. He captured Takshaka and was about to kill him when a sage named Astika intervened and convinced Janamejaya to stop the genocide.

Tamas—darkness, inertia, heaviness, stubbornness, lazy, steadfast; one of the three *gunas*.

Tantra—a spiritual discipline in which one weaves together, as if on a loom, the cosmic principles of male and female in order to transcend duality; from *tan* = stretch + *tra* = to cross over or protect.

Tanumanasi—thinning out of the mind; from *tanu* = thinning or stretching + *man* = mind.
The third *bhumika*.

Tapas—heat, discipline. One of the five *niyamas*, or personal observances, described by Patanjali in the Yoga Sutra. Also, along with *svadhyaya* (study of the Self) and *Ishvara-pranidhana* (devotion to God), one of the three constituents of Patanjali's *kriya yoga*.

Thakurji—Thakur is a royal title meaning "Lord or little prince." *Thakurji* is often used as an affectionate name for the personal form of Krishna that one worships as a *murti* and performs *seva* to.

Tilak(a)—a mark (usually temporary, not a permanent tattoo) placed on the forehead or sometimes other parts of the body of a devotee to indicate which deity or *sampradaya* (spiritual lineage) they follow. The *tilak* that followers of Vishnu wear is an abstract form of Vishnu's foot, made of two vertical lines in the center of the forehead. Followers of Shiva wear three horizontal lines across their forehead, with or without a red dot; sometimes a crescent moon is included. Lines can be made of clay or sandalwood paste or other substances sacred to a particular deity. The *bindi* (dot) that Indian women wear over their third-eye center is a tilak with many meanings, depending on the woman wearing it.

Titiksha—endurance and patience. A calm acceptance of the conditions of life that cannot be changed, because they are out of our control. One of the six virtues (*shadsampat*) that must be cultivated for *shubheccha*, the first *bhumika*, to arise.

Trataka—steadfast gazing at one object without blinking; one of the *shatkarma kriyas* (six cleansing actions) described in the Hatha Yoga Pradipika.

Trinity—there are two major holy trinities referred to in Hinduism: Brahma (creator), Vishnu (sustainer), and Shiva (destroyer); and *Brahman* (the Divine, absolute impersonal), *Ishvara* (the Supreme Lord, Krishna, *Adipurusha*, *Paramatman*), and *Maya* (the Lord's agent of manifestation working by means of the three *gunas*). The Hindu trinity could be viewed as corresponding to the Christian holy trinity: Father (*Brahman*), Son (*Ishvara*), and Holy Spirit (*Maya*).

Turiya—the fourth. *Samadhi*, a state, beyond the normal three states of consciousness—*jagrat* (waking), *swapna* (dreaming), and *sushupti* (deep sleep). Turiya = total nondual enlightenment. The seventh and final *bhumika*.

Ujjayi—victorious.

Uma—a benevolent Hindu goddess, the second wife of Lord Shiva (she was Sati in a previous incarnation). *Uma* = light. She is known as the Lady of Light, the Lady of the Mountains, the White Goddess, and in Tibetan Buddhism as White Tara. She is depicted as beautiful and benignly powerful. She is also called Parvati and Gauri.

Uparathi—true mental poise; from *upa* = the way + *rati* = special form of affection. *Uparathi* is one of the six virtues (*shadsampat*) that must be cultivated for *shubheccha*, the first *bhumika*, to arise.

Vaikuntha—the place of eternal bliss, the heavenly realms of Vishnu. Also called Vishnuloka.

Vairagya—dispassion, detachment, renunciation; a state of being free of attachment to materialistic life. Letting go of feelings of pride, aversion, and fear associated with the egoic obsession with I, me, and mine; from *vai* = to dry + *raga* = passion, interest. According to the sage Vasishtha, *vairagya* is one of the four means to cultivate *shubheccha*, the first *bhumika*.

Vaishnav(a)—a devotee of Vishnu or of one of his *avatars* (Rama, Krishna).

Vaishnavism—the worship of the Hindu god Vishnu and his *avatars*.

Vajroli mudra—a hatha yoga practice that requires the yogi to draw the female ejaculation up through his penis from the vagina of a female yogini.

Vallabhacharya (1478-1531) the last of the five great *acharyas* of Vedanta. He descends from the Rudra lineage of Vishnu Swami. He is the founder of the Pushtimarg, the Path of Grace—holding the philosophical view of *shuddhadvaita* (pure nondualism), perceiving all of existence as Divine.

Valmiki—author of the Ramayana and the Yoga Vasishtha. The Ramayana is the first epic poem in Sanskrit literature. It consists of twenty-four thousand verses, in seven cantos, and tells the story of Rama, the seventh *avatar* of Lord Vishnu, who was born at the end of the second age, or Treta Yuga. The Yoga Vasishtha is a text containing twenty-nine thousand verses structured as a discussion between a young prince Rama and his teacher, the sage Vasishtha.

Van (also ban)—forest.

Varna—caste, order, type, or class. The framework used in Vedic Indian society to group people. There are four classes in the Indian caste system: *Brahmins* (priests, philosophers, intellectuals, teachers), *Kshatriyas* (protectors, guardians, rulers, administrators, warriors), *Vaishyas* (artisans, merchants, tradesmen, farmers) and *Shudras* (workers).

Vasana—perfuming. The subtle seeds of desire. Predispositions, habituations of the *jiva*. *Vasanas* influence which latent *samskaras* are set in motion.

Vasishtha—one of the seven great *rishis* of India. Considered to be the first sage or proponent of the Vedanta School of philosophy. His philosophy is expounded upon in the ancient scripture the Yoga Vasishtha, written by the poet Valmiki.

Vayu—wind, air.

Veda—from *vid* = to know. The Vedas are the most ancient compilation of Hindu knowledge. There are four Vedas: Rig, Yajur, Sama, and Atharva.

Vedanta—the end of the Vedas. Philosophical school that probes into the nature of God (or *Brahman*), individual souls, and the material world and their relationship to each other.

Vicharana—right inquiry; from *vi* = correct + *charana* = seeking. The second *bhumika* according to the Yoga Vasishtha. When you process this virtue, you find yourself in the right place at the right time and are able to progress on the spiritual path.

Vijaya—one of the gatekeepers, along with his brother, Jaya, of Vaikuntha, the heavenly abode of Lord Vishnu. Because of a curse by the Four Kumaras, Vijaya and Jaya had to take birth three times as demons who are killed by different avatars of Vishnu. In Satya Yuga, Vijaya is Hiranyaksha, who is killed by Varaha; in Treta Yuga, he is Kumbhakarna and is killed by Rama; and in the Dvapara Yuga, he is Dantavakra and is killed by Krishna.

Vimana—a spaceship, a flying machine described in many ancient Sanskrit scriptures as a flying car or a celestial chariot. *Vimanas* were the favored mode of travel by many demigods and *rishis*. Vimanas were of different types and capacities. Some could travel through air, some through space, and some through time. Some vimanas were huge, opulent, floating palaces, with the capacity to teleport thousands of people to distant planets and other dimensions, while others were small crafts, able to travel at such high speeds that they disappeared from normal sight. *Vimana* = traversing, or to have been measured out; from *vi* = separate + *mati* = he measures.

Vimukti—a special kind of liberation that is given to the pure *bhakta* whose only desire is to render loving service to Krishna; from *vi* = separate + *mukti* = liberation. *Vimukti* goes beyond the five types of liberation: *sayuja* (becoming one with God); *salokya*, in which the soul goes to heaven; *sarupya*, in which the soul gets a God-like body; *samipya*, in which the soul gets to be near God; and *sarshti*, in which the soul obtains God's six opulences (knowledge, wealth, fame, strength, beauty, and renunciation).

Vina (also veena)—an ancient Indian plucked string instrument. The goddess Sarasvati and the immortal sage Narada Muni are the most celebrated *vina* virtuosos.

Vinyasa—to place in order in a special way, with meaning and intention; from *vi* = to order or separate + *nyasa* = to place.

Virabhadra—the fiercest, most vengeful, destructive warrior aspect of Lord Shiva; from *vira* = hero + *bhadra* = friend.

Vishnu—the preserver in the Hindu trinity, or *trimurti*, of Brahma, Vishnu, and Shiva. Vishnu incarnates on Earth in his *avatar* form to bring balance whenever evil is on the rise. Most scholars and religious leaders agree that there are ten primary avatars of Vishnu: Matsya (fish), Kurma (tortoise), Varaha (boar), Narasimha (half-man, half-lion), Vamana (dwarf), Parashurama (warrior), Rama, Krishna, Buddha, and Kalki (yet to come); some include Jesus as well.

Vishuddha chakra—pure, poison-free, the throat *chakra*.

Viveka—discrimination, the wisdom to discern the difference between what is real and what is unreal or temporary; from *vi* = to separate + *eka* = one. *Viveka* is a virtue enabling a person to separate the one (real) from the many (unreal) and to see the one (real) in the many (unreal). According to the sage Vasishtha, viveka is one of the four means necessary to cultivate *shubheccha*, the first *bhumika*.

Vraj (also Braj)—the area in North India where Krishna lived as a child and young adult, nowadays known as Mathura District.

Vrajbhasha (also Brajbhasha)—the ancient language spoken by Krishna, predating modern Hindi. It is still spoken in the Vraj (also Braj) area of North India today. The contemporary Pushtimarga saint Shyamdas spoke this language eloquently.

Vrajbhashi (also Brajbhashi)—a resident of Vraj (also Braj).

Vrindavan— one of the oldest sacred cities in India. *Vrinda* refers to a type of basil plant also known as tulsi, and *van* = forest. Vrindavan is one of the twelve ancient forests that existed during the time Krishna lived and spent his young adult years as a spellbinder to cows and enchanter of the *gopis*. The twelve forests are collectively known as Vraj (also Braj).

Vyasa—ancient sage, author of the Vedas, the Mahabharata, the Bhagavad Gita, and the Shrimad Bhagavatam. He is the father of Shukadev. Vyasa is also known as Vedavyasa and is considered the founder of the philosophy known as Vedanta.

Yagna—a Hindu ritual sacrifice that involves feeding a sacred fire to appease and win the favor of Agni, the fire god, in order to attain a specific objective. Traditionally, animals were fed to the fire, as well as ghee, rice, and vegetables.

Yaksha—nature spirit.

Yamas—restrictions. Patanjali, in the Yoga Sutra, lists five *yamas*, or ways to restrict your behavior in regard to others: *ahimsa* (nonharming), *satya* (truthfulness), *asteya* (nonstealing), *brahmacharya* (not sexually abusing others), and *aparigraha* (greedlessness).

Yamuna—one of the two most revered rivers in India, the other being the Ganga. Each river bestows special gifts to the sincere devotee: Gangaji grants liberation (*moksha*), while Yamunaji grants devotion (*bhakti*).

Yantra—a symbolic form of a deity, a magical geometric form used to cast a spell or as an aid to meditation.

Yatra—a journey, a pilgrimage usually performed with a religious or spiritual intent. A *banyatra* is a forest journey.

Yoga—divine union, to remember God, God-realization, Self-realization, *samadhi*, the ultimate eternal reality; from *yuj* = to yoke, to join together. The state of joining, connection, re-connection, or remembrance of God. The word *Yoga*, with an upper case "Y," pertains to the state of divine union. When spelled with a lower case "y," it pertains to the practices done to bring about the state of Yoga.

Yoga nidra—yogic sleep, a state of consciousness between waking and sleeping, like the "going to sleep" stage, typically induced by guided meditation or *shavasana*.

Yoga Sutra—a scripture compiled by the Indian sage Patanjali, who organized the philosophy of yoga into 195 *sutras* (threads or terse verses), contained in four *padas* (chapters).

Yoga Vasishtha—an ancient philosophical scripture written by Valmiki. The text is structured as a teaching given to the young prince Rama by his teacher, the sage Vasishtha, on the nature of reality. The viewpoint is one of Advaita Vedanta.

Yogi—one who practices yoga or who has attained enlightenment or the remembrance of God, the reconnection to the Divine Supreme Person.

Yudhishthira—the elder brother of Arjuna who becomes king after the battle of Kurukshetra. The son of the god Dharma and the princess Kunti. *Yudhishthira* = one who is steady amid conflict; from *yuddha* = war + *sthira* = steady.

Yuga—an age, period, or cycle of time; from *yuj* = to join or yoke. According to Hinduism, there are four yugas: Satya, Treta, Dvapara, and Kali. We are currently in the Kali Yuga.

Acknowledgments

For a writer to know that a piece works, they must read it out loud to someone before finalizing. It can be difficult to find the right person who will provide such a favor. You don't want a friend who will sit through the reading and at the end tell you, "It's great!" That is not helpful. You need someone who is going to be a harsh critic and not afraid to tell you when something doesn't work. Yes, this can be an unnerving experience for the writer as well as for the listener, both of whom must patiently sit through the process. I owe a debt of gratitude to **David Life** for playing this role, giving me his listening time, his scrutiny, and fearless, unapologetic, often severe, but always brilliant commentary.

Thank you to **David Life** for the design and layout of the book.

I am extremely grateful to **Jaimie Epstein** for her masterful final edits to the manuscripts for both volume 1 and 2. It was an honor to work together with her on this book.

Appreciation to artist **Frederick Gladding Kahl** for creating the glass sculpture *Apsara,* which appears on the cover and frontispiece of both volumes.

Thank you to my dear friends **Paul Gopal Steinberg, Kathleen Hunt, Katya Grineva, Martyna Eder-Febre, Ally Gopi Buxton, Rachel Bennet**, and **Jai Uttal** who kindly took the time to read through the initial versions of many of these pieces and provide important edit suggestions as well as supportive commentary.

I owe a debt of gratitude to the **Jivamukti Yoga Global community of teachers and students**, especially **Camilla Kamala Veen, Hari Mulukutla,** and **Karoline Straubinger** for their continuous interest in my writings. Their encouragement compelled me to bring this book to publication.

Thank you to my daughter **Tia Town** for her patience with me while I worked to complete this book.

I bow to my holy teachers—**Randy Hall, Shri Brahmananda Sarasvati, Swami Nirmalananda, Shri K. Pattabhi Jois, Shyamdas,** and **Shri Milan Baba Goswami**—who have guided my spiritual path and encouraged my study of the ancient wisdom teachings found in scripture. They continue to teach me the meaning and application of compassion toward others and most importantly how bhakti, loving devotion to God, is the essential quest in life.

All glories to **Shri Krishna**, the one who pulls the strings.

About the Author

Sharon Gannon is a polymath who excels in many artistic disciplines as well as being an animal rights vegan activist. She is a Krishna bhakta, and best known as the co-creator, along with David Life, of the Jivamukti Yoga method; jivamuktiyoga.com.

Lightning Source UK Ltd.
Milton Keynes UK
UKHW020649230622
404860UK00008B/484

9 798210 359315